THE UPPER ROOM

Disciplines

2009

UPPER
ROOM BOOKS®
NASHVILLE

An Outline for Small-Group Use of Disciplines

Here is a simple plan for a one-hour, weekly group meeting based on reading Disciplines. One person may act as convener every week, or the role can rotate among group members. You may want to light a white Christ candle each week to signal the beginning of your time together.

Opening

Convener: Let us come into the presence of God.

Others: Lord Jesus Christ, thank you for being with us. Let us hear your word to us as we speak to one another.

Scripture

Convener reads the scripture suggested for that day in Disciplines. After a one- or two-minute silence, convener asks: What did you hear God saying to you in this passage? What response does this call for? (Group members respond in turn or as led.)

Reflection

- What scripture passage(s) and meditation(s) from this week was (were) particularly meaningful for you? Why? (Group members respond in turn or as led.)
- What actions were you nudged to take in response to the week's meditations? (Group members respond in turn or as led.)
- Where were you challenged in your discipleship this week? How did you respond to the challenge? (Group members respond in turn or as led.)

Praying Together

Convener says: Based on today's discussion, what people and situations do you want us to pray for now and in the coming week? Convener or other volunteer then prays about the concerns named.

Departing

Convener says: Let us go in peace to serve God and our neighbors in all that we do.

Adapted from The Upper Room Daily Devotional Guide, January–February 2001. © 2000 The Upper Room. Used by permission.

THE UPPER ROOM DISCIPLINES 2009
© 2009 by Upper Room Books®. All rights reserved.

The Upper Room Web site: http://www.upperroom.org

Cover design: Left Coast Design, Portland, Oregon
Cover photo: Denis Tangney/iStockphoto.com
First printing: 2008

The week of February 23–March 1 was published in *Disciplines* 2003.

The weeks of July 20–26 and August 24–30 were published in *Disciplines* 2000.

ISBN: 978-0-8358-9928-4
Printed in the United States of America

CONTENTS

An Outline for Small-Group Use of *Disciplines* 3

Foreword 11
Helen R. Neinast

January 1–4 13
This Little Light of Mine
Janet Wolf

January 5–11 17
Baptism of the Lord
Robert V. Dodd

January 12–18 24
Knowing God, Known by God
Victoria Rebeck

January 19–25 31
Get Ready
John W. Bardsley

January 26–February 1 38
Living as Covenant People
Gerard Marks

February 2–8 45
The Healer of Brokenness
Beth A. Palm

February 9–15 52
Living into Grace
Johnny R. Sears

February 16–22 59
Transformation
Myrtle E. Felkner

February 23–March 1 66

Gracious Water, Gracious God
Terrell M. McDaniel

March 2–8 73

Faith, Grace, and Surprises
Curtis S. Ackley

March 9–15 80

Looking Beyond Labels
William Stillman

March 16–22 87

The Cure for Death
Bob Kaylor

March 23–29 94

Lessons from *The Heart of Darkness*
Pamela D. Couture

March 30–April 5 101

"Reel" Jesus: Life with Our Lord
Ellen Hamilton Fenter

April 6–12 108

The Road to Resurrection
Dan R. Dick

April 13–19 115

Strength in Community
Timothy B. Warner

April 20–26 122

Peace with God, Peace through God
Twila M. Belk

April 27–May 3 129

God's All-Embracing Care
Juan Bek

May 4–10 136
Abiding in God
Ann Freeman Price

May 11–17 143
Love as a Verb
Elaine Puckett

May 18–24 150
The Spirit of God in Our Lives
Akiiki Daisy Kabagarama

May 25–31 157
Voices On Fire
Frank Ramirez

June 1–7 164
God in Three Persons
Emily M. Akin

June 8–14 171
Seeds of Faith
Marilyn Dickson

June 15–21 178
God's Pursuit . . . Our Response
Laura Flippen Tenzel

June 22–28 185
Trust in Times of Trial
Jacob S. Dharmaraj

June 29–July 5 192
Steadfast Presence, Sufficient Grace
Barbara J. Lindgren

July 6–12 199
Claimed by God
Melody C. Porter

July 13–19 206

The Blessing of Identity
Robert Roth

July 20–26 213

Imagine That
Mary Donovan Turner

July 27–August 2 220

True Sorrow Brings Forgiveness and New Life
Leona Ellis

August 3–9 227

In the Thickets by the Jordan
Austin B. Tucker

August 10–16 234

Wisdom
Janet Casterline

August 17–23 241

Strength Amid Changes
Marvin D. Arnpriester

August 24–30 248

Love's Many Facets
F. Dean Lueking

August 31–September 6 255

Wisdom, Compassion, and Faith
Albert Isteero

September 7–13 262

Navigation Systems
Jeff Taylor

September 14–20 269

Greatness
Brian K. Bauknight

September 21–27 276
Choices
Susan Hibbins

September 28–October 4 284
The Blameless Life
Paul Moots

October 5–11 291
Light at the End of the Tunnel
Soozung Sa Rankin

October 12–18 298
Out of Weakness, Strength and Service
H. Sharon Howell

October 19–25 305
Discipleship and Vulnerability
Jennifer S. Graves

October 26–November 1 312
Blessed Assurance, Heaven Is Mine
Timothy J. Nadeau

November 2–8 319
Unforgettable Themes
Chris Thron

November 9–15 326
Perseverance by the Grace of God
Heather Morris

November 16–22 333
Blessed Assurance, Heaven Is Mine
Laurie Hays Coffman

November 23–29 340
An Honest Faith
Enuma Okoro

November 30–December 6 347
Way Makers
F. Douglas Powe Jr

December 7–13 354
Joy Anchored in God's Love
Jonette Gay

December 14–20 361
Finding Fulfillment
Larry G. Jent

December 21–27 368
Responding to God's Gifts
Sam Clark

December 28–31 375
Overwhelmed with Joy
Beth A. Richardson

The Revised Common Lectionary for 2009 379

FOREWORD

"INSIDE YOURSELF YOU SHOULDN'T BE RUNNING ALL THE TIME."
That's Tina Turner, rock and soul superstar, quoting a Trappist monk.

An astute observation and wise counsel, these words echo God's invitation to each of us: "Be still and know that I am God." God waits to meet us in silence and solitude; times of silence deepen our knowledge and experience of God. But God also meets us in the everyday tumble of our lives; for those times when we must be on the run, God keeps pace with us. Whether our prayer time is spent in silken quiet or amid ragged noise, God does seek us out. God is faithful; God finds us wherever we are.

Disciplines offers a way for you to make time and space for God: to still yourself, to meditate on scripture, to pray, and to listen to God. Each week, *Disciplines* features scriptures from the Revised Common Lectionary, a guide or table of readings used weekly in public worship. Each week a spiritual leader or writer reflects on a different set of scriptures, explores their meaning, and suggests a way to meditate and pray. This daily practice of scripture reading, reflection, and prayer is a powerful means of grace and spiritual growth.

There are countless ways to approach a daily discipline of scripture reading and prayer. Quiet time in the morning can be calming and centering for you; this may be the best time for study and prayer. Or, you may need time in the evening to pause, reflect, and pray. You may decide to read *Disciplines* just before you exercise; prayer and meditation are sometimes deepest when people swim, walk, or run. No matter what form your spiritual discipline takes, God begins with you wherever and however you begin.

This year marks the fiftieth anniversary of *Disciplines*. As you read scriptures, reflect on your faith, and pray throughout the year ahead, remember that you are in good company: thousands of believers all over the world have read these same scriptures; reflected on the mysteries of this same faith; and prayed to this same God, the God who hungers for your company and who waits for you today.

— Helen R. Neinast
Author and Consultant • Upper Room Books

This Little Light of Mine

JANUARY 1–4, 2009 • JANET WOLF

THURSDAY, JANUARY 1 ～ *Read Revelation 21:1-6a*

See, the home of God is among mortals." What an astonishing declaration. God is at home among us. God is not waiting to pull us out of this world into some faraway escape world. God's home is here, among us. It is in this life, on this earth, that we are to search for signs of God's glory.

As we begin this new year, we celebrate the many places we have seen God's glory shining. I think of South Africa where the prisoner of twenty-seven years became the president; where the first official act of the government was to abolish the death penalty; where the constitution guarantees rights for all God's children, including those of any sexual orientation; where the language of the church was moved into the streets as reconciliation took on flesh.

We have seen God's glory in the nonviolent movements for change in the Philippines and Poland, Tiananmen Square and Indonesia. We've seen it in the US civil rights movement of the 1950s and '60s as people the world labeled nobodies became sources of light and life, blessing and transforming a nation. We've seen it in congregations who keep on loving when loving is hard to do, who hope in defiance of despair and death, who practice resurrection and give flesh to forgiveness. We see it as this new year dawns. We see it in our own lives when despair gives way to hope and pain is transformed into joy.

Revelation is a testament to the promise of God's presence in places where the promise is not yet realized.

My eyes and your eyes have seen the glory of the coming of the Lord!

Community organizer, college professor, and elder in the Tennessee Annual Conference of the United Methodist Church; living in Nashville, Tennessee

Eugene Peterson in *The Message and Contemplative Prayer* helps us hear the message of these verses. "The mystery is that . . . [both outsiders and insiders] stand on the same ground before God." We were trying to pull together a Christmas play, and our own congregation's little Joseph had made it a most challenging task. Nevertheless, someone decided our Joseph would be included. He and I would sit up front to remind folks when to come and go. Little Joseph was not enthused: "Ain't coming to no stupid Christmas play. I got better things to do, hah! My mama's taking me to the Christmas parade."

It seemed unlikely that Joseph's mama, a single mother with four boys and two part-time jobs, could take Joseph to the parade. So I tried again: "If you're not here, the angels might stay too long. The shepherds might forget to show up. We can't do it without you!" Joseph's parting words were these: "Ain't coming to no stupid Christmas play."

But he did come, early even, and was wonderfully helpful getting the youngest children into their costumes. Then one of the older kids hollered: "Thought you weren't coming to no stupid Christmas play?" My heart sank, sure this would do Joseph in. But Joseph just turned and declared: "Course I'm gonna show up. They can't even do it without me!"

What might it mean for us to change the way we tell and live the stories of God among us so that outsiders become central? How might we begin?

As we move into a new year, we stumble into the wideness of God's mercy, the extravagance of God's grace. Matthew's epiphany story is a reminder that it was folks outside the official story that searched for, found and worshiped this child Jesus. Often the people we label outsiders, the "unchurched," evangelize the "churched" if we listen. Our congregation learned to be church from folks who are homeless; people coming out of prison and overcoming domestic violence; little kids wandering in without adults, struggling with the hard stuff of racism and poverty.

We have also learned by changing our social location, not waiting for people to come to us but moving ourselves into the streets and the prisons. Several of us have worked together to offer graduate theology courses inside the maximum security prison, with half of the students coming from the inside and half from a local seminary.

Two other classes are offered in minimum security prisons, again with half of the students from the inside and half from local colleges, congregations, and the community. We have discovered that doing theology inside the prison, learning about criminal justice behind the walls, changes our understandings, challenges our stereotypes, and moves us into a partnership that redefines prison ministry from the inside out.

How does our social location limit our understanding of the gospel good news? How might we relocate ourselves to listen to and learn from "God's poor"? [Psalm 72]

And having been warned in a dream not to return to Herod, they left for their own country by another road.

Keb Mo sings a song titled "There's More Than One Way Home." It is a reminder of this epiphany experience. Having encountered King Jesus, the magi do not go back to King Herod. They go home by another way. The powerful presence of this One called Jesus compels them to resist the path defined by Herod. Herod may have called them in for a secret meeting and sent them out with orders to return, but the manifestation of God's glory requires them to work out a different way home.

From the beginning, the nearness of God's kingdom clashes with all other kingdoms. That's why Herod is frightened and so many others with him. The coming of Jesus marks a decisive shift in the universe, a challenge to all other powers. Then and now, the powers that be meet resistance with oppression and violence. Herod's response will mean that Jesus begins life as a refugee, an illegal alien, his family on the run in Africa; it means that hundreds of children will be killed and Rachel will refuse to be consoled.

We see the shadow of the cross from the beginning of the story. What does it mean to worship this One who reorders the world and our steps, to find another way home?

What changes need to happen in our lives, in the life of our congregations, communities, and nation, in order for us to follow the path of God's kingdom?

Baptism of the Lord

JANUARY 5–11, 2009 • ROBERT V. DODD

MONDAY, JANUARY 5 ~ *Read Genesis 1:1-2*

Justin, our oldest son, was a precocious six-year-old when he asked me, "How did God create the heavens and the earth?" While I was struggling to come up with a detailed theological explanation, his face brightened with insight as he announced, "I know! God's got powers." He had answered his own question.

Hebrews 11:3 tells us, "By faith we understand that the worlds were prepared by the word of God." Nobody was there to witness and record this event. Our belief that God created everything that exists is based on divine revelation. It cannot be proven scientifically, and it does not need to be. Scripture tells us, "In the beginning God created the heavens and the earth."

Material realities can help us experience spiritual realities. Celtic Christians sometimes asked, "Can you see the mountain beyond the mountain?" They were aware that we simultaneously live in two worlds: the physical and the spiritual. We baptize with water to acknowledge the One who gives us life both physically and spiritually.

God created all things, both seen and unseen, by the power of the Word. What God says comes true. How does God do that? In the words of my son, "God's got powers."

Almighty God, you spoke the worlds into being by the power of your word. Let me hear you speaking to my heart. Amen.

An ordained elder in the Western North Carolina Conference of the United Methodist Church, and author of many books, articles, and Bible study materials

The ancient Hebrews believed that their world was covered by a transparent dome that they called the firmament. Beyond this dome was a watery chaos, referred to as "the deep". Genesis says the spirit of God, like a mighty wind, swept over the waters. Water, wind, and spirit are often closely associated in scripture. Each represents God's active presence in the world.

Water and spirit are interwoven throughout the Bible, from the watery chaos beyond the heavenly firmament in the Genesis creation story to the river of the water of life flowing from the throne of God in Revelation 22.

Light and darkness are also scriptural themes. God spoke light into being and separated it from darkness. Scripture says, "And there was evening, and there was morning—the first day" (Gen. 1:5). Today we tend to think of the twenty-four hour day as beginning with morning and moving toward the evening. But Genesis describes the daily cycle as beginning at sunset and moving through the night to the dawning of a new morning.

God brought existence out of nonexistence and established order out of chaos. The ancients lived in a world where they believed that their continued survival depended upon the outcome of conflicts between various warring gods. But Genesis affirms that God has established a certain amount of predictability in the natural world. Spring follows winter, summer follows spring, and fall follows summer. If you plant apple seeds you will get an apple tree, not a peach tree. If you plant wheat, you will get a crop of wheat instead of corn. You really do reap what you sow. This ordering is God's gift to us. Without it, there would be no life.

Creator God, thank you for this amazing world in which we live and for the wild and wonderful, highly complex way in which all life can be used for our good and your greater glory. Amen.

As I stand out on our deck overlooking the woods in our backyard and in neighboring yards, the crisp air refreshes and invigorates me. Beyond the trees and rolling hills I can hear the muffled sounds of commuter traffic. Somewhere in the distance a lone crow calls to its mate. The early morning sun shines its golden rays through the last remaining multicolored leaves still clinging to the trees. Their beauty reminds me of stained-glass windows and the canopy of trees provides a cathedral-like place that calls me to worship God. A prayer of thanksgiving wells up from within me. Psalm 29 reminds us that the God of creation continues to be active in creation. I experience God's handiwork in my own backyard.

The psalm is an evocative and powerful reminder that God is the rule of life, the one who appears in our world to rule with strength, to give us life, and to bestow the order that brings us peace and security.

When Aaron, our youngest son, was a preschooler, he sought to understand the world around him by often asking me questions similar to these:

"Who made the trees?" he would ask.

"God made the trees," I would answer.

"Who made the roads?" he would ask.

"Workers made the roads," I would respond.

"God made the workers," he would wisely conclude.

God who created us and continues to be involved in creation desires cooperation with the Spirit in the creative process.

Breathe on me, God. Fill me with life. Breathe into my spirit your Holy Spirit, so that my life may in every possible way bring glory to your holy name. Amen.

In Ephesus the apostle Paul encountered some disciples who had been baptized by John the baptizer. He sensed that there was something incomplete about them and asked, "Did you receive the Holy Spirit when you became believers?" Their response indicated that they did not realize God's Spirit could be experienced in such a personal way. So Paul laid his hands on them and prayed for them. As a result they were filled with the Holy Spirit. They experienced profound worship too deep for words. They prophesied, making clear, understandable, and powerful declarations of faith.

For these believers the baptism of John indicated their repentance and desire to live a life of obedience to God's will. But Paul reminded them that John's baptism pointed them to the one who would come after him, meaning Jesus. John had said to the crowds, "I baptize with water, but one who is coming after me will baptize you with the Holy Spirit" (see John 1:29-34).

Sometimes we have a sense that something is missing in our life. Even if our life has gone well, we may still feel incomplete. Ironically, church life can be spiritually draining, if we get caught up in the multiple responsibilities and activities generated by committee meetings, planning sessions, leadership enlistment, membership cultivation, funding strategies, the maintenance of facilities, and so on.

The believers baptized by John had done all the right things. But they were still spiritually incomplete. So Paul introduced them to the one who could complete their faith by the power of the Holy Spirit. It may be that we too need Paul's instruction to deepen our faith and our discipleship.

Lord, forgive me when I try to follow you in my own strength and through my own ingenuity. Enable me, instead, to rely on the strength and guidance of your Holy Spirit. Amen.

John the baptizer proved to be a controversial figure who captured the people's attention. Calling people to repentance and faithfulness, he emerged from the wilderness having existed on a diet of locusts and wild honey, with the smell of the wilderness on his body and the fire of God in his eyes. He wore a camel's hair robe and leather belt. And the crowds came out in droves to see and hear him.

John challenged people to repent and be baptized with water in the Jordan River. His primary purpose was to prepare them for the one who would come after him, one who was greater than John in every way. John saw himself as a messenger sent to prepare the way of the Lord. He said, "I have baptized you with water; but he will baptize you with the Holy Spirit." John's ministry was only a prelude to the main event. John was clear that what Jesus could do was far superior to what he could do.

The water of baptism is a sign of activity in an inner spiritual dimension. We baptize with water as a reminder of the one who baptizes with the Holy Spirit. Jesus saturates our soul with an awareness of God's presence, inundating us with the fire of God's love. This is not a second act of grace but a continuation of the love of God that has already been made available to us through Jesus Christ.

The baptism of Jesus lays claim to us, and our baptism becomes a call to follow Jesus as good disciples and faithful servants. God's Spirit continually cleanses, refreshes, renews, transforms, and empowers us.

Lord Jesus, fill me with your Holy Spirit and empower me to be your true disciple in every area of my life. Amen.

Jesus came from Nazareth to be baptized by John. At first John hesitated and said, "You shouldn't be baptized by me. I need to be baptized by you." (See Matthew 3:14.) But Jesus insisted, and after he came up out of the water, the heavens opened and the Spirit came down on him like a dove. Matthew adds that the Spirit rested on him: this was not a temporary thing, but a permanent anointing. Then a voice from heaven spoke and said to Jesus, "You are my Son, the Beloved; with you I am well pleased." What an amazing affirmation of Jesus' true identity. What a powerful anointing for the ministry that Jesus was about to begin. What tremendous spiritual fortification for the trials and tribulations that he would all too soon face.

Every baptized believer has been initiated into the church universal and anointed for ministry. Some believers are called to the ordained ministry, but all believers are call to some ministry. The baptism of Jesus brings attention to God's affirmation of us as God's children and our anointing for ministry.

When he was a youth, one of my friends responded to an altar call at a revival service. Asked why he had come forward he said, "Because I want to do something great for God." According to popular thinking in those days, doing something great for God meant that you might have been called to be a preacher or a missionary. There seemed to be few other available options. But today we understand that there are many ways to serve God.

Jesus' baptism revealed who he truly was—God's beloved son. Our baptism reveals who we truly are—children of God, called to serve.

Lord Jesus, you call us to serve you in many different ways. Our baptism is our commissioning for ministry. Help us to understand our calling more clearly and to serve you with strength and joy. Amen.

In order to swim you must learn to trust the water's natural buoyancy to support you. Instead of fighting the water, you must give in to it. You can't become a good swimmer by staying on dry land or by remaining in the shallows where you can touch bottom. Eventually you have to get into water over your head.

Water is a recurring theme in our lives: the water of the womb in which we were nurtured prior to birth, the water of baptism that acknowledges spiritual birth and growth, and the water in which we learn to swim. Jesus said, "No one can enter the kingdom of God without being born of water and Spirit" (John 3:5). Water facilitates physical birth and indicates spiritual birth.

Sometimes the baptism of Jesus involves pain and suffering. (See Mark 10:33-34, 38.) Opposition, difficulties, trials, and tribulations often follow spiritual breakthroughs. Immediately after his baptism, Jesus was driven by the Spirit into the wilderness where he was tempted by the devil (see Matt. 4:1).

As the result of injuries sustained in an automobile accident some years ago, I live with chronic pain each day. Because prayer has always been a vital part of my life and ministry, learning to live with pain and to pray my way through pain has been the greatest challenge of my life. I have found that when I try to cope with unrelenting and often excruciating pain, it helps to have a variety of spiritual coping strategies available. At different times one approach may be more effective than another. The important thing is that I keep on praying, that I not give up.

No matter how overwhelming life becomes, God is greater than all our difficulties. The psalm says that God is mighty, and this mighty God gives us strength and peace.

Lord Jesus, give me a spirit of prayer for the meeting of my needs and the needs of others, so that my inner life will be strengthened for the tasks at hand. Amen.

Knowing God, Known by God

JANUARY 12–18, 2009 • VICTORIA REBECK

MONDAY, JANUARY 12 ~ *Read 1 Samuel 3:1-20*

All of us hear voices. The voices tell us what we "should" do. "You should major in business so that your earning potential will be great." "You should keep your opinions to yourself." "You shouldn't rock the boat."

The voices can rise to a confusing cacophony. Their sound and fury offer no wisdom. If we can lie still and quiet, we might hear the voice of God. The wise ones in our lives will not tell us what we "should" do. They will urge us, the way Eli counseled Samuel, to remain hushed and listen for God's voice. In the still and quiet places of our hearts, we are more likely to hear God.

And we may be surprised at what we hear. God may give us consolation, or we may be discomfited. We may hear a word of encouragement to help us through a hard time. Or God may speak a word of challenge to us, showing us some new direction in which we need to go.

It is always a risk—a real risk—to listen carefully to God. Yet that risk is grounded in faith, and in the love of a God who desires for us a faithful and abundant life. Whatever God tells us, God's word to us will be truth. Unlike other voices that try to confine us, God's voice is a call to liberation. Hear the call to freedom in Christ that allows you to be true to yourself and to be the person God calls you to be.

O breath of life, blow like a wind across the noisy voices that storm my landscapes. Calm me so that I may discern the power of your presence. Amen.

An ordained deacon in the United Methodist Church, director of communications for the Minnesota Annual Conference of the United Methodist Church, and appointed to Edgewater Emmanuel United Methodist Church in Minneapolis, Minnesota

The psalmist tells us that God knows us, spiritually, mentally, and physically—inside and out. This can be a frightening thought! Each of us has dark, shadowy corners of our souls. We do not look at these corners ourselves. Even less do we want God to be poking around in them!

A vague or gnawing sense of shame and unease brings these dark corners to mind, even though we try hard not to think about them. There's the time we lied to someone to avoid the consequences of something we did. There's the time we passed along a rumor about someone, though we know we'd feel betrayed if that person did the same to us. We have other shames too painful to acknowledge.

We do not want to look into those corners ourselves and do not mention them in prayer to God. Yet God has already visited these dark and lonely places. God has dwelt in them and explored them. God has shined God's light on them. And yet, God loves us and desires no less to be in relationship with us.

God, far more than we understand, claims us, loves us, and cares for us. Such knowledge can be too wonderful, too fearsome, for us. Yet it can also give us strength to acknowledge these places and to visit them ourselves. God has already been there; they are made safe by God's redeeming love and so they cannot hurt us. In fact, walking with God through our pain and regret disables their power over us. God will make us whole.

God, you have searched me and known me. Lead me through the dark corners and bright rooms with your power and love, so that I might experience a more perfect union with you. Amen.

We are indeed fearfully and wonderfully made. How does the heart know to continue beating? The lungs to draw repeated breaths? The invisible DNA to make a fingernail, or the curve of an ear, a pancreas, a wristbone? The sheer engineering is mind-boggling.

The fact that we have minds that can be boggled is also awe-inspiring. My mind can take my thoughts, string them into sentences, and move my hand across a keyboard to make symbols that another can read. Someone else's mind can do calculus. Another can look at a sweater and figure out how to knit one just like it. Many can imagine what someone else might be thinking and feeling and find just the right words or actions to comfort, encourage, or challenge.

Even when our bodies or minds deteriorate from illness or age, we are reminded no less of how simultaneously fragile and robust our bodies are. God breathed into each of us the breath of life, and that life does not easily abandon these earthen vessels we call our bodies.

The life force that made each one of us in all our intricacy, as well as other living beings and the world in which we live, is greater than the sum of all these created beings. Beyond the span of our own lives, beyond everything we can imagine, God is. There is nothing that can overcome or devalue us because God is greater than all. At the same time, God cares enough for each one of us to design the invisible parts that make us who we are. Truly God is awe-inspiring!

God, you are both great and accessible, both powerful and gentle. I praise your mighty love. Amen.

Freedom in Christ truly is radical. United with God through Christ's birth, death, and resurrection, we need not worry if we've performed the right rituals or said the right prayers. We need only be ourselves. With a love greater than she knew existed, a mother loves her newborn child, who has done nothing to win her affection. In a similar way God loves each of God's children. No earning or proving is necessary to attract God's profound love.

John Wesley, the founder of the Methodist movement, spoke of God's "prevenient" grace. One way to understand this is to say that God chose to love us before we chose God. Yet we do have a choice in that relationship. God invites us into a covenant with God. We can know what that looks like to some extent when we consider the marriage covenant. Two people voluntarily enter into a special relationship with each other. Although each maintains his or her unique identity, when making choices both must consider the well-being and feelings of the other.

In the ideal covenant, each member remains free to be himself or herself. Further, each member helps the other to be his or her best self. All things are lawful. But are they beneficial? Do they benefit oneself, one's partner in the covenant, or the communities in which we live and work and refresh ourselves?

Freedom in Christ is a freedom to make choices that allow us to grow into our "perfect" selves, that is, the whole, spiritually mature people God intends us to be. In making choices, day to day, we grow more deeply into the covenant God has made with us.

God, help me to use my freedom in Christ to make choices that bring me and others closer to you. Amen.

I was about twelve when a few of my peers experimented with smoking. Others didn't, quoting from First Corinthians: "The body is the temple of the Holy Spirit."

Now that I am well past my teen years, I ponder the meaning of the sentence, "Do you not know that your body is a temple of the Holy Spirit within you, which you have from God, and that you are not your own?"

A temple is a place of worship. What do we do to worship God? We get ourselves to worship services in our faith communities. We assume postures of prayer or praise. We sing.

The temple described here is that of the Holy Spirit. In Genesis, God breathes the breath of life (in-spiration) into the nostrils of the first person. It is a holy spirit, a holy inspiration, that is breathed into us. When we are still and quiet and take in breaths, we are breathing in the very holy inspiration that gives us life. Such breathing gives us both our physical and our spiritual vitality.

Further, the Holy Spirit dwells within this temple. How do we make our lives hospitable dwelling places for the Holy Spirit?

These temples are not our own but are from God. We did not create ourselves. These temples are a gift from God where we can experience the mystery of the in-breathing of the Holy Spirit.

In a quiet place, sit still and be aware of your inhaling and exhaling. With every breath, think of God's Spirit filling you with God's grace and empowering you to share God's love in the world.

For good or for ill, the trappings of Christianity saturate Western culture. Christmas is perhaps celebrated most by the retail industry, which begins observing it sometime in October. Couples who are not at all religious seek out a pretty church to host their wedding ceremony. Rock stars in sexually provocative clothing wear jewel-encrusted crosses around their necks.

The pervasiveness of Christian culture works against the faithful. In the West, the church has been tamed and cowed, overly familiar and cliché. At best, we Christians have not allowed God and the body of Christ to transform our lives. At the worst, shady broadcast preachers invoke God's name to fleece the flock.

Can anything good come out of the church? Most likely, your church is a place where people do their best to be Christlike. They may fail sometimes, but they also grow and reach out with love for each other and their neighbors, particularly those in need. At the Communion table, you experience the grace of God. Through the body of Christ you experience hope.

Do you share grace and hope with your neighbor? When your friends come to you seeking supportive kindness, do you invite them to "come and see"? Perhaps past church experiences have discouraged them. But you have something valuable to offer: a community of caring people, inspiring worship, and a God who transforms lives.

Philip invited a skeptical Nathanael to come and meet Jesus for himself. Don't keep Jesus to yourself! Invite others to "come and see!"

God, help me and my faith community to reflect your love, and point me to other people with whom I can share that love. Amen.

Among the early Christians were Jews who would hear this story and think of their patriarch Jacob. Jacob gained power in his clan partly because he cheated, tricking his father into giving him his blessing. He was the first Israelite, God's chosen; yet in him there was deceit.

That Jesus called Nathanael "an Israelite in whom there is no deceit" is a sign to the listener of the story that God is renewing God's people. This is not about Christians and Jews and who is superior; not at all! It is about how, from time to time, God moves to renew God's people. The author of the Gospel of John is saying that Jesus was bringing about renewal.

The last verse in this reading also evokes Jacob's story. Jacob slept in Beer-sheba and met God in a dream. God was accompanied by a retinue of messengers (angels) who ascended and descended a ladder from earth to heaven (Gen. 28:10-17). In John's Gospel, Jesus says that God's angels will ascend and descend upon the Son of Man. This gate into heaven is an image of renewal, of a new relationship with God. God stands ready to renew us as well. The gate to that renewal is Jesus. Entering that gate means turning away from old habits and practices and starting along a new and perhaps unfamiliar path. Nathanael responded to Philip's invitation to "come and see." In so doing Nathanael hears Jesus' promise that he would see even greater things.

Are we ready for this? Are we ready to "come and see"?

Dear God, renew me today and guide my steps along your path. Amen.

Get Ready

JANUARY 19–25, 2009 • JOHN W. BARDSLEY

MONDAY, JANUARY 19 ∽ *Read Jonah 3:1-5, 10*

God points to coming events through prophecy and by speaking directly to us. Sometimes we don't hear the voice crying out to us. Sometimes we listen to our more pressing needs. We focus more on what we *think* our priorities are.

In the cartoon *Non Sequitur*, a man stands on a street corner with a sign: "The end is near!" A man on the opposite corner also has a sign: "The world ended and you're still in denial!"

When God speaks we get a reality check. Jonah did. God told Jonah to carry God's message of destruction to Nineveh; Jonah ran away. He met up with a big fish, and God saved him by having the fish spit up Jonah on the beach. When God spoke to Jonah the second time, Jonah obeyed! He went to the corrupt city of Nineveh and told them what God had said: "Forty days more and Nineveh shall be overthrown."

That's when Jonah got an even bigger surprise. Nineveh *responded* to God's words by repenting and believing in God! God had intended Nineveh's destruction. God hadn't planned for Nineveh's repentance. *But God changed God's mind.*

God spared the city. This moment is electric. It says something very important about God: God is not an uncaring, unreasonable tyrant. God is able to change, to respond to repentance with forgiveness and protection.

God, thank you for your great mercy toward Nineveh and toward me. Help me to listen for your word, to hear you when you speak, and to respond to your judgment with repentance and belief. Amen.

Writer, woodworker, and retired United Methodist minister; currently serving as interim pastor of Valley View United Methodist Church in Jonesborough, Tennessee

January 19–25, 2009   31

Trust and calm assurance. Try feeling that—or believing it—during times of trouble and turmoil. With God on one side of us and evil on the other, we sometimes don't know where to turn. This psalm is a good refuge. In this psalm we find company and reassurance.

Faith and patience can be elusive. To show us a way through hard times, the psalmist focuses on the power and love of God. In Psalm 62:5-7, a long list of words testifies to the scope and strength of God's power and love. God is our hope, our rock, our salvation, and our deliverance. God is our honor and our refuge. For the psalmist and for us, just going through this litany of God's roles in our lives is reassuring and comforting.

When our world seems to be "just on the edge," when we as individuals and as a community feel weak and fearful, we can sing with the psalmist, "Power belongs to God, and steadfast love belongs to you, O LORD." Because God is powerful and loving, we can live in hope, with full confidence in God. In the middle of our self-doubt, God is there. Powerful and loving, the God we know is always ready to rescue us, to save us, to give us refuge and hope. Surely we must praise God for the care God showers on us. Give thanks to God, for God is compassionate, strong, and faithful.

Read Psalm 62:5-7 slowly, as a prayer. Focus on the words "my soul waits in silence" to begin your prayer. When you feel stilled and quieted, take a few moments to linger over each of the descriptions given to God in the psalm: hope . . . rock . . . salvation . . . fortress . . . deliverance . . . honor . . . rock . . . refuge. Take one of the images with you and carry it throughout your day.

Psalm 62:8-10 is an eloquent confession of faith from someone who has had a personal experience with the divine. Sometimes, the psalmist has heard God in the silence of prayer and meditation; at other times, the events of the day speak for God. The psalmist is encouraged by God and knows God's love and power. We living in the twenty-first century need to know God in this way too.

The cosmic battle between God and our enemies for the allegiance of our souls is chronic. It encompasses all that would tempt and destroy us. God's opponents would have us believe that our destiny lies within our own mind, body, and spirit, that we have no time for God in our frenetic high-tech world.

In the comic *Peanuts*, Lucy holds up a large heart and says: "This, Linus, is a picture of the human heart! One side is filled with hate and the other side with love. These two forces are constantly at war with each other." Linus replies, "I think I know what you mean. I can feel them fighting."

No doubt the psalmist had felt them fighting too. Forces of chaos and disorder may tear at our faith and our sense of being in God's care. This, however, is not enough to tear us from God. Our God protects and defends us.

Whatever the troubles and temptations around us might be, the psalmist asserts that our deliverance rests in God. There is much out there—in our world, in our nation, and in our personal lives—that can distract us from God and God's love. We must strengthen our prayer life so that our confidence in a steadfast and loving God will remain strong.

 O God, help me remember that you are my rock. Be my rock and my salvation today and forever. Amen.

When life is overwhelming, people respond in a variety of ways. Some say, "Oh, that's life." Others sigh in resignation, "No one ever said life was fair." Still others turn to the Psalms for comfort and confidence.

The conflict between right and wrong, between good and evil, has as its prize the souls of God's people. God understands how attractive temptations can be. Even Jesus understood what it was to be tempted.

Some have said that we live with one foot on earth, the other in heaven. And some days it feels as if that is true. We want to know God and to follow God. But sometimes the world, with its busyness and its obsession with money and power, threatens to tug us away from God. Our trust, which the psalmist says should at all times be in God, is redirected toward things and people who are less than trustworthy.

Yet even as we long for the things of the world, even as we seek out values that could destroy us, we continue to yearn for God. It is against this backdrop that the psalmist makes two important statements about God. Our God, the psalmist says, is both powerful and loving. The importance of this for our lives is evident if we try to imagine God as having one of these qualities without the other. To believe that God is powerful but not loving makes God no more than a tyrant. To believe that God is loving without being powerful reduces God to sentimentality. But our God, Psalm 62 says, is both loving and powerful. God is our best refuge and hope.

God of love and power, you are my refuge and my hope. May I know your presence with me throughout the day. Amen.

Corinth was the largest city in ancient Greece. As the richest port it commanded the leading naval power of its time. The city was filled with dislocated people—people who had come from other places without strong identities who were seeking to better themselves by getting rich and gaining social status.

This is the city to which Paul has written his letter. His words most likely were new to the Corinthians; they probably confused the Corinthians as much as they confuse us today. This passage in particular is full of odd pronouncements from Paul. It is hard to explain and harder still to draw counsel from it.

We do know that Paul's writing reflects his belief that the second coming of Christ was very near; that background helps put some of the things he wrote in context. But what does the passage mean for us, who still live in expectation of God's reign but do so two thousand years later?

Paul's words are a guide for what some people call "detached involvement." By this, Paul meant that we do not withdraw from the social structures of the world, but we clearly understand these structures as temporary, provisional. Knowing that the world as we know it is passing away gives us a chance to avoid becoming trapped by the world. We can be in the world but not *of* it.

To prepare for Christ's second coming, we must take care that we are not co-opted by the values of the world around us. We must stay awake and aware to be certain our allegiance is to God and not to the powers of this world. Paul says we have been bought with a price. The present world is passing away. We must glorify God and prepare for Christ's second coming.

Lord, help me live as your faithful disciple, today and every day of my life. Prepare me for the life that is to come. Amen.

Paul writes with strong conviction that it won't be long before Christ returns. Paul notes that the physical world "is passing away." It is time to put our lives in order.

When we examine the circumstances of the world around us, Paul's counsel can seem quite contemporary: wildfires race across the West Coast of the United States; snow and ice storms ravage the mid-West; political turmoil tears up many parts of the world; genocide is killing thousands.

Paul was correct in saying that the present form of the world is passing away. Yet Paul wrote two thousand years ago, and he was concerned only about how Christians were to live in the short time left. He didn't advise them how to act for the "long haul" because he never expected the long haul to be an issue. But we can surmise from Paul how we today, living in the long haul, are to do.

Drawing wisdom for the long haul from Paul's letter is not so direct as it might be—behave as though we have no wife or husband, get rid of all our possessions. Paul's words do translate to us in another way. He is right in that the faith does place a demand on us and our possessions. Faith demands that we examine whether our possessions dictate our loyalty, our way of life. Are we too much invested in what we have to realize that these things are only that— passing and provisional things?

If we are too tied to this world, Paul says, our trust is misplaced. We are not ready to see Christ revealed in this world and we will never be, until we allow our God—and not our possessions—to determine who we are.

Lord, help me to recognize your appearance in the world. Make me ready to hear your voice and to know what I must do to respond. Amen.

Confusion surrounds us! There are so many circumstances in this world that beg for justice, for healing, for mercy. As it is in our world, so it was in the world of John and Jesus.

John the Baptist was a catalyst. After John was arrested, Jesus went to Galilee to proclaim the good news: "The time is fulfilled, and the kingdom of God has come near; repent, and believe in the good news." His words are rays of light that follow the dark of the storm. But the passage is clear: Jesus is not just one more in a long line of prophets. Jesus is both the one who proclaims *and* the one who is proclaimed. He does not merely proclaim the kingdom of God—he *brings* the kingdom of God.

So Jesus' call to the disciples is powerful and authoritative. The disciples respond, this passage notes, without hesitation. Mark says nothing about the disciples' motivation for following Jesus. Nothing in the passage tells us why Simon, Andrew, James, and John answered Jesus' call by packing up and going with him.

The disciples act on faith. But theirs is not a faith that understands or appreciates what is happening. Theirs is a faith that simply responds to a plain and straightforward call. This call will eventually provide them with more questions than answers, but it is a call from Jesus. Because it is Jesus calling them, they respond immediately, asking not questions.

We also have the opportunity to hear Jesus' call and to respond. In this time of Epiphany, God breaks into our world and our lives with a power that disrupts our day-to-day living. God reorders our values and our very comfortable lives. God has made the call and given us the faith we need to respond.

In the midst of our everyday lives, God breaks in. This is the good news: we are called each day anew to follow Jesus.

God, we know you keep your promises. Help us to remember this while we answer the call to follow Christ. Amen.

Living as Covenant People

JANUARY 26–FEBRUARY 1, 2009 • GERARD MARKS

MONDAY, JANUARY 26 ~ *Read Psalm 111:1-3*

Psalm 111 is a joyous invitation to praise God. The New Revised Standard Version of the Bible says in verse 2 that the works of God are so great they are "studied" by the faithful. But the New International Version translates it this way: "Great are the works of the LORD; they are pondered by all who delight in them." To ponder means to contemplate, leisurely and unhurried. It is part of delighting in God.

There follows in the psalm a litany of reasons why praising God is the most sensible and logical thing to do: great are the works of God, glorious are our Creator's deeds, God's righteousness endures forever, the Lord is gracious and compassionate. Read verses 1-6 again slowly, and ponder. As you do this, list your own reasons for spending unhurried time in praise of our God. C. S. Lewis, the great apologist for the faith, argues in his *Reflections on the Psalms* that we most certainly ought to praise God because "praise not merely expresses but completes the enjoyment."

When we lived in Japan, my wife taught English to a class of older Japanese women. Every year these women vacationed overseas, mainly in Europe. The visits became the topic of conversation for some weeks after their return. During one discussion, Yoriko-san remarked that whenever she experienced something new and wonderful on one of these visits, she "always wanted to thank something." Only one or two in the group were Christians, but they all agreed that life's blessings deserved thanksgiving and praise. Likewise, we are compelled, as we ponder God's gifts, to join in delighted praise to God.

Sit quietly for a moment and begin to compose your own psalm of praise. Keep it in mind as you go through the day, and add to it.

Retired New Zealand Baptist minister who served in local churches, international congregations, and as General Secretary of his denomination; living in Tauranga, New Zealand

A song of great celebration, Psalm 111 praises the covenant God has made with us. It is a covenant, the psalmist says with assurance, of which God is "ever mindful," to which God is always faithful, and for which we give thanks.

The Creator's goodness is not something arbitrary, determined by a divine mood swing. God has entered into a covenant with us. The word most often associated with covenant in our Bible is *law*. Law, however, is not the most helpful translation of the Hebrew Torah. The original Hebrew included a note of kindly guidance and direction for living. God's intention in entering into this covenant with us is not only to help us find life at its very best but also to invite us into a partnership to establish the reign of God here on earth. As Paul wrote, "So the law is holy, and the commandment is holy, righteous and good" (Rom. 7:12).

God's great works, glorious deeds, graciousness, compassion, provision, and power all express the love of our Creator. They are powerful evidence that we can depend on God keeping faithfully to the promises in the covenant. Our God is not hidden. Our God is in plain sight—and great are the works of God among us.

All God's precepts are trustworthy. And, because we have been loved by a God who is faithful to all promises, we keep these precepts with "faithfulness and uprightness." Surely God's praise does endure forever.

Carved above the door leading into Cambridge University's Cavendish laboratory are these words from Psalm 111:2: "Great are the works of the Lord." The laboratory's first director, James Clerk Maxwell, in 1874, insisted on this inscription. Maxwell discovered electromagnetism; he was also a committed Christian. He believed the work done in the laboratory reflected the works of God. How are you discovering the works of God in your life and through what you do?

In a covenant, both parties commit to each other. The relationship between two people can be a covenant when each agrees to a commitment that will include mutual care and faithfulness to the other. God takes the initiative in establishing a covenant with us. God will provide for and protect us, we must covenant to hear God's word and trust ourselves to God's revealed will.

But how are we to know God's will? That was Israel's question. Many of the surrounding nations practiced sorcery, divination, witchcraft, and spells. Some spoke with mediums and consulted the dead—practices detested by the people of the one true God. But the question remained: how would they know God's will?

God would provide them with a prophet and, in time, a succession of prophets who would speak in God's name. "I will put my words in the mouth of the prophet, who shall speak to them everything that I command. Anyone who does not heed the words the prophet shall speak in my name, I myself will hold accountable."

If we are to be the covenant people of God today, we must listen carefully to the revealed word of God and just as carefully build our lives on that word. We live in the years following the life, death, and resurrection of Jesus, the greatest of all God's prophets. He is the image of God, the perfect representation of the Creator. If we immerse ourselves in the life and teaching of Jesus, we will hear and know the word of God.

Creator God, you have spoken. But am I listening? Teach me to wait on you, listen to you, and hunger for your word more than for anything else in life. Amen.

A number of us reading these words today might be regarded as serving in the role of a modern-day prophet, especially if we are among those who bring the word of God to congregations each week. The final words in today's reading are very direct: "Any prophet who speaks in the name of other gods, or who presumes to speak in my name a word that I have not command the prophet to speak—that prophet shall die."

How, then, do we heed this warning and discern what word God is telling us to bring? With so much at stake, how do we listen wholeheartedly to what God is telling us?

I was a pastor in Baptist churches most of my life, and I grew up believing that scripture was God's word. Period. End of story. But over the last twenty years, I have been introduced to the miracle of solitude and directed silent retreats. For someone like me— an evangelical, extroverted and programmed person—the experience of silence was indeed a miracle. During my very first seven-day silent retreat, God spoke to my life in a way that I had never known before.

An experience of silence does not negate the Bible as God's word, but I found that God also speaks the word to us in silent meditation. Be prepared: whether in silence or by other means, if we listen, God will speak.

When you reflect on those times when God spoke to you, what have you learned? What disciplines enable you to hear God's word?

Perhaps the most surprising part of this story is discovering that the man possessed by the evil spirit was in the synagogue on the Sabbath. Was he part of the congregation, a demented soul who wandered in desperate for help, or was the spirit in the man intending to be disruptive? We are not told.

What we are told is that Jesus taught with unusual authority—an authority even greater than the scribes, the most important and knowledgeable teachers in Israel. Jesus had authority because his teaching came from God. The evil spirit could no longer be silent. It challenged Jesus, who in turn commanded it to leave the man. We can only begin to imagine the stunned reaction of the congregation as the man shook violently and the spirit left him with a great shriek!

The people had never seen the like before—a teacher with such authority that evil spirits fled. Mark says that Jesus' fame (some translate this as "the reports about him") spread throughout the surrounding regions of Galilee.

A new era is ushered in. As Jesus described it, the reign of God comes close at hand. But has this anything to do with covenant? Absolutely. The covenant promise is that, in addition to marveling at the miracles of Jesus, we also join in the rest of his mission, by working to create a world of justice, generosity, and compassion.

What is my commitment to God's agenda in the world? What parts of my life witness to my faith? What parts of my witness need to be strengthened?

Idolatry and sacrifice to the gods was commonplace in ancient life. So it is not surprising that the question arose: Should Christians eat such meat, or for that matter, any meat, because its origin was always unclear? The church in Jerusalem had sent a letter urging all Christians to abstain. (See Acts 15:29.)

However, the issue was still a live one. Some Christians were convinced that to eat such meat was to expose themselves to malevolent spirits. Others were equally convinced that there was only the one God and the one Lord, Jesus, who had freed them from all superstition and fear.

This might, to us in the present day, seem an outdated and irrelevant issue. But, in fact, Paul's teaching here has great relevance. In speaking of care for those who are weaker or those who hold different ideas than others, Paul invokes an important principle: In the Christian community, love takes precedence over an individual's liberty to say or do whatever he or she wants. Paul says we should take account of how our actions affect others and honor the feelings of other community members.

Paul is not saying that we should avoid conflict or stifle discussion about differences in the community. He only asks that each member of the faith community be taken seriously, treated with respect, and shown compassion.

Paul's philosophy is summed up in Romans 15: "We who are strong ought to bear with the failings of the weak and not to please ourselves" (NIV).

Lord, how much time and energy do I spend trying to win arguments? Sometimes in my determination to put people right, I am plain wrong. Help me to be compassionate toward those whose opinions differ from mine. Amen.

It is unlikely that many of us will find ourselves in a situation even close to that which the Christians in Corinth found themselves. But before we move on, let us look again at the first verse in this passage: "Knowledge puffs up, but love builds up."

Decades ago when I was a new pastor serving in my first church in New Zealand, I met a Croatian couple. Rokko, the husband, had been a freedom fighter in his own country and came to New Zealand as a political refugee. New Zealand was a land of opportunity for him, and his priority was to buy land and build his family a home.

Rokko made a deposit on some land, pitched a tent and lived there while he paid the remainder of the mortgage and saved for a house. However, local laws did not allow him and his family to live in a tent in the middle of the city! I was able to help the couple with representation that eventually reached the prime minister. In the end they were offered a tiny but affordable apartment that still allowed them to save for their dream home.

Rokko and his family invited me and my family to their home one day to express their gratitude, producing a bottle of wine and chocolate biscuits. It would have cost them almost a week's housekeeping! I was a Baptist, and without thinking I said, "I'm sorry, but I don't drink wine." I cringe every time I recall my appalling thoughtlessness.

Some principles need to take second place to sensitivity and love. I learned Paul's message to the Corinthians that day, and I have not forgotten it.

Sometimes we offend more by style than by substance. When has this happened to you? When have you offended someone in this way? How do Paul's principle and Jesus' teachings inform your relationships with others?

The Healer of Brokenness

FEBRUARY 2–8, 2009 • BETH A. PALM

MONDAY, FEBRUARY 2 ~ *Read Isaiah 40:21-28*

Isaiah's message sounds somewhat like a parent talking to a child stressing the importance of long-held teachings. The reading begins with what we might say today as, "How many times have I told you . . . ," "Don't you know by now . . . ," etc. Isaiah stresses the timeless truths that God is powerful, sitting "enthroned" above the earth, equal to no one, the "everlasting God," and "the Creator of the ends of the earth."

Sometimes a reminder God's character helps us reset our perspectives. Perhaps Isaiah felt his readers needed a bit of a "talking to," an attitude adjustment. Isaiah might have been trying to lift their eyes from their own narrow view and look toward God to see the bigger picture. We all meet people who seem to have turned their eyes inward or downward and can only see things from one perspective. Sometimes we find we are the ones with our eyes turned toward self instead of toward God. Many times when our focus is turned inward, negative attitudes, misunderstandings, and impasses in communication cloud relationships.

Today's scripture helps us remember to notice where our eyes are focused. What might change if we lift our eyes, stop complaining, and look to the everlasting God, the Creator? If we hold our gaze on God and resist the urge to turn it back toward ourselves, how might we experience the Holy One in the circumstances of our lives?

Almighty God, fix my eyes on you, the creator of all, the author of my life. Teach me to look to you always. Fill me with your loving Spirit as I interact with others. Amen.

Writer, retreat leader, and spiritual director; completing certification in spiritual formation as a layperson in the United Methodist Church; living in Rockford, Illinois

Today's passage was the first I highlighted, as a youth, in my Bible. I found it when I was sixteen after stumbling, collapsing actually, when my father died. My world stopped. I floundered. I fell. I didn't know how I'd ever rise again. Weary? Tired? Most definitely, and in a way I didn't think was humanly possible.

The fact that God's word said that "Even youths grow tired and weary" told me that God was aware of my struggle. God knew the pain I was suffering as a sixteen-year-old longing for her dad. Even if I didn't understand how, God was present and would help me. A glimmer of hope from Isaiah's ancient words penetrated all the pain that surrounded me. I received Isaiah's passionate proclamation that our "LORD is the everlasting God." God's help and loving relationship is available to persons of all ages.

I've imagined how things would have been different if I hadn't had access to the Bible and teachers about the truths of God's character when my life shattered. I don't believe I'd still be alive to tell the story now. I can't imagine dealing with that pain without knowing God. I needed the love and support of God's people as I walked through the healing process. The world's options for coping with that kind of pain would have led me to destruction. Instead, I experienced the process of healing, and my spirit found freedom to soar with the eagles.

Everlasting God, thank you for reaching out to us when we stumble and fall. We are grateful for the strength you give us. Fill us with your healing spirit. Amen.

Reeling from the pain of a shattered heart caused at various times by differing circumstances, I've clung to the promise found in today's reading that God "heals the brokenhearted." Given time and tools of healing, I've experienced God's tending of my wounds. I've also witnessed God minister in others' lives and seen their mended hearts eventually proclaim joy that rises with their healing. God incorporates the gifts of healing tools of counselors, pastors, support groups, prayer groups, and the medical community to help heal our brokenness in life. With the gift of God's unfailing love, a heart and soul that has experienced intense pain can be transformed to a stage of healing where an individual can experience joy again.

The psalmist proclaims that the same Lord that has numbered the stars and is mighty in power will be faithful to bind our wounds. The feelings of brokenness are powerful, but God's love and care for us is unfailing. In time, our brokenness can mend in stages when we allow God into our pain and into our healing process. A broken heart needs a Savior, a healer, the Great Physician who can come to us with just the right salve to tend to our brokenness. Any number of factors in our journey through life can leave us brokenhearted. Yet, we are blessed to have a God whose "understanding has no limit." No matter the source of our pain, God as Healer comes with the tools to bind our wounds.

God, open our hearts to receive your healing. May we not resist help when we are in need. Give us courage to reach for the resources you put before us. Hear my prayers as I lift to you those I know who are brokenhearted and in need of your healing grace. Amen.

Today's psalm is full of praise for God who is mighty and amazing in power, love, and healing. The psalmist calls us to praise. The question is, "How can I praise if I'm still one who is brokenhearted?" In many psalms, both expressions of sorrow and praise exist in the same verse. Can someone recover from a wounded heart and return with an attitude of praise? Yes, because God's presence is at work in the person. Otherwise, it doesn't make sense.

A broken life might logically lead to an angry person, a person who believes she or he has good reasons to be bitter. A person can get stuck in a life ruled by those feelings, continually resisting the healing process, and avoiding God's healing. Often, however, people who have experienced tragic experiences don't remain in anger and bitterness. Instead, at some point, they come to experience transformation that leads to experiences of authentic praise.

When God is part of the healing process, people who are in the midst of difficult times *do* find strength to praise; they find the strength to praise, with a joyous voice. When you know in your own soul that you'd never be whole again without the power of God bringing you to a new day, praise can be a natural response to God's care.

Bring the music, sing, and dance. Praise the Lord and give God the glory. The healer is in our midst.

Listen to your favorite praise music or hymns. Sing along. Move to the Spirit. Express yourself in a way that authentically releases praise from your soul. Spend time today in adoration of God, the healer of broken hearts.

The morning news was on the television as my family prepared for the day. The anchor of the show was on location in a foreign country. I didn't notice what country or what religious building she was about to tour. My attention focused on the program when the highly esteemed American journalist asked the guide how she should present herself to be respectful.

In the country from which she was reporting, all women were required to cover their heads with scarves. She was asking questions to be certain she was wearing the scarf correctly before she entered the sacred building. She wisely showed humble respect as a guest in a new culture in a holy setting and became like her hosts, instead of insisting they become like her. By doing so, her respect opened doors for sharing life stories and spreading understanding among people.

I was impressed by her graciousness and thought of today's reading. Paul said he "became like a Jew, to win the Jews . . . became weak, to win the weak" doing so "for the sake of the gospel," that he may "share in its blessings" (NIV). Paul's manner of sharing the gospel and the newswoman's gracious way of entering a new area paved the way for each of them to hear others' stories and to tell their own stories.

By showing their respect, permission and trust were laid as a foundation for relationships to form and more stories to be shared. I believe Paul's message rings as true today as it did to the people of Corinth. Respectful relating and learning about one another opens doors to transforming relationships.

Gracious God, help us to look at one another through your eyes. Open our hearts to receive each other's stories. Help us today to approach someone we don't know, not as a stranger, but as a friend of yours we haven't met yet. Amen.

Today's passage from Mark's Gospel recounts the story of Jesus and the disciples returning to the home of Simon and Andrew after teaching in the synagogue. The scripture relates that the entire town came in the evening to the house and Jesus continued to heal many. Can you imagine the entire town coming to your house at the end of a long day of ministry wanting something from you? How would you receive them? How do you envision Jesus received them?

I imagine he welcomed them with warmth, compassion, and a healing touch. Jesus focused on the one in need. To do that, Jesus had to rely on the strength of God to meet the unrelenting requests with continual grace.

How do we meet the demands of the many while maintaining our compassion for the individual? Without respite and nourishment, our souls will dry up, and stress will break us apart. Our fast-paced world beckons us never to stop, but Jesus' ministry demonstrates another kind of leadership. Notice the scripture says that "all the sick" came and that "Jesus healed many." He didn't meet everyone's needs pressing in on him. He stopped to rest.

Throughout the Gospels, Jesus shows us how to balance the needs of ministry with needs for prayer and respite.

Think about the importance of rest, of balance, of nurturing others *and* nurturing yourself. Both body and spirit have ways of telling you it is time to stop, rest, and pray. What would it mean for you to listen to these signals—and then to stop, rest, and pray?

Choose a favorite spiritual practice, prayer, or retreat place to visit. Plan a deliberate time to meet with God in a quiet place to nourish your soul and ready you for a new day on your journey with Jesus.

I tiptoed down our creaky stairs, hoping not to wake the rest of my sleeping family. Like Jesus in today's Bible passage, I felt drawn in the early morning hours to seek God's presence in a quiet place. I hungered for time spent alone before meeting the demands of the day. Jesus' outdoor sanctuary was a mountain; mine is my backyard. Gently rocking in my swing, I listened to the birds, took in the sights of the garden, and prayerfully dwelt in the presence of God.

For me, the beginning of the new day spent outdoors envelops me with the gift of peace God offers. This peace refuels my spirit in the midst of the many demands of life. The dawning of a new day and the quietness of the morning that begins filling with the praise of songbirds and the work of bees is a holy time.

Soon the demands of ministry and responsibilities will come looking for Jesus and for me. My daughter often finds me out on the patio and comes out pajama-clad and sleepy-eyed saying, "Mom, I wondered where you were." I hear the words echoing hers of the disciples who searched for Jesus saying, "Everyone is looking for you." The day's needs begin begging for attention. Jesus is filled from his time in solitude and ready to meet the day. Jesus shows the anxious disciples with their pressing tasks the importance of prayerful solitude to equip themselves before they embark on the ministry ahead.

Where do you find peace and strength for the day ahead of you? Is there a specific place or time that calls you to quiet and solitude? What strengthens and renews you?

Try greeting the morning before the noise of the day or saying good-night to God outside in the quiet of the moon and the stars. Look around you; listen; notice the sounds, smells, and sights of creation. Meditate on what you notice and how it speaks to you of God's presence with you this day.

Living into Grace

FEBRUARY 9–15, 2009 • JOHNNY R. SEARS

MONDAY, FEBRUARY 9 ~ *Read 2 Kings 5:1-14*

In his book *Thoughts in Solitude*, Thomas Merton asks, "What is the use of praying if at the very moment of prayer, we have so little confidence in God that we are too busy planning our own kind of answer to prayer?"

I respond to problems by analyzing the situation and trying to "figure it out." This useful ability has its shadow side. I can put myself under a lot of stress looking for the big solution to a problem. Often, I imagine the solution will involve some heroic effort or change on my part.

What I've learned—more accurately, what I'm still learning—on my journey, is that I usually just need to let go of my need to fix it myself and to face the particular burden with faith. Then, I simply take that next, small step, and then the next one, and so forth until one day I realize that the issue I was struggling with has faded away. At that point, I look back and revel at the cumulative power of several "little graces" that God has granted.

Naaman got exactly what he was seeking—his leprosy was cured. He also got a practical lesson in humility and gained a new faith in the God of Israel. Yet, he nearly missed out on being healed because he had already decided for himself how his healing should take place. He came very close to missing out on his healing altogether.

To assume we know what our healing should look like is to put ourselves in the place of God. Prayer is all about trust. Without trust, our prayers are nothing more than self-help exercises.

God of great patience, forgive my need to be in control. Grant me the wisdom to wait for the power of your ever-present grace to reveal itself. Amen.

Husband and father, ordained deacon of Midway Baptist Church in Midway, Kentucky, retreat leader for Merton Institute, compliance manager for Lexmark International, Inc.

I believe many of the ills of the world today—wars, political division, social unrest, the "culture wars," even marital problems result from a failure to listen. Many have observed that the root of the gospel message is essentially relational: to love God and neighbor. A vital aspect of all healthy relationships is good communication, which requires listening. Prayer itself has more to do with listening to God than the other way around.

So . . . it would seem listening is a fundamental aspect of living the Christian life. Yet in our culture, the emphasis is on asserting our own message rather than listening to one another. Speaking up is a good thing but if no one's listening, what does it matter? In many current political situations, for instance, special interest groups use their financial influence to "shout" over one another while the mainstream public is fed up because it seems no one is listening to us.

Great leaders surround themselves with people who will speak truth to them and will take time to listen to that truth—even if they disagree. Naaman demonstrated his leadership and wisdom when he heeded the advice of his servants. What's more, he did this even while he was "in a rage." As a result, he was healed. Not taking time to listen is a guaranteed way to limit God's activity in our lives.

In the ministry of the church, we put a lot of emphasis on words—spoken and written. But do we give enough space to listening? People truly are longing to be heard. Perhaps the best gift we can offer a hurting world is deep, holy listening.

Loving God, teach me to listen with the ears of the heart. Amen.

Jesus commanded the leper, "Be made clean!" And indeed, the leprosy left him; but it appears Jesus had more than that in mind. Jesus' desire for us is complete restoration and wholeness. According to the law, the leper needed to present himself to the priests and offer a sacrifice in order to reenter society and be restored to the community. Without that, his leprosy may have been gone but he would remain ceremonially unclean and, therefore, an outcast.

The man was given all he needed for full restoration—he just needed to follow through. I wonder if he ever did, or if he settled for partial healing. The scriptures don't tell us if he followed through. What we do know is that he began to talk about his healing freely—despite being instructed not to by Jesus. It's easy to judge him for this; but if you think about it, you could hardly blame him. Who wouldn't want to tell everyone they saw about such an experience? It seems like a fairly natural reaction to me. Perhaps Jesus wanted the man's new life—a potentially transformed life—to speak for itself.

The real work of healing comes in integrating those encounters with Christ into everyday life and allowing them to transform our very being. Otherwise, we eventually default to our pre-encounter status quo. I wonder how many times Christ has spoken the words, "Be clean!" to me, giving me what I needed for healing, and I, instead settled for partial healing. Too often I have been content to talk about God's healing rather than allow it to really change my life in ways that made the words unnecessary. When that happens, I stunt the fullness of the cleansing God wants to give.

Christ the healer, I pray that you will cleanse me and that I receive it in full—obediently presenting my offering, my life, as witness. Amen.

Guilt is a powerful motivator. Churches and parents throughout the ages have mastered the art of social engineering through the use of guilt. Chances are that you've employed the proverbial guilt trip on many occasions in your own life.

All kidding aside, guilt does serve an important purpose. Indeed, guilty feelings help us recognize our mistakes and draw us to genuine repentance. It becomes an instrument of the healing and growth process when it drives us to examine ourselves and deal with the issues that cause unhealthy behaviors.

But when we hold on to our guilt and internalize it, we transform it into shame, and shame serves no helpful purpose. Shame makes us feel unlovable. It builds a wall that cuts us off from God and from others—the very opposite of what God desires!

Christians often say that God loves us unconditionally, but we rarely live as though we truly believe that. Instead, we somehow convince ourselves that we need to fix our own mistakes and brokenness before we can come to God. But it is God's grace that heals us. Our job is simply to keep ourselves open to it. Distancing ourselves from God by refusing to let go of our guilt only leaves us mired in our own mess. How can we live a life of joy and peace if we refuse to believe that God loves us just as we are?

The psalmist testifies that God's love is infinitely greater than God's anger and that each new day holds the promise of a fresh start. Imagine the freedom of living into that promise! It might just be enough to turn our mourning into dancing.

What keeps you from truly believing that God loves you unconditionally? What would it take for you to release that to God?

This psalm of praise and thanksgiving invites others to join in (v. 4). The heading of Psalm 30 reads, "A Song at the dedication of the temple." Although that was not the original occasion for the writing of the psalm, it was eventually employed to commemorate the purification of the temple in 164 BCE during the Maccabean revolt. This use illustrates the importance of practicing gratitude as individuals and as communities.

Gratitude, an essential quality in a life of faith; allows us to see beyond ourselves. Gratitude helps us to recognize our dependence on the provision of God, who is always faithful. In fact, the primary function of worship and religious ceremonies is to remember God's faithfulness and give thanks.

Sadly, we are conditioned to be unsatisfied and ungrateful. Every day, we are bombarded by images and messages that tell us our lives are incomplete, unhappy, and unfulfilled. In many ways, our economy depends on this lack of contentment because it makes us good consumers.

In such an atmosphere we can quickly become self-absorbed and unable to see the goodness of God working all around us. So, we need gratefulness. But a life of gratitude does not happen by accident. It must be cultivated. Like the Israelites, we must incorporate regular practices into our lives that train our hearts to be thankful.

Ask God to show you ways to practice gratitude on a daily basis. Consider memorizing some verses from a psalm to recite each morning.

Given the devotion around the world to sports, Paul's athletic metaphor is quite relevant to us. Becoming a world-class athlete requires single-minded dedication, discipline, and sacrifice. These aspects we understand and celebrate. Who isn't inspired by the human-interest stories on TV about athletes who have overcome tremendous obstacles and achieved greatness?

So when Paul speaks of running a race to win, he's speaking our language. But the real question for people of faith is this: Which race are you running? Are you in the proverbial rat race or the kingdom race? The race you choose determines what you devote yourself to because the rat race and kingdom race have many opposing values. Consider the lists below:

Rat-race values	Kingdom values
Busyness	Living an unhurried rhythm
Self-sufficiency	Intimacy and trust
Individualism	Community
Consumerism	Simplicity and contentment
Competitiveness	Humility

Living by one set of values closes us off from God. Living by the other opens us up to receive the full abundance of God's grace. Consequently, the manner in which you run will differ depending on the race you choose. Many of us, perhaps subconsciously, live under the illusion that we are capable of running both races at the same time. This double-mindedness creates internal turmoil and tension as the two value systems collide.

Rat-race values are so embedded in much of the world around us that it is extremely difficult to avoid falling into those behaviors. Still, as Christians we can demonstrate to a hurting world that there is an alternative to the rat race—one that leads to an imperishable prize.

In your daily life, which race do you choose most often? Why? What impact does this have on your life and those of others?

Busyness is an important value in the rat race because we've somehow come to believe that our value as a person is related to our level of productivity. Just ask someone how they've been and frequently the response will be, "Busy!" We wear it like a badge of honor.

I believe busyness is a significant threat to our spiritual well-being today. Our lives are fragmented and overcommitted. At our frantic pace, we rarely stop and evaluate why we do what we do or whether or not our activity is producing the kind of fruit God desires. If we're not careful, years can go by and leave us wondering what has happened to our lives. Paul warned us not to run aimlessly but, in many cases that seems like exactly what we're doing.

Structure, routine, and rhythm provide the stability necessary for growth and health. This rhythm and routine are key aspects of the Rule of Benedict that has guided the lives of many monastic communities throughout the centuries.

The antidote to busyness is to structure our lives around an intentional rhythm. Rhythm is steady, deliberate, and meaningful without being rigid and overburdening. It shapes and forms us slowly, little by little. Our primary task is to show up faithfully day by day. This creates space for grace to work in our lives as we put our trust in God to grow us rather than trying to achieve it on our own.

Without rhythm, we might miss out on truly living the life that God has provided and disqualify ourselves from the kingdom race.

Think about your daily patterns. Where do you see a natural rhythm? What small steps can you take to create regular space for grace? What can you do now to make today a real sabbath day?

Transformation

FEBRUARY 16–22, 2009 • MYRTLE E. FELKNER

MONDAY, FEBRUARY 16 ～ *Read 2 Kings 2:1-12*

These last few days of winter in Iowa find the farmers checking their tractors, repairing the corn planters, getting ready for spring's field work. Elisha, the farmer in our scripture, must have felt that same sense of anticipation as he plowed his fields.

Then along came Elijah and threw his mantle over Elisha. Elisha knew immediately that this put an end to plowing. Elijah, that intrepid man of God, had indicated that Elisha would be his disciple and successor. Elisha knew this call was both immediate and sacred; he would not return to farming.

Eli learned from Elijah and stayed with him on the difficult journey from Gilgal to the Jordan. Bound to Elijah when he accepted God's call to be a prophet, he saw in Elijah's ascent into heaven the very face of God.

The power of the transfiguration comes to us in a myriad of ways.

I experience God's glory and power in the thunderstorm. I know God's encompassing compassion as I watch my toddler grandchild, legally blind from birth, explore the dimensions of his world. God is revealed in the love that binds me to this green land.

The magnificence of Elijah's transfiguration evoked in Elisha both terror and joy. Elisha is torn by the grief of Elijah's leaving but astounded by the power of this moment. Elisha, the one so long dependent on his teacher, now becomes the one who will work and speak for God. Elisha answered God's call after Elijah's transformation. We can do no less.

God's self-revelation awaits. Pray that you will be receptive to God's presence today as God transforms your life.

Christian educator and author, active in the ministries of Faith United Methodist Church in Centerville and of the Iowa Conference; living in Centerville, Iowa

At dusk one evening a mother raccoon emerged from under a shed, leading her four young cubs to snuff in the grass beneath my birdbath. One young raccoon climbed the maple tree until he came to the attached wire clothesline. Hanging upside down, this little cub "walked" the clothesline until he came to the bird feeders that hung on the wire. He reached out a paw, grasped the feeder, and tilted it to one side. Sunflower seeds cascaded to the ground. Satisfied, he crabbed back along the wire, found purchase on the tree, and joined his siblings in feasting on the seeds.

A deer stepped from the timber and paused to watch the raccoons, ears lifted in alert attention. Just then my telephone rang. The clamor sent the animals scurrying. The deer bounded back to the timber, and the raccoons scurried to hide in the branches of the maple tree. I laughed aloud in delight. That bandit raccoon was welcome to the seed. The gift to me was an experience of God's wondrous creativity and sense of humor!

Psalm 50 declares, "Out of Zion, the perfection of beauty, God shines forth." In sudden and unexpected ways, God breaks into our lives with power, joy, and wonder. Sometimes God's in-breaking comes with great noise. Other times, God appears in quiet and solitude. Either way, we experience God, and our world shifts.

God was revealed to me in the antics of the animals, in the resourcefulness of those nuisance raccoons, in the beauty and grace of the doe. With the psalmist, I can rejoice that God breaks into my life with joy and wonder.

Eternal and loving God, may I see today that you shine forth in the perfection of beauty. May my gratitude for your world be my offering to you. Amen.

My husband and I were flying our light aircraft over the Midwest right after a rain shower. The sun came out and, as we flew across the landscape, every puddle and pond caught the rays of the sun and reflected them to us. The psalm suggests that just as every bit of collected water reflected the sun that day, so must we faithfully reflect to the world around us God's light shining in us. To be part of God's creation means there can be no half measures: we cannot forget God or give our mouth "free rein for evil."

Prejudice, gossip, untruths and insincerity are foreign to those who love God. All that we say, all that we do must reflect God as surely as those puddles threw the sunlight back into our faces over Kansas.

Moments like the one I experienced flying over the Midwest are beautiful moments. And they are critical because of their power to change lives. Through God, our ordinary days are made extraordinary. So we can call on God in our days of trouble. We can bring our thanksgivings as sacrifices to honor God. God has come into our lives with power and life-changing clarity. This is the psalmist's joyous message.

We see our world drenched with light. And God is the source, the bringer of light and life.

God of light and mercy, break into my life today. Forgive me when I have ignored the light that is in my brother or sister. Grant me the courage to be your disciple. Help me to be open to your powerful presence and to give you thanks. Amen.

I chuckled as I watched the new spring calves playing "king of the mountain" on a mound of dirt near the edge of the timber. Not so many years ago our young children played the same game there. It does seem as though a "top dog" gene thrives among all God's creatures—human and animal!

Paul found out that some folks in Corinth, the city where he had worked with such energy and faithfulness, now suspect him of self-commendation. Paul hastens to deny and correct this impression. He is no top dog, not what some would call a "peddler of God's word." Instead, he speaks to the people of Corinth sincerely in Christ. His words are bold: "For we do not proclaim ourselves; we proclaim Jesus Christ as Lord and ourselves as your slaves for Jesus' sake."

Paul insists that the same God who created light from darkness, who created the universe itself, is shining that holy light into the hearts of those who accept and believe in Jesus. Paul takes no credit for this transformation in their lives, but acknowledges the grace and power of God.

Paul leaves us no wiggle room, does he? We who have received the light of Jesus Christ in our hearts are bound to reflect that light. God's love and grace are best seen through those who serve, those who love with purity, and those on whose tongues we hear only praise of God through Jesus Christ.

On days we feel we're on top of the mountain, on days we feel fragile and low, Paul's words encourage us with their testimony that God's divine splendor is always near to us. God's light shines on us, sustaining us and keeping us faithful.

Loving God, help us be faithful witnesses to your love and power, that others may come to see your light shining through us. Amen.

Early in 2 Corinthians 4 Paul declares himself a slave to the Corinthians for Jesus' sake. Even after much persecution Paul has not lost heart; he is willing to hang in there in order that the gospel of Jesus Christ might come alive in the people of Corinth. Paul warns again that there can be no self-righteousness in us; by Jesus' life and death we are all shown to be of value to God and are to be nurtured through God's love and grace.

The light to which Paul witnesses shines on all people, all the time. Paul reminds us that this light shines out of darkness and that it illuminates the hearts of all believers, no matter who or where they are.

My Danish immigrant father loved meeting the many different people of his new country. He threw back his head in laughter as he told us of his early experiences in America. He was delighted with his own contribution to this melting pot of races and religions. He sang lustily in church and field, read his Bible every day, and lived a life of hardship and friendship.

Today our global family is ever more closely tied together. What affects our sisters and brothers in Africa or New Zealand, Iran or Sweden, Palestine or Jerusalem most certainly affects all of humankind. Paul's words both reproach us and challenge us. They reassure us that, though the battle for faith is real, the light of Christ illumines our way and keeps us on the path.

Though we live in a different world than Paul did, one thing is still clear: God strengthens us so we do not lose heart. What might this mean for you as you go about your life and work today?

Peter, James, and John have gone with Jesus to a high mountain. The events there happened six days after Jesus' remarkable disclosure that he must suffer greatly, be rejected and killed, and finally rise again. Earlier, Jesus had asked the disciples, "Who do you say that I am?" Peter had answered fervently, "You are the Messiah." But even Peter—bold and fervent—was surprised at the transfiguration of Jesus.

As a teacher I am aware that most of us need to hear new information several times before we internalize and remember it. This, however, was not new information for Peter. That Jesus was the Messiah was an often-repeated truth, but it became obvious that the disciples had not yet internalized this information. Peter, James, and John needed the dramatic sight of the transfiguration of Jesus in order to get the message: Jesus was truly divine and truly human, Son of God and Son of Man. Seeing Jesus transfigured made it all real to the beloved three. The shining white garments of Jesus were a sign of his divinity. The voice of God was heard from the cloud.

These words from the cloud are reminiscent of the words God spoke at Jesus' baptism. But there is one difference: At the transfiguration, God states emphatically, "This is my Son, the Beloved; listen to him!" The message is straightforward: The disciples have watched Jesus' deeds, but they have not understood his words. Focused on the glory and work of Jesus, they have missed the meaning of his words: Jesus must suffer in order to triumph. There is no glory without the cross.

In whom do you see God at work today? How have you been a witness to God's presence? How can you use the gifts that God has given you to transform part of your world today?

TRANSFIGURATION SUNDAY

If I've told you once, I've told you a hundred times: don't squeeze the bread," a mother scolded the toddler riding in her grocery cart. Sometimes children are distracted and just don't listen well. So it was with Peter, James, and John. God spoke to them from a cloud on the mountain, not only identifying Jesus as the Beloved but admonishing the disciples, "Listen to him!" The transfiguration of Jesus must have been a powerful message; the words and deeds of Jesus were those of God the Almighty. It was time to listen up. All that Jesus spoke and taught and did was God-made-known.

But Peter and James and John are puzzled. First God tells them to listen to Jesus, and then Jesus warns them to say nothing about his transfiguration until after he rose from the dead. How, why, where, when, what—all these questions must have flooded their minds. Questions continue to plague the disciples as Jesus goes from that place to Capernaum, where he continues to heal, teach, and reveal God's will.

The transfiguration of the church is yet to happen. We see signs of that possibility in the happiness of children as they explore God's word, in earnest youth in the throes of growing up, in adults who care and serve, in the elderly whose wisdom sustains us.

Like the disciples, we too have questions, and sometimes we too are afraid to ask them. We may spend our lifetime searching for understanding, but the answers are there. Jesus has told us and shown us—a hundred times.

Come, Jesus, reveal God to me, to my church, and to the world. Transform me so that I may listen and understand. Amen.

Gracious Water, Gracious God

FEBRUARY 23–MARCH 1, 2009 • TERRELL M. MCDANIEL

MONDAY, FEBRUARY 23 ~ *Read Genesis 9:8-17*

God seems to love using water as a symbol in covenants with earth creatures. Water, one of the strongest elements known, cannot be destroyed by normal means. It can only change form—from liquid to solid to gas. Yet it can, on occasion, cause great destruction: by flood, as it did in Noah's day, or one drop at a time until a canyon is formed.

On the other hand, water seems to be quite gentle and obedient to God's will. It meanders downhill finding its own way, respecting obstacles in its path until it finds a way around or through them. Water portrays the perfect balance of power and passive acceptance—the ingredients of serenity. Perhaps that is why we often feel so comforted in its presence.

Don't forget that water is also the mystical, essential "stuff" of life itself. It heals, cleans, and nourishes. It covers most of the earth and is the main component of our own bodies! Water protects us in the womb and replenishes us as we live each day.

It is no accident that God chooses water and light—two elements of life-giving power—as the central symbols for the new covenant with us: the light of the world, reflected through something common—earthly but powerful—to reveal the possibilities of a world reconciled with God.

If you don't see a rainbow today, sip a tall glass of water. Enjoy the blessing of having your thirst quenched and your body refreshed. Express your praise and gratitude for the blessings of the earth, those of the spirit, and the life-giving, mystical connection between the two.

Clinical and corporate psychologist; attends Belmont United Methodist Church, Nashville and New Community Church, Hendersonville, Tennessee

God reveals to us the divine desire for reconciliation with God's children. And although we often read this passage as symbolic of God's covenant with us humans, we are reminded that it is a covenant made with all the earth. Every time God mentions humanity, all the other living creatures and the earth itself also are mentioned. This is no small matter: If you read the passage aloud, you cannot help but notice this emphasis on inclusion in God's promise. We are a part of something bigger, and we must view ourselves in the context of a living world in which God is in loving control.

This point has not been lost on the sparrow (Matt. 10:29), a happy creature whose bird-sized brain rests assured that God is looking out for him or her. But we humans, with our impressive neo-cortex, are a more complicated matter. We have the potential to be God's helpers in extending grace and righteousness to the world, but we become alienated. We seem to have more difficulty than the rest of nature in accepting God's grace to us and thus feeling the joy of true reconciliation—reconciliation not just with God but with nature, one another, and the rest of God's family.

Jesus taught us that we must be like the sparrow. If so, perhaps we could find happiness. Today's passage reminds us of a God who desires to be in relationship and to celebrate an everlasting covenant where no one—and no thing on earth—is left out. To live in such communion is our heart's desire. So why can't we let go and let our heads believe?

God, I suffer when I am disconnected from you and the rest of our family. Thank you for your love for me and for your commitment to help me be whole through reconciliation. Amen.

On this special day we celebrate our connection to the earth; but we also experience, in concrete terms, the humility of our earthly limitations.

While most of nature rests securely in God's loving arms, humans seem restless. Realizing our potential, we long to do more than live out our lives on earth. We yearn to actualize our spirits, to realize the promise of our ability to think and feel, and to find immortality. Ironically, we end up feeling alienated, acting primarily in disobedience to God's way.

To say, "I come from ashes, and to ashes I will return" in the Ash Wednesday ceremony is not to degrade the earth, for the earth is God's blessing to us. The earth is our partner in God's creation and covenant. Instead of indicting us, being "grounded" by our earthly nature is a good place to start our journey toward reconciliation with God. Being made of ashes, we must reach outside of our physical world for the power to be more.

Today's passage reveals that, once reconciled, we can become "the righteousness of God" on earth, no less! Imagine! To become a living instrument of God's grace! However, as Jesus demonstrated to us, this kind of greatness is born only of humility. We begin our journey from the lowly place of dirt, ashes, and water.

Tonight accept and appreciate the sense of water's gentle touch as you wash off the cross of ashes. Pledge to respond in good conscience in the coming days to God's movement of reconciliation in your life.

Show me your ways, O LORD" (NIV). The psalmist is certainly responding in good conscience as he implores God to show him God's ways and to teach him God's paths.

What is the way of the Lord? I'm not sure that anyone can really define it in its entirety. It's big . . . really big—like God is. It's profound, elegant, simple, and right in front of our noses. We see it in scripture, the structure of DNA, a child's laugh, a sunset, broccoli. (Yes, broccoli!)

For instance, we would do well to follow the example of water (described on Monday) for following the path that God has set out for us. We can learn from water if we are humble enough. Consider the carving of a canyon one drop at a time, signifying both power and passive acceptance.

But living humbly is the problem, isn't it? At least it is for me. I may have some profound moments when I feel close to God, humble, expectant, open, thankful. But a lot of my life is spent being full of myself. I get wrapped up in and react to events. And while I am fretting, I miss the green in the broccoli, the beauty in the sunset, or the moment (ah, that moment!) of hearing my own child's laughter.

Embarrassing as it is to admit, God shows me the way; and I ignore it. And when I try to live by the way, I inevitably blow it. I think that the psalmist knows this about himself too, because he asks for mercy, love, and forgiveness. Thankfully we need not rely on our own perfection but on God's love for us in order to live in God's covenant.

I was born of earth and water, but on my own I cannot even be as obedient as they. Have mercy on me, and according to your love remember me. My hope is in you, O Lord. Amen.

A ll the ways of the LORD are loving and faithful for those who keep the demands of his covenant" (NIV). Uh-oh. I'm in trouble. "According to your love, remember me, for you are good, O LORD." Whew. Thank goodness for God's grace.

I believe that grace is a big part of the way, and it seems the psalmist shares my perception. Grace is a goodness, a connectedness, an acceptance drenched in love and inseparable from God. It is powerful and reflected in everything God has made. Most important, grace is so abundant that it flows over us like water, quenching our thirst and making us clean, fresh, and whole.

And, oh boy, do we ever need it. We need it extended to us. We need it to heal us. Ultimately we need to reflect it through us toward everyone and everything else with which we have contact. We just can't quite make grace happen on our own, though. So we become alienated. We struggle. We allow ourselves to be put to shame, as was the psalmist.

Here is where Jesus Christ comes in. He literally embodies grace and extends it gladly. He teaches us to live with, by, and for grace. He reconciles us with God and loves us because of, and in spite of, our humanness. Jesus "went the distance" for us because he knew we needed hope and salvation. He does these things not because he knows the way but because he is the way.

From ashes I have come and to ashes I will return, but to you, O Lord, I lift up my soul.

Breathe normally in meditation, but as you inhale, humbly pray, "Teach me your ways, O Lord." As you exhale, allow yourself to feel God's grace flow over you.

For those of us baptized as youths or adults, our excitement about acknowledging God's grace is mixed with some concern about the future. What changes will our newfound profession of faith require of us? Exactly how are we to handle things differently now that we have submitted to God's will (or at least committed to learn how to do so)? How do we learn to rely on grace?

It is reassuring to know that Jesus must have experienced some of the same concern as he looked to his future. In his traditional role as part of the Godhead, dealing with this old world might have been a snap. But in human skin, it is likely that Jesus felt some of the same anxiety—and maybe even some of the resistance—that you or I might feel about facing our futures.

Yet despite any anxiety or resistance Jesus might have felt, he submitted to the Father's plan, communing with our world through baptism with earth's water. As soon as he emerged, Jesus, the human, got to feel the exhilaration of the Father's approval! Not long after, he also got a heavy dose of temptation. Later he began to translate his commitment into action.

Once again water is central to the covenant, a soothing balm for our worries. It serves as an earthy reminder of God's gentle, indestructible, and powerful gift of grace, and of God's promise to be with us as we fulfill the missions of our lives.

Today remember your baptism. How might you rely on grace to get you through today's trials?

O God, how I want you to be pleased with me! But I fear what is in store for me if I truly submit to your will. Please help me to rely on you, your promises, and your grace. Amen.

FIRST SUNDAY IN LENT

I just realized what I like about this passage. Although we are in the first week of the Lenten season, this passage gives away the ending.

You and I are the beneficiaries of a most gracious deal. The problem is that on our own we can't live up to our end of the bargain. Miraculously our benefactor paid our debt by sending the Son, who taught us how to live. What's more, the Son defeated death for us so that we may be permanently reconciled with God, living forever in communion. The water of our baptism symbolizes the extraordinary grace that is synonymous with God's way. Praise be to God, the author of this miraculous love!

It has been an honor to have you with me each day of this special week. The presence of your spirit and the awareness of your journey were a blessing to me as I wrote. Whether this is your first Lenten season or your one hundredth, I would like, in the words of Paul (2 Cor. 5:20), to "entreat" you on behalf of Christ, be reconciled to God. God waits patiently and lovingly for your commitment. Drink in the blessings of grace that fall on you like rain each day, and seek to be humble, mindful, and obedient to your Lord. And I look forward to hearing the miraculous stories of how God used you, an humble servant, as an instrument of God's perfect righteousness and outrageous grace.

God, Father, Mother of all the earth, I accept your incredible gift of grace and, most important, the sacrifice of Christ Jesus when he defeated death so that I may have eternal life. I pray that I might understand more each day how to be mindful, thankful, and obedient to your will. Amen.

Faith, Grace, and Surprises

MARCH 2–8, 2009 • CURTIS S. ACKLEY

MONDAY, MARCH 2 ~ *Read Genesis 17:1-4*

Abram was ninety-nine years old. He and his wife Sarai, herself ninety years old, had been faithful to God through all these years. But promise after promise that he would produce more heirs than the grains of sand hadn't yet happened; so perhaps his "twilight years" would be different from those he had first contemplated.

What must he and Sarai make of the remarkable words of God in this story? The idea that at their great age they would become critical to the great history of their faith must have left them both incredulous. It's interesting that they laughed about it. It was an odd promise, but maybe their laughter was born not from giddy belief that God's promise would come true.

The real mystery of God's calling is that God sees qualities in each of us that may make little sense to us. Abram and Sarai knew that they had messed up many times in their lives. The scriptures are full of colorful stories that highlight their foibles. But that didn't matter so much to God: what God wanted most was their complete belief and trust. Without it, they couldn't have imagined the role that they would play in God's unfolding story. Without their trust, the promise might have remained just that—only a promise.

Once in a while something—or someone—surprises us and puts us on a new path. Can you recall a time when your life was changed by a surprise? How did you experience God as you tried to respond to the unexpected in your life?

Minister and executive of the Western Reserve Association, Ohio Conference of the United Church of Christ; an active member of Pilgrim United Church of Christ in Cleveland, Ohio

As Abram and Sarai begin their new adventure, God renames them. Now Abram will be known forevermore as Abraham ("ancestor of a multitude"), and Sarai is given the name Sarah ("woman of high rank"). It is an important moment in their lives, even though it comes at such an advanced age. God is inviting them to become someone totally new and to live into a vision of a nation yet unborn.

No doubt, the nine months of Sarah's pregnancy must have given them both time to begin to imagine themselves as the ones God saw them to be. Clearly, they lived up to their new names, and all of Hebrew and Christian history grows out of that miracle.

How powerful it is to embrace a name! God claims us by naming us: "I have called you by name, you are mine" (Isa. 43:1). We claim the best in children when we shape them by naming their good qualities and behaviors. We claim parts of ourselves that we want and own by naming them. There is real power in saying, "I am competent and caring," instead of using negative words like, "I am simply no good at this, and I can't do it!"

Might a Lenten discipline emerge for you from this line of thinking? What is your most positive aspiration for yourself? If you could select a name for yourself, what would it be? Can you imagine being called that name by God? What would it be like to "adopt" that name for the remainder of Lent?

Take some prayer time to bring yourself quietly into God's presence. Imagine that God comes to you, and invites you into a surprising new chapter in your life. By what name do you hear God calling you? What does it feel like to be loved that deeply?

Iam fascinated by the curiosity of children. Watching a young child examine a new toy carefully, trying to figure it out, reminds me of my own childhood. As the preacher's kid, I was often the subject of my dad's newsletter columns. He wrote one about me as a three-year-old, in which he pointed out my propensity to double my questions. "What's in it and what makes it go?" apparently was the standard formula. One day, I pressed these two questions while in my dad's care. The object of my questions was the produce scale. He stooped down, carefully explaining the device, and in the process he tore the paper bag that was on the scale, sending oranges rolling in every direction. While the chuckling folks behind him helped gather the oranges, I remained silent for a bit. When all the oranges had been gathered, I happily piped up again, "What's in it and what makes it go?"

"That," he wrote, "is when we left!"

Paul, explaining faith and grace, as opposed to law and judgment, gets straight to the point. If our life in God depends on the law, he says, we're in big trouble. But if faith is real, then grace happens; the transformation of life moves from generation to generation. Paul's logic is unswerving; his conclusion is inescapable.

What's in it? Grace. Freedom. The transformation of our world. And what makes it go? Our faith that the promise has come to all the children of Abraham and Sarah.

Grace is what's in it, and faith is what makes it go.

Today I offer you every ounce of my faith, God. I don't understand the mystery of your love, but you have promised that my faith is enough to lead me to grace. For that, I give you thanks, and I share this joy with others. Amen.

Jimmy showed up that morning at our church in his wheelchair, wearing the best clothes he owned. He had come with about a half dozen other residents of the group home in our area that serves developmentally challenged adults. He took great joy in the liturgy; his ear-to-ear smile made that clear. But his disease-ravaged body kept his muscles from doing what he wanted to do.

One Sunday something odd happened. The usual smooth transition into the Prayer of Our Savior wasn't going so smoothly. Listening carefully, I realized that, word by struggling word, it was Jimmy's voice setting the pace of the prayer. Breathing instinctively, as one body, each member of the congregation was following his lead, word by word.

Jimmy had studied all week so he could participate, we learned later. On his way out that day, he signaled me to get down on one knee in front of him, and I heard him say, "I . . . want . . . to . . . join . . . this . . . church!" We cried as we heard him make his statement of faith—faith in God and faith in us to support his journey.

A month later, Jimmy came forward to say his vows. We had a candlelighting ceremony at the altar that day. Two ushers prepared to lift Jimmy's chair up the uninviting step at the chancel so he could light his candle. "No!" he said. "I want to walk!" With one usher supporting each arm, he made his way out of his chair to the altar. As the congregation sang "This Little Light of Mine," there was no flame brighter than Jimmy's spirit. And his smile was reflected in the faces of his church family, the community that Jimmy's own joy had transformed.

How have you experienced the words of the psalm, "For he did not despise the affliction of the afflicted"? Who in your life reminds you of God's great deliverance?

For Abraham, the physical evidence all pointed the other way. Everything about his life said it couldn't possibly be true. But he had the words "from a reliable source" that he would be the father of many nations. So, turning aside all arguments to the contrary, he clung to his hope against hope that what he believed in his heart was true.

How hard it is for us sometimes to do that! We hit a rough patch in life. A friend says, "You know it will work out—has God ever abandoned you before?" In the middle of our own despair, it's sometimes hard to believe that. It can be hard to remember what it's like to be so caught up in hope and possibility.

But, just as it was for Abraham and Sarah, the way forward is a path lit by hope and abundance—not scarcity and fear. The church I belong to is itself a testament to that kind of hope. Fifteen years ago, down to only a handful of members in a declining part of inner-city Cleveland, the church's future looked very bleak. The pastor who came to serve saw evidence to point to the impossibility of its survival. But out of this handful of people grew a vision of a welcoming, open, and affirming community committed to peace. Today its five hundred members are transforming the community, even as they are themselves transformed by a vision rooted in hope. "I'm not done with this church or with you," God seems to say. Hoping against hope, the people of Pilgrim Church prove it every day.

When in your life have you felt hopeless? Who spoke to you in those moments? How was God present to you? What can you learn from having been through those moments? What will strengthen your own "hope against hope" in the future?

Needle's Eye is a mountain pass a few miles from the border between Arizona and New Mexico. If you come from the West Coast, as I did, you will have traveled through miles of scrubland and desert before you come to it. I arrived on a bicycle, two weeks into a coast-to-coast trip the year I turned fifty. Grinding uphill for hours, you can see the peak the entire time. You traverse switchback after switchback. Your eyes are sore from days of hot, brown scrubland. The end of the climb seems to taunt you because at each turn, the road doubles back yet again. It was at lunchtime that, jelly legs and all, I finally managed to park my bike at the top.

I surprised even myself, because I got there without walking my bike. Speaking to a friend who made it up ahead of me, I stammered out something about how maybe we should build three booths or something, referring to the mountaintop in the story of the Transfiguration. I did the final quarter mile up and came to the most incredible downhill I experienced on the trip. Desert scrubland gave way to verdant, fragrant pine forest. On this side, the mountain caught the clouds and their life-giving rain. The temperature dropped 20 degrees as I flew down the hill. To this day I remember that moment as a great transformation for me.

That challenge became a metaphor for life. I underestimated that day's impact on my life. The disciples too might have missed the point of their mountaintop experience with Jesus. He took them up the mountain to prepare them for their ministry after he was gone. Later on, they must have recognized the transfiguration as their turning point as well.

What mountaintop experiences have you had? What did you heard God saying to you in those moments?

SECOND SUNDAY IN LENT

The events on the mountain were no doubt riveting. Peter was left stammering, wanting to mark the event with a booth. Certainly the vision of Jesus talking with Moses and Elijah is not the stuff of everyday life. Yet God's voice interrupts Peter's terror and awe, and tells him to pay attention to the present. "This is my Son, the Beloved; listen to him!" says God. Simply marking this moment as important is not enough. Pay attention! This isn't about Moses and Elijah. It is about Jesus. Don't miss the point.

How much the disciples must have wanted to stay put, to see if they could make sense out of all of this. But Jesus calls them down the mountain again, and even swears them to secrecy about what they've seen. This experience was for them, and not everyone else just yet. There is still work to do, and that work is down the mountain.

There's a balance at stake in all of this. Abraham and Sarah become father and mother of untold generations of the faithful— but their faith happens in each individual moment. The psalmist reminds us that God loves us all—and is not put off by our afflictions. Jesus shows the disciples the majesty of what is about to unfold and how it will transcend even deepest tragedy—but he calls them down the mountain again into the days that unfold in the final steps of Jesus' earthbound journey.

In every moment with God comes the transcendent—the possibility of touching the fringes of heaven. And in the same moment comes the imminent, the close-enough-to-touch-it life that happens as God's love unfolds.

God, as you call me to the mountains of my faith, give me the strength to climb, the faith to perceive, and the wisdom to follow you. Help me be prepared to see your glory in every moment of this day. Amen.

Looking Beyond Labels

MARCH 9–15, 2009 • WILLIAM STILLMAN

MONDAY, MARCH 9 ~ *Read 1 Corinthians 1:18-25*

On my way to the post office one day, I passed by a large antique mall. I felt drawn to it, so I stopped in on the way home. Walking three floors of crafts, antiques, and just plain junk, I kept wondering why I was there. Twice I said, either out loud or to myself, "Okay, show me what I'm supposed to see." Each time, I turned a corner and saw an image of Christ, a vintage picture, or a plaque. I interpreted these as simple synchronicities.

Finally, I bought a book. I had wondered if I was supposed to stumble upon an artifact of mystical relevance or bump into someone I knew, but nothing stunning had happened. As I was leaving, an older couple walked in with their son, a man with Down syndrome. The son stopped, looked at me, and gave me his greeting. I smiled broadly and said, "Good morning," in return. Looking up, I noticed a sign on the wall behind him reminding us of the "Christ" in Christmas. In that moment, I realized the peaceful greeting the man and I exchanged was precisely what we each required of the world.

The moment reminded me that we must cherish small, quiet instances and not be so intent on seeking something more spectacular than real life itself. Paul gave this same reminder to the Corinthians when he redirected them from demanding signs and wisdom. We, Paul says, proclaim Christ crucified—the antithesis of all that.

Christ made the moment between me and the man at the market possible. Christ gives us not the signs or wisdom we demand, but instead blesses us with his presence in our everyday lives.

God, let me look not to signs or to wisdom but to you. Amen.

Autism self-advocate, speaker, and author of Autism and the God Connection *and* The Soul of Autism; *see* www.williamstillman.com

One afternoon, I visited my grandmother at her retirement home apartment. She was then in her early nineties and, like some other elderly citizens of that age, she felt despondent about her "purpose" in life. She was increasingly frustrated; she didn't feel as though she was contributing anything to anyone, and she openly wondered why she was still among the living. After lunch, we sat on her couch facing the window of her third-floor apartment with its expansive view of a verdant hillside. We spoke of spiritual things, angels, and dreams; and, for the first time, she shared that she was now having dreams that seemed increasingly profound though she could not recall specific details; some included a reunion with my grandfather who had passed thirty-five years earlier.

Turning to look back out the window, we both saw a vivid rainbow arc that stretched across the skyline, then faded, and reemerged several times. It was so beautiful and unexpected, we immediately rose to our feet and went out on the balcony to view the arc in its entirety, tracing its tail that ended in the field across the street.

After lamenting that she doesn't know why she's still here at ninety-three, we decided that if she hadn't lived so long, she wouldn't have seen the breathtaking rainbow. She said she'd never seen one like it before. She expressed gratitude for the rainbow and interpreted it as a spiritual sign, which somewhat surprised me. It was a very blessed and touching moment.

The beginning of Psalm 19 praises the glories of God evident in God's handiwork. "There is no speech, nor are there words," the psalmist says, yet God's glories are proclaimed and call out to us all. In this Lenten season, we are given moments like these so that we may listen—and hear—with our hearts.

Today, open my eyes and ears to the glories that are all around me, God. Keep me mindful of you and of your son, Jesus.

Recently I had the pleasure of making a presentation to an audience that included several persons with disabilities. Among them was a gentleman named Donald who sat in the very first row with his support aide. Donald, by all appearances, is someone who challenges popular notions about competence, impairment, and intellect. Throughout my speech, Donald would intermittently rock, make vocalizations, and stand spontaneously in front of the room. To the casual observer, this might have been chalked up to stereotypical "behaviors." But my host made it clear that Donald's "behaviors" were in fact his intentional communications with us.

My host pointed out that when in my lecture I talked passionately about hidden intelligence, Donald began reacting, supporting me in ways only he could by rocking and vocalizing his clarion approval. My lecture began to feel, at times, like an old-time revival! When I asked for a volunteer to imitate a physical rocking movement, Donald rose up and stood next to me—he knew he could demonstrate this kind of rocking best! I gave a reading, and Donald stood beside me again, allowing me to stroke his back gently as he listened intently. Every time I extended my hand to Donald, he accepted it lovingly.

Despite his support aide telling me Donald would likely not be able to tolerate a day-long presentation, Donald was a full participant in the entire meeting. In fact, Donald was a great teacher for me and for the others who were there that day. We just had to find our way toward his ways of communication, to learn from him on his terms.

Paul in his letter to the Corinthians makes a similar claim for Jesus: Christ crucified can be a stumbling block to some. But when we accept Jesus' own peculiar power and wisdom, we understand that God's weakness is stronger than our strength could ever be.

Lord, your ways are different from our ways. Teach us to learn from you and from others you place in our path today. Amen.

Imagine growing up across the street from an active playground and being completely invisible. As the oldest of four boys, I became aware of my differences at an early age. My brothers played with children who didn't even know they *had* an older brother. I was a nonentity, in the seclusion of my own company. Asperger's Syndrome (mild autism) frequently kept me from understanding unwritten social skills and developing friendships,

In adolescence, I was an easy target for abuse from my peers, and for years I endured physical harassment, verbal lacerations, and public humiliation. It was a dark era in my life—one that fueled hopelessness, deep depression, and post-traumatic stress disorder. It wasn't until I was a young adult that I rediscovered the spirituality I had blocked because I resented God for not rescuing me.

During this reawakening, I had a powerful dream. In the dream, all of my adversaries were seated at a very long table. They were seated, but I—interestingly enough—was standing. I walked behind them and, one by one, leaned down to kiss each on the cheek in an act of forgiveness. After that dream, I was healed. I was never again plagued by nightmares of abuse. I awakened to a full understanding of the power, the beauty, and the importance of forgiveness in our lives.

The commandments in Exodus may appear to have nothing to do with forgiveness and everything to do with rules and restrictions. But God's commands have at heart a concern for right relationships—between us and God and among ourselves in the human community. These "rules" help us order our lives in a covenant where no one is abused or exploited, where all are valued and respected.

When these commands are ignored, relationships get broken. And when that happens, forgiveness is the only way back to the commandments—to true community and communion with God.

God, keep me under the care and direction of your commandments. Amen.

The youngest of my four brothers took his life last year. He had several times considered terminating his pain but he was afraid of being banished to hell if he killed himself. I wrestled with this: If God is love, does it make sense that those souls most vulnerable and conflicted, yet lacking fortitude to persevere, would be given over to eternal damnation?

Then one night I awakened from a dream that graced me with a very different understanding of "hell." Rather than seeing hell as a place of suffering to be endured forever by human souls, I saw hell as more self-styled and self-made, full of the negative emotions and situations we create. Hell is the confines of our own remorse, revenge, and other addictive emotions that keep us spiritually stunted. This hell numbs the soul and blocks it from the illuminating light of truth.

In my dream, as I soared above this hellish place, I saw other souls who shared my realization. These souls began to rise. I don't believe the God my brother now knows is a punitive, wrathful God; I believe my brother has met the God who offers salvation and a safe harbor. In my heart I know that God is mentoring and counseling my brother, and all the confusing questions he held about life have been met with gracious resolve.

The strength of Torah—God's instruction and law—is not unlike the strength that comes after we experience a revelation similar to the one in my dream. God's teachings—demanding and generous at the same time—bring purpose and understanding to human life. The law of the Lord does revive the soul, make the simple wise, and give joy to the heart.

I know in my own heart that my brother, with God's help, has now found his way, even as we will find ours.

God of grace, guide us and all whom we love along your way. Amen.

Often when I speak in public, I conclude with a story from my book *Autism and the God Connection* about ladybugs and how they came to bear on my life and on the life of another family. I won't recount the story here; the important thing to know is that Native Americans consider the ladybug to be a symbol of trust. The ladybug encourages people to release their frustration and anxiety, and to trust in the Great Spirit.

Curiously, more often than not, after I tell my ladybug story, ladybugs tend to *appear*! One cold March, my hosts called me out of the auditorium where I had just told the anecdote about ladybugs to show me a chandelier—covered in ladybugs. There it was—a reminder to trust.

After another speech, I was approached by a woman whose eyes welled with tears. In her hand was a paper towel; she had ducked into the ladies' room after my presentation, and awaiting her there was a single ladybug, with the singular message, "Trust."

Seeing unexpected ladybugs is a small thing that carries a big message. We too carry small things that hold great meaning for us, that remind us of who we are and who God is. Our trust in God—and our reminder to trust always in God—has its firm basis in the first verse of Exodus 20: "I am the LORD your God, who brought you out of the land of Egypt, out of the house of slavery." God is trustworthy, the scripture says, and we honor God by exchanging worry for trust. People sometimes carry things or hold an image in their minds to remind them to trust God. Some keep a small cross in their pocket. Some memorize a favorite scripture and keep it close. Others carry a stone to touch as a reminder. I look for ladybugs.

"I am the LORD your God." Remember that—by whatever means comes to you. Remember that, and give thanks.

Lord, my God, thank you for redeeming me. Let me always trust in you. Amen.

THIRD SUNDAY IN LENT

The story of Jesus chasing the money changers out of the Temple portrays a vivid and definitive act of zeal that got the attention of Jesus' disciples and of Jesus' detractors. Jesus says little, but both groups feel that his action indicates something important about his true identity.

Seeing what Jesus has done, the disciples immediately connect his act with the fulfillment of the scriptures about the coming Messiah. The others, seeing the same act, don't make that connection; they oppose him. The whole Gospel of John focuses on claims about who Jesus is and the world's response—or lack of it. Jesus' action connects him to the fulfillment of scripture, and it connects the disciples to Jesus as Messiah. Sometimes it is action and not words that make this strong connection between us and scripture, between us and God.

I saw a beautiful example of this kind of unspoken connection in the action of a young girl with autism who, at the age of eight, didn't speak and had only recently begun to walk. At a social gathering after church, the girl ambled her way through the crowd. She honed in on an older gentleman who was engaged in conversation and silently she slipped her hand into his. The man gently disengaged her hand and continued his conversation, but the girl again placed her hand in his. By this time, the man had finished his conversation. He stood there alone, holding Elena's hand until her mother came to retrieve her. The older man asked the girl's name, and the mother told him, "Elena." With tears in his eyes, the man explained that his wife's name was Elena, and that very day was a difficult one for him—it was the anniversary of his wife's passing.

Jesus' act cleared the Temple and revealed him as Messiah. Elena's act revealed the love of this Jesus, our Messiah, to a grieving man and showed him that he was not alone.

Reveal yourself to me, O Lord. May I act today on the love you give me. Amen.

The Cure for Death

MARCH 16-22, 2009 • BOB KAYLOR

MONDAY, MARCH 16 ～ *Read Numbers 21:4-6*

I've never been bitten by a snake, but that doesn't stop me from being a raging ophidiophobiac—one who fears those slithering reptiles. As an officer in the infantry prior to my call to ministry, I had a few close encounters with rattlers in the woods, including unknowingly stepping over a coiled five-footer once while on a patrol. My medic, who saw my near misstep, told me later how lucky I was that it hadn't nailed me. "He'd a messed you up bad, sir," he said matter-of-factly.

It's hard to imagine a worse ophidiophobic nightmare than in today's reading. The Israelites are complaining again. All along the journey from Egypt, God had been miraculously supplying them with food and water. Rather than enjoy God's abundant provision, however, they whined about the menu. In response to their complaints, God sent "poisonous serpents" into the desert camp. I'm thinking they stopped worrying about food pretty quickly after that!

We may want to question God's harsh judgment here, but focus instead on the symbolic nature of the snake. Some ancient rabbis viewed snakes as an ironic form of retribution. The serpent, cursed and made to eat dust for his deception, accepted his fate without complaint. How ironic, then, for the uncomplaining serpent to be punishment to people who did nothing but complain. In Numbers the snakes were a vivid call for the people to embrace humility and turn from complaint to gratitude.

What are you complaining about these days? How could you turn your complaints into opportunities to trust God?

Pastor of Park City Community United Methodist Church in Park City, Utah, and senior writer for Homiletics

I was flipping channels recently and came across a documentary about a man who catches poisonous snakes and "milks" their venom for use in treating snakebite victims. The harvested venom is used to make antivenin which, when injected into the victim, helps build antibodies to neutralize the effect of the toxic bite. The irony is that while snake venom can kill, it can also heal.

The first antivenin was developed by French scientist Albert Calmette of the Pasteur Institute in 1895, but long before that many ancient cultures used the symbol of the snake to represent death or life, depending on the context. In Greek mythology, for example, the rod of Asclepius featured a snake coiled around a staff as a symbol of the healing arts—the shedding of a snake's skin symbolizing rebirth and the staff symbolizing authority. The caduceus, a popular symbol of the medical profession today, incorporates this ancient symbol.

The ancient Israelites were directed to look at a similar snake on a stake in order to heal the snakebites they were enduring as a result of their sin. The plague of serpents seemed to have the desired effect of convicting the people of their self-serving ways (21:7). In response to their repentance, God instructed Moses to make a bronze snake and put it on a pole so that when the people looked up at it their potentially fatal snakebites would be healed (21:8). The cure for snakes was a snake.

Whether the snake is a symbol of death or life depends on human choice. When the Israelites looked inward and downward in self-interest and sin, the snakes killed. When they looked up at the snake that God provided as an antidote, they lived. God judges the sin that leads to death, but God also provides the way of healing and new life. It's our choice as to where we will fix our attention.

Lord God, forgive me when I look downward at my own self-gratification. Help me to look to you for life. Amen.

The bronze serpent that Moses constructed at God's command would eventually be used both to judge and to heal. A problem arose, however, when the people began to worship the snake as an idol. Symbols themselves are not to be worshiped. Instead, they point to a higher truth. In John 3, Jesus borrowed the symbol of the serpent to describe his own mission and then offered an entirely new symbol that would point to God's plan of healing for the whole world.

The phrase "lifted up" has a double meaning in John 3:14. In one sense it is a royal metaphor for the exaltation of a king or ruler, while in another more literal sense it refers to the death of Jesus. For John, the crucifixion is the royal coronation of Jesus as Lord and king, and the cross is his throne. From the vantage point of the cross, Jesus would become the agent of healing for a world assailed by sin and death. The cross would be the new symbol of healing and hope for everyone.

If the cure for snakes was a snake, then the cure for death, according to Jesus, was his own death. The cross and resurrection represent God's victory over sin and God's triumph over death (3:16). It is through Jesus' death that we truly experience life. The "eternal life" that Jesus refers to in this passage means much more than immortality or life after physical death. "Eternal life" instead describes the "abundant life" we can live in the present because of his victory over the effects of sin and death (John 10:10). Belief in Christ frees us to live new and reborn lives right now, looking ahead in the love and grace of God instead of looking back and wallowing in the guilt of the past (John 3:3).

Jesus' words of life are good news. God can turn even an instrument of pain and death into a symbol of new, abundant, and eternal life!

Spend some time focusing on a cross, and write down what the symbol means to you.

My grandparents lived on a small farm, and I loved spending my boyhood summers there. While it was always great to be there, certain places on the farm I feared to tread. One such place was the dark and foreboding basement of the barn. Pap would send me out there to fetch a tool or some twine, and I'd always act as though it was no big deal; but inside I was squeamish.

The worst part of the whole experience was reaching through the cobwebs to find the light switch and flicking it on. The sudden burst of light would set off an instant flurry of activity as bats, rats, cats, spiders, snakes, and who knows what else made for the corners and crevices to get out of the light. After I caught my breath, I'd quickly grab what I needed and beat feet out of there!

One of the recurring themes of John's Gospel has to do with light and darkness of the spiritual kind. Like flicking on a bright bulb in a dark room, Jesus entered the world and exposed the darkness of human sin to the light of God's love. Jesus understood, however, that people often love the dark corners too, preferring to do their evil deeds out of God's sight (3:19). Those who believe in Jesus, by contrast, "come to the light" and are unafraid to have their lives exposed because they have been forgiven and "do what is true" (3:21).

We can't hide from God. The light of God's revelation in Christ exposes the whole world and illuminates the path to the abundant and eternal life. We can continue hiding in the corners, or we can choose to be clearly seen for who we are and what we can become with God's help.

Spend some time reflecting on some of the dark corners of your life. Ask God to shine the light of forgiveness and renewal on those dark places.

I always get a kick out of those diet commercials that show some gravitationally challenged individual going from flab to fab because they popped a pill or began eating bird-sized portions of prepackaged, calorie-stripped food. The before-and-after pictures of these folks are dramatic, but they always come with the disclaimer, "Results may vary." Truth is, regardless of your diet plan, you still have to work hard if you want to look good in bike shorts or a swimsuit.

Today's reading describes an even more stunning before-and-after scenario—that of spiritually dead people becoming alive again. Writing to the Ephesians, Paul (or another writer—scholars debate the authorship) begins by reminding them of the past. They were "dead" because of the "trespasses and sins" they lived in, following "everyone else" in the pursuit of earthly and self-gratifying pleasures (2:1-3). Gorging on their own self-indulgence, humans quickly become separated from God and begin to die spiritually. For Paul, the line from *Sixth Sense* "I see dead people" isn't just a part of a movie dialogue—it's the human condition.

But, says Paul, there is hope even for the dried-up, decaying, and decomposing spirits of overindulged sinners, and that hope comes at God's initiative. Human willpower can't overcome sin—only the mercy, love, and grace of God can change the picture. The change from life "in this world" to a life with Christ in the "heavenly places" isn't simply a future promise but a present reality. We change our focus, our hope, and our outlook when we offer ourselves to Christ. (John 2:4-7) Our gratitude for God's gift is not passive; it is active and vital—full of good works. This gift of salvation isn't meant to be analyzed. It is meant to be lived with gratitude, praise, and worship.

Once again, the cure for death is a death. The way of Christ is the way of life.

Merciful God, I thank you for your gift of new life in Christ. Help me to be more like Christ each day. Amen.

Having given his readers a description of the process one undergoes to move from the death of sin to new life in Christ, Paul moves quickly to reveal the operative principle that makes it all possible. For Paul, God's salvation is a gift of God, offered without strings and disclaimers. To receive it, one only needs to respond through faith. Grace is God's unmerited favor toward us—the fact that God loves us deeply in spite of our tendency to pull away from God in our sin. Rather than threaten or cajole us into love, God chooses instead to offer us grace. Faith, then, is simply saying yes to God's offer. This love is not something we earn or can boast about. It is free.

But while we don't earn God's grace, we do respond actively to this gift. Paul makes it clear that we are not only saved *from* something—the old life of sin and the effects of death—we are also saved *for* something: new life and the good works that come from knowing God. We do not earn salvation, but the evidence of our salvation is always bound up in the things we do for God and for others. To put it another way, God's grace always comes to us on its way to someone else!

The beautiful lyrics of this passage, then, lead us from analyzing God's grace to worshiping God energetically for it. In this way, our very lives—the way we live every day—are an act of gratitude for God's grace and salvation.

Think about someone who could use God's message of grace and healing today. Ask God to help you find ways to share the experience of grace in your own life with someone who needs it.

Fourth Sunday in Lent

One Sunday a couple of years back I woke up feeling pretty lousy with a stomach bug. Being a preacher, however, and being too self-important to want to take a morning off and let my lay leader handle it, I decided to tough it out and headed to the church even though I had spent much of the early morning hours quite sick. Halfway through my sermon the room started spinning. I had to excuse myself to make a very quick but wobbly run to the restroom. Without missing a beat, my lay leader stepped in and finished the service. So much for being indispensable.

An ER doctor in the congregation stopped by the house later and hooked me up to an IV, which helped a lot, though what he said helped me even more: "Next time, stay home. God will still show up even if you're not there." He said it with a smile, but the message really stuck with me.

Psalm 107 is a song of thanks to God for always showing up. "Steadfast love" is the psalmist's way of describing it.

There are times when all of us need to stop and rest, recognizing the symptoms of pride and self-interest that can lay us out and lead to a slow spiritual death. It's then that we need to look to God for a fresh infusion of God's love.

The final word is not our sin or our suffering. The final word is God's grace. This is the good news: when we ask, God always shows up.

Gracious God, thank you for your steadfast love toward me. Help me to live in your grace every day. Amen.

Lessons from *The Heart of Darkness*

MARCH 23–29, 2009 • PAMELA D. COUTURE

MONDAY, MARCH 23 ~ **Read John 12:20-26**

What does it mean to "serve Jesus and follow him"? Anticipating the crucifixion, we must be struck with the truth that following Jesus means dying for him, in figurative or literal ways.

Many Christians contemplate the symbolic meaning in this passage: we die small deaths, and even large ones, because our faith dictates one path of life rather than another. But many Christians around the world must grapple with the literal meaning of dying for Jesus, living in war-torn areas where being a Christian means putting one's life at risk.

I spent January 2008 researching peacemaking practices in Democratic Republic of the Congo (DRC). There, Christians literally risk their lives to follow Jesus. I interviewed Congolese Christians whose witness to their faith strengthened mine.

Bishop Kenneth Carder speaks of "the mysterious coexistence of the destruction and amazing grace." In the DRC, where Christians experience the destruction of war and its aftermath, an amazing grace exists. There, where violence and corruption ostensibly pervade every aspect of society, evidence abounds of God's image in human beings and of Congolese Christians being made perfect in love.

This experience raised for me questions about my faith journey. Perhaps it does for you too. How have we been called to die with Jesus, either figuratively or literally? Where have we found grace amidst destruction?

God, allow us to see the reality of your grace in the middle of pain and destruction. Amen.

Vice President for Academic Affairs, and Dean, professor of practical theology at Saint Paul School of Theology in Kansas City, Missouri

The war in Democratic Republic of the Congo was at its worst between 1997 and 1999. Seven African nations participated directly in the fighting and up to twenty nations from around the world were involved in the supply of arms and the black market sale of Congolese natural resources. In 1999 South Africa brokered a peace agreement among the African nations. But local militia groups, commonly known as the Mayi-Mayi, were not included in the peace agreement. In 2004 the government asked the leaders of the DCR's United Methodist Church to convene a peace conference that would bring the Mayi-Mayi to the peace table.

The most powerful leader of one of the militia groups refused to participate. This leader lived in a cave, protected by six barriers of armed guards. A United Methodist district superintendent who had come from the same village as this leader was asked by his bishop to go and talk with him. It was a dangerous trip, but when the district superintendent finally came face-to-face with the man, the leader extracted from him the most difficult promise that a person can be asked to make. The leader would come to the negotiations, but the minister had to guarantee the leader's safety with the lives of his own family. He was required to give his family's names and to sign a document stating he understood that if any harm came to the leader, all his family would be killed.

"Now my soul is troubled. And what should I say—'Father save me from this hour'"? In his courage, this United Methodist pastor decided to risk his life and the lives of his loved ones to bring peace and save the lives of others. How does the courage of this pastor witness to you? What is the most courageous act you have undertaken because of your faith? What are your deepest fears about what being a Christian might require of you?

Loving God, do not ask us to suffer unnecessarily. But when we must suffer, be with us. Amen.

The most anguished laments of war come from innocent victims, especially refugees and those displaced within their own country. People who must leave all they own are vulnerable victims whose cries, we believe, are heard by Jesus.

The members of one United Methodist family fled the fighting until they reached the banks of the Congo River, which they could not cross. The rebels talked to the family trapped by the river, and they realized the father was bilingual. They wanted him to work as their interpreter. He had understood his Christian faith meant he was to renounce war; but as he realized the possibility of an end to the war, he decided he would be an interpreter for the rebels. But the rebels with whom he was traveling were attacked; he was the lone survivor. Hearing that everyone had been killed in the attack, his family believed him to be dead also.

Instead, the man had been taken to a hospital far away from the war zone. He spent two years recovering from his wounds. Because he had registered as an internally displaced person, the church knew he was alive. When his family finally made its way through the bush away from the war zone to safety, they also registered as internally displaced persons with the church. It was then they learned that their husband and father was not dead but alive!

This story is repeated in different circumstances throughout the world where war creates refugees and internally displaced persons. We can be confident that Jesus as the high priest laments, with "prayers and supplications, with loud cries and tears," the sufferings of the innocent victims of war. Whether we are in danger zones or safe zones, we can join our cries with his, allowing our anguish to be placed in the palm of God's hand.

Suffering Jesus, because of your anguish, you understand our deepest suffering. Make your comfort known to all who join their cries to yours. Amen.

The district superintendent described in Tuesday's meditation personifies obedience. The displaced family in yesterday's story and others like them portray acute suffering. But the courage of these people in living their lives also exemplifies "being made perfect" in love. They have loved the gift of life enough to fight for it, to affirm it, to risk it in order to make possible a life for themselves and for their families. In obedience and suffering, love is wrought.

One Congolese citizen was in the United States at the outbreak of the war in his home area; he could not return. So he went to a part of the country that was receiving refugees and worked on the church's behalf to organize getting food, water, and shelter for people. He coordinated the contributions of Congolese congregations toward the refugee crisis, and he worked with the church to distribute aid offered by the United Methodist Committee on Relief.

Distributing food is a unique act of love because food is the basis for life. When the church can distribute food, it can allay one of people's most primal fears—that of going hungry—as a way of helping people come to peace. When sources of food are close at hand, peace may be sustained.

Jesus frequently distributed food. The actions of his life in distributing food to the hungry are grafted onto the actions of his death. As one who was made perfect in his suffering, Jesus' actions are uniquely represented when we reenact his death in sacramental feeding at the Lord's Table. When we witness any act of feeding, we are empirically verifying that humanity can be made perfect in love.

How have you provided food or been provided with food in the last week? In what circumstances have you seen people being fed in the last week? Can you discern in these scenes examples of people "being made perfect in love"?

Christ Jesus, help us seek our perfection as we feed one another in love. Amen.

War generally does not erupt without reason. Wars are fought for unjust and just causes. But war is a symptom of power, corruption, injustice, and oppression. Yet war-torn people also know that life beyond war must also be won.

After war, enemies must face one another and rebuild relationships. The Congolese United Methodist Church has been active in conflict resolution and reconciliation. One Congolese pastor, educated in conflict resolution at Africa University, made his way after the war to an area where both congregations and families had been torn apart. First, he visited to get a sense of the situation. Later, he returned with another pastor to stay for a month, developing trust and talking with people. In a month of work he was able to help people talk about their differences and train local leaders in conflict resolution work.

Conflict resolution work is a sign of hope in Democratic Republic of the Congo, but it is not always successful. The atrocities of war have left people physically maimed from war wounds and psychologically scarred from sexual violation. The resilience of the human spirit is powerfully evident when people whose family members have been killed or violated are able to sit with those who have perpetrated these crimes. It is prayer and faith in action that enable this to happen. Prayer and faith in action are at the heart of this kind of reconciliation.

The plea, "Wash me thoroughly from my iniquity, and cleanse me from my sin," is not a vacant, hollow plea in war-torn areas. It is a cry from the bottom of the heart.

As we witness confession and reconciliation in the world's war-torn places, we must consider those parts of our own souls that need to be washed and cleansed. Lent is the time to prepare ourselves, to examine ourselves, and to ask God to cleanse us from our sin and disobedience.

"God of all peoples, wash me from my iniquity, cleanse me from my sin." Amen.

People who anguish deeply also often know great joy. It's easy to go to church in Congo, even without an interpreter, because the joy of the singing and dancing carries everyone into full participation in the service. Every church has its drums—round, hollowed tree trunks with holes that create vibrations—and other instruments that contribute to complex African rhythms.

One Sunday I attended worship at a small congregation in a township. The one-room church was a mud hut with a thatched roof and benches for seats. Children filled nearly half the church. Adult men and women made up the other half. Village children crowded the church's windows to watch what was happening inside.

The children stared. A *muzingu*—a white person—was in church. They clearly had never seen such a person. When I was introduced, I told the children that my skin was just like theirs—that after the service they could touch it for themselves. They did.

Several musical groups performed. An *a cappella* group of five men sang biblical songs and set a beat to the drum with a dance step. A little boy who looked to be about two years old came down the center aisle and looked up at the adult men. He began to tap his feet in imitation of them, finding the rhythm until soon he was dancing along. He couldn't have been walking for long, but he was already participating in the musical offerings of the church.

The joy of music and dancing our faith was joined to the happiness of being one family in Christ, where a right spirit could be renewed in all of us. What worship experiences do you recall that lifted your heart in joy? When has your heart been lifted by a social and spiritual connection with others in worship? Where do you yearn for God to restore joy in your life?

Dear God, restore to me the joy of your salvation and sustain in me a willing spirit. Amen.

FIFTH SUNDAY IN LENT

In the time I spent in Democratic Republic of the Congo, I saw and heard powerful testimonies to what it means to have the law of God written on one's heart. Some of the testimonies had to do with overcoming hardship, but others had to do with the joy of living.

I visited several hospitals in Congo. The wire cot beds had been painted in some previous decade, and the chipped parts showed their age. Sometimes the cots were covered with boards and foam mattresses. The foam was often stained with blood. Mattresses covered with vinyl were usually torn. There were few sheets to cover the beds; those few had to be washed by hand. Medicines and medical supplies were scarce. Food for the patients was brought in by their families.

In the midst of this scene of want, one ward stood out as a testimony to life: the maternity ward. As a way of expressing and honoring life, Congolese mothers dress their newborns in the finest knit layettes—white, pink, blue, green. The mothers were exuberant about their babies. The joy of the mothers in the maternity wards was contagious. It was an affirmation of life, of the basic belief that it is worth it to bring life into the world.

This is a scene that proclaims the presence of a God who forgives iniquity and remembers sin no more. Many of these mothers had desperate stories to tell, but like the men and the boy dancing in church, at this moment, joy overcame despair.

Joy helps us know what life will be like when the law of God is truly written on our hearts, when we truly live in covenant with God. When have you observed such joy in the lives of others that you know you've seen the face of a forgiving and loving God? What joys in your own life reflect the presence of God's covenant in your heart?

Reveal to me your covenant, O God, that I may know your ways. Amen.

"Reel" Jesus: Life with Our Lord

MARCH 30–APRIL 5, 2009 • ELLEN HAMILTON FENTER

MONDAY, MARCH 30 ～ *Read Psalm 31:9-16*

To put myself in mind of this last week before Easter, I spent time reviewing Holy Week scenes from an array of films about Jesus, beginning with 1907's silent movie *Ben Hur: A Tale of the Christ* and advancing to 2004's panegyric *The Passion of the Christ.* I remembered the grandeur of DeMille's epic savior, the radical singer of director Norman Jewison's film *Jesus Christ Superstar*, the raw honesty of Scorsese's man of constant sorrow in *The Last Temptation of Christ.*

Every generation of filmmakers creates its own picture of Jesus. Films of the 1900s entertained audiences with a technicolor Christ, reflecting the emerging belief that society had nowhere to go but up. After two world wars, a remake of *Ben Hur* presented the story of one man's quest for domination amidst brief encounters with a Jesus whose face was never seen. The 1970s delivered a network television miniseries *Messiah*; and in film's most violence-saturated era, Mel Gibson depicted Jesus' passion in stark and shocking terms.

The psalmist, telling of his own suffering and sorrow, captures the sufferings of Christ in moving terms. Psalm 31 speaks of failing strength, of bones that waste away, of a life spent with sorrow.

The days ahead for Jesus will be the hardest days of his life. So when the psalmist, who is in dire straits, says, "I trust in you, O LORD," we are struck by his steady—almost stubborn—faith. It sounds like the steady faith of Jesus.

This psalm points to a portrait of Jesus that stands true to the witness of the Bible and true to the tests of time.

God, may I transcend my own conceptions of Jesus so that I may see my savior through the lens of the Bible. Amen.

United Methodist pastor; native of New Mexico; founder and counselor, The Center for Pastoral Counseling & Spiritual Wellness in El Paso, Texas

A scene in *Jesus Christ Superstar* depicts Jesus trying to get away for just a few minutes of peace. But as he makes his way through the hills above Jerusalem, lepers come pouring from the rocky crevices, begging to be healed. Jesus is shown reeling under the pressure until he finally shouts at them to heal themselves.

It was a controversial scene. People don't want to believe Jesus could lose it like that. After all, he walked on water. People don't want to believe that their minister or others who care for them could lose it like that either. But this is "prime time" in the church, just a few days before Holy Week. Many ministers and church leaders have been preparing for this season for months: directing choirs, making costumes, designing media, preparing food, writing sermons.

And in the midst of all that, the normal duties of life continue. Whether we are busy clergy or busy laity, the scripture has a message for us. Mark says that just before the most trying and deadly time of Christ's life, he went out to Bethany with the twelve. And then there is a period. A period. End of sentence. In my Bible there's even a big space before the next word appears. This suggests to me that Jesus took a break, that he took some time to be with friends in Bethany.

I admonish you, brothers and sisters, to observe the space between the sentences from time to time. Jesus took time apart just before the greatest challenge of his life. We should too. In the busyness of Easter preparations, we must take time to focus on our faith, on the Holy Spirit, and on the nature of this Jesus we would follow.

God, still my soul and let me become attentive to Jesus. Even as he is praised by those who will later reject him, keep us from the mistake of holding to our own images of Jesus. Redirect our hearts so that we may understand his place in our lives. Amen.

My first summer at divinity school, my theology professor showed a clip from Monty Python's *Life of Brian*. It parodied Jesus delivering the Sermon on the Mount. People on the far side of the hill misheard the sermon and thought Jesus said, "Blessed are the cheese makers" instead of "Blessed are the *peacemakers*."

I was shocked. I didn't understand how an educated Christian professor could use a parody of Jesus' life as a teaching tool. Monty Python and Christian theology seemed incongruous.

Years later, I began to realize that I, like many in the church, tend to strain on satire while swallowing dogma whole. The more I thought about it, the more I began to understand what my professor was trying to do. He was demonstrating how holding incongruous concepts together can be a source of truth.

Mark's account of Jesus' trial before the high priest is an example of two incongruous concepts colliding. Jesus, God's son and our truth, stands in the midst of religious people who are not religious at all— their actions and their motives are actually quite profane.

The collision between the mind-set of the high priests and the witness of Jesus' life resulted in an interchange that might have sounded like this: The road to the cross is a bridge to eternity. "Ha!" This cannot be true. Darkness cannot overwhelm the light. "Ha!" They hear this with complete misunderstanding. "I am [the Messiah]; and you will see Son of Man, seated at the right hand of the Power," Jesus finally says. "Ha!" The priests and scribes responded. "That is blasphemy."

Sound ridiculous? Perhaps, though only from a human point of view.

God, grant me the humility to accept when I don't get it, the freedom to laugh when I do, and the wisdom to keep my mouth shut otherwise. Amen.

I grew up watching westerns, a film genre that gave me a firm understanding of good guys, bad guys, and how to tell the difference. That is, until Clint Eastwood's *Unforgiven* reshuffled the deck of good and evil, casting cowboys as villains, harlots as heroines, and vigilante justice as—well, justice.

I experience a similar dissonance reading the dramatic interplay between key figures during the last week of Jesus' life. Judas comes across as a jerk when he condemns Mary's anointing of her Lord; yet I hear a vindicating defense as he avows solidarity with the poor. And there's Pilate, who is damned if he does and damned if he doesn't.

There's Peter too. At age twelve I delivered my first solo, *I Would Be True*, with gut-wrenching conviction that came on the heels of a sermon that warned about Peter's denials, "Beware the crowing of the cock!" Yet Peter had been christened *the rock on which the church will be built*.

Within these most brutal scenarios we meet real people in real time dealing with real life, and it gets messy. White hats and black hats are abandoned; self-interest and self-survival take precedent. Axiomatically, we hear the most stunning of confessions from the most unlikely of people—a Roman centurion, one who might easily have been among those who hurled insults but is the one the scriptures chose to make the simple confession, "Truly this man was God's Son!" (Matt. 27:54).

The stories leading up to the crucifixion of Christ are stories of real people, people not unlike you and me, struggling to understand Jesus and his passion, even as they witnessed it.

God, help me see your works and hear your words in these days before Holy Week. Teach me to navigate the murky waters of life, fixing my gaze on you. Amen.

Untold numbers of Bible scholars have spent untold hours of investigation trying to figure out just what Mark 14:51 is all about. One of the leading explanations of the young man who fled the garden naked is that Mark, the attributed author of this Gospel, is observing a practice common to ancient times in which a writer would plant clues in the text regarding his identity—not unlike Stephen King's habit of sneaking in and out of his movies. The question is, why here and why naked?

There is a moment of deep insight in *Shrek 3* when the lovable ogre, who has learned he is soon to be a father, falls into troubled dreams over his anxieties concerning parenthood. The end of his nocturnal wanderings comes when he sees himself standing naked in front of his wife and friends and realizes they see him for what and who he really is.

I spend a great deal of my ministry counseling others, so I am aware that such a dream is not all that unusual. And, while it says a lot about the dreamer, it also says something about what being naked represents: being exposed, vulnerable, or found out.

If someone compiled a top-ten list of the Bible's saddest verses, Mark 14:50, "All of them deserted him and fled," would surely be included.

The Last Supper scene of *Jesus Christ Superstar* finds the disciples focused, as usual, on all the wrong things: themselves. As Jesus serves up the meal he says to them, *The end . . . is just a little harder, when brought about by friends.*

Two thousand years later, this naked truth rips at my gut, exposes my own complicity, calls me to bare it all. In crucial moments I too have fled Jesus. Yet owning this hard truth is the only way I can return to the One I have left. God's mercy—and only that—can close the distance I have made between us.

Forgive me; forgive me; forgive me, Lord.

Watching movies about Jesus, I realize that developing a screenplay based on the life of Christ must be a real challenge. After all, most folks know the hero dies at the end. So it is tempting to assume that everything that comes before the big finish is just filler. Perhaps that's why *The Passion of the Christ* begins with Gethsemane. I find this type of thinking dangerous.

We must be careful lest we focus so completely on the crucifixion of Christ that we fail to appreciate the quality of the life that came before it. If Jesus' death on the cross was all that needed to happen so my sins could be forgiven and I could go to heaven, why didn't they just do the deed the day after his bar mitzvah?

Hyperbole noted, my answer to that question is that the day-to-day life of Jesus is *in some ways* as important as his death. From his life we learn how to be people on planet earth. We observe a man who comprehends the mystery of the whole equation, who sees the big picture. And because of the profundity of that life, he was marked to be killed.

In a *Peanuts* cartoon, Charlie Brown tells Lucy they must stop fighting and find a kinder way to resolve their conflicts. He tells her that the planet is filled with people hurting each other, that it's possible they as children can make a new world order. Lucy listens for a minute and then, *POW!* She slams him to the ground and walks away saying, *I had to hit him quick, he was beginning to make sense*.

Jesus made sense. He makes sense. He peacefully, lovingly, obediently, gracefully, and intentionally lived his days so that when they were done, we would have the template for the kind of life God envisioned *in the beginning*.

Lord, make me like you. Amen.

PALM/PASSION SUNDAY

There's a funky little coffeehouse in Taos, New Mexico, called *The Bean*. They make the best breakfast burritos in the world. When I manage to get up to the northern part of the state, my ritual includes dropping by for a leisurely brunch accompanied by first-rate people-watching.

A few weeks ago while I stood in line there I became aware of a certain *electricity* in the air. The people around me seemed brighter and more alert than usual, and the guy working the counter was a bit flustered as the couple in front of me placed their order.

Before long the pair turned around, and I found myself within spitting distance of two famous movie stars. A million thoughts went through my mind as I took in the experience. I considered saying all the silly things people say to celebrities but vetoed the idea and did nothing but gape.

In retrospect I realized that what I had really wanted was for them to talk to me. I suppose I thought it would be a kind of validation if these superstars considered me interesting enough to engage in a little conversation. But the sad reality is they looked right through me as they left the place.

People loved celebrities as much two thousand years ago as they do now, and that's one reason so many of them lined the red carpet to see Jesus as he entered Jerusalem on a donkey. They waved palms and shouted hosannas, and I'm guessing that each person in the crowd hoped deep within that this famous man about whom they had heard such remarkable tales would notice him or her.

They didn't know it then, but he had. He's noticed you too. And me. He's even started up a conversation with each of us, with all of us. It began with the greatest word: *Shalom.*

Thank you, dear Jesus, for knowing me, for loving me, for calling me by name. Amen.

The Road to Resurrection

APRIL 6–12, 2009 • DAN R. DICK

MONDAY, APRIL 6 ~ *Read Isaiah 42:1-9*

Ambivalence: the state of holding conflicting or contradictory feelings or emotions in tension. Excitement and fear at beginning a new job; terror and joy when the car narrowly misses hitting your child; the pride and embarrassment competing as you receive an award—these are all familiar experiences of ambivalence.

Holy Week is a time of deep ambivalence in the Christian heart and mind. The prophet Isaiah paints a glorious picture of God's power and protection in today's reading, and yet we know what is to come for the suffering servant of God. How deeply ambivalent Jesus must have felt following the triumphal entry into Jerusalem—riding into the city in power, facing abject powerlessness. Heading toward eternal glory by way of soul-wrenching sorrow and suffering. Saying good-bye to disciples and friends so that the will of God might be fulfilled. Long before Jesus' own flesh was torn, his heart and psyche were torn by conflicting and contradictory feelings. The path to resurrection and new life required passage through devastation and death.

Yet the grace-filled message through this Holy Week is simply this: life is fraught with contradictions and conflict. But through it all, in every dark and demanding place, God is with us. This is the God who places within us the Holy Spirit that we might not be crushed, might not faint or fear. We may walk as Jesus walked, facing terrible torments, but we will never walk alone.

Gracious God, help me be aware of your presence as I travel through these days of Holy Week. May I experience some of the pain Jesus felt that I might celebrate his glory as well. Amen.

Research Coordinator for the United Methodist Church's General Board of Discipleship, living with his wife Barbara in Nashville, Tennessee

O God, do not be far from me; O my God, make haste to help me.

My grandmother was a champion pray-er. She could pray for twenty minutes without taking a breath. Raised in a stolid King James, Southern Baptist congregation, her prayers were liberally seasoned with *thee*, *thou*, and dozens of words ending in *-eth* (as in *sinneth, faileth*, and *disappointeth*). Her prayers were intimidating in scope, scale, and content. However, when she suffered a series of strokes, her prayers became very simple, sincere, and direct. I remember holding her hand in the hospital while she whispered, simply, "O God, help me; O Jesus, comfort me." In the face of deepest need, all pretense disappeared; and the honest childlike prayers emerged.

The psalmists model pietistic prayers, but they also know how to cut through all the poetry to get to the heart of the matter. In the midst of lofty verse the heart song is often heard: *save me, rescue me, hear me, do not forsake me.* God is the source of salvation, protection, comfort, and victory. In our greatest need, we turn most humbly and openly to God.

Psalm 71 reminds us what it might have been like for Jesus in his last week on earth, knowing of the great trials he would have to endure, and finding solace and comfort in God's great power and grace. If ever Jesus needed to feel God's presence and guiding hand, it was never greater than this week in Jerusalem. We know how the story will end; but for those who stood in uncertainty and wonder, it was so important to have a God who served as "a rock of refuge, a strong fortress," to protect them from what must surely come.

O Lord, I need a rock and a refuge, a safe place to come when the pressures and demands of life grow too great. Receive me, rescue me, and restore me, that I might go forth to share your praise and good news. Amen.

Do you think Jesus ever considered running away? We know he didn't, and even though he asked God to lift the burden from him, the usual picture of Jesus is that he faced his torments and torture with stoic courage. However, it would be very human and understandable that he would have considered escaping the awful fate to come.

Courage sometimes comes not in facing the actual punishment but in quelling the demons and fears of the mind. Our anticipation of punishment is many times worse than the punishment itself, and the sense of dread can eat away at our resolve. Many people say that waiting is the hardest part of any bad experience. People dread going to the dentist more than they actually fear the experience. Most people spend only twenty minutes in the dentist's chair, but they worry about it for days in advance.

This midpoint of the Holy Week must have been a torturous time for Jesus, knowing what was to come and having to stay focused and calm. Surrounded by disciples and friends that hadn't quite grasped the severity of the situation, Jesus must have felt very lonely during this time. It is not unreasonable to assume he might have considered a retreat into the hills.

Few of us will face anything remotely resembling the situation Jesus encountered in Jerusalem. Yet, because he faced his fears and endured his fate, he stands as a shining beacon of hope and inspiration to those who follow him. We too are surrounded by a mighty cloud of witnesses—Jesus chief among them—who give us courage, strength, and hope in the face of any and all adversity.

Great and wondrous God, please give me the strength and courage I need to be faithful in all situations, especially in those times when life seems most bleak and terrible. Remind me of Jesus' example when I lose heart. Amen.

MAUNDY THURSDAY

The sacrament of Holy Communion is indeed a special celebration, to be entered into reverently and humbly, but I wonder if the way we celebrate it today is truly what Jesus intended? What must it have been like for Jesus on that last night with his friends before his torture, death, and resurrection? He looked upon the faces of the men (and perhaps women) that meant the most to him and knew he had to leave them behind. There is strong evidence that he lacked confidence that they understood what would happen and that they would need to carry on his work after he was gone. It must have been a heart-wrenching time. How to say good-bye?

Paul's brief description of the last supper doesn't institute a sacrament, but instead consecrates as sacred the ordinary and every day. Bread was the staple of every meal. In hard times when meat and vegetables were in short supply, grain sustained the community. Jesus took bread and broke it and said, "This is my body." In a similar way, wine was the lifeblood of every community. Often, water was not safe to drink, and milk was in short supply, as was the juice of various fruits. Wine was generally in abundant supply. Jesus took the cup of wine and said, "This cup is the new covenant in my blood." Then he said an amazing thing: "As often as you eat this bread and drink the cup, you proclaim the Lord's death until he comes." In other words, every time we eat bread or drink wine it reminds us of Christ, our Christian discipleship, and the message entrusted into our care—that Jesus Christ is Lord. Every meal should be a Communion meal, bringing to mind who we are, whose we are, and why we are called to be the body of Christ!

Holy and loving God, make Christ real to me each and every day. In the goodness of daily bread, in the thirst-quenching refreshment of the cup, make me mindful of Christ's presence. Amen.

GOOD FRIDAY

The modern church often tends to race through Good Friday to get to Easter. The desire to celebrate rebirth and resurrection is strong. We face so many pressures, demands, and disappointments in our daily lives. Who wants to dwell on the sad and solemn? It is much more appealing to focus our attention on victory and triumph.

But we diminish the true power of Easter if we ignore the meaning of Good Friday. We are familiar with Judas' betrayal, Jesus' arrest, Peter's denials, and Jesus' interrogation by the high priest and Pontius Pilate. We cringe at the picture of Jesus, sentenced to death, flogged, dragging his cross to Golgotha, where he is nailed to the cross and lifted to die hanging as a common criminal. Ending with the humiliating test to see if he is dead—being pierced like so much meat—Jesus is then laid in a tomb, and, to all earthly appearances, the story ends.

But the power of Good Friday rests in the answer to Pilate's question to Jesus in John 18:38*a*: "What is truth?" Is truth the earthly powers that defy God? Is truth the ability to silence the prophetic Word? Is truth the violence that attempts to dissuade others from hearing the good news? Is truth believing that death can end God's will for the world? No. In all things God's truth prevails. The real truth is that nothing on earth or in heaven can silence the true Word, the good news of Jesus Christ. Even the most evil intentions and acts cannot change that. The truth is that God so loved this world that Jesus was sent that all might have redemption and know God's love. Even in the deepest darkness, God's light still shines.

So often, O Lord, my soul feels wrapped in darkness. Shine the light of your gracious love and healing on me, that others might see and know that you are the source. Amen.

But mortals die, and are laid low; humans expire, and where are they?

I always imagine the disciples on this blackest and most hopeless Saturday morning, huddling together, trying to figure out what to do. In my mind's eye I see scared and distressed men and women, and in my mind's ear I hear a never-ending refrain of "yes, but . . . " "Jesus said he would return—yes, but dead is dead." "Jesus told us all this was God's will—yes, but we saw him flogged and crucified and buried." Jesus told us to have faith and trust—yes, but he isn't here now, is he?"

The broken, battered corpse of the carpenter's son from Nazareth could not possibly have been what Jesus' followers expected to end up with at the close of three years' teaching, preaching, and healing. How could they recover from such a tragedy? Everything they worked for was suddenly sealed away in the earth, perhaps never to return.

All of us have known despair and disappointment in our lives, but few of us can relate to the abject devastation the disciples felt when their Master and Teacher was ripped away from them. More than losing a friend or a brother, they lost their mission and purpose in life. They had given everything to follow Jesus—leaving home, family, trade, and possessions. They had one simple identity: they were the followers of Jesus. Then, all that was gone.

It is invaluable to seek to understand what the disciples felt in the time between the crucifixion and resurrection of Jesus. In this time we gain insight into what life might be like without God, without hope, without purpose, and without a future. It is in this deep darkness that we are prepared for the blinding brilliance of Easter morn.

Be still, my soul, help me in my dark places, where my faith is attacked, O Lord, and my hope is weakest. Protect me in the difficult days that I might live toward a resurrected heart and spirit. Amen.

EASTER SUNDAY

The greatest joy I have ever known in my life came at the birth of my son, Joshua. On that day, in that moment, nothing else mattered. My little boy was born; goodness and light and hope and promise filled my life. I was startled to realize that I had never known a love so great as the love I felt at his birth. It was—and is—a transforming, sustaining, and empowering love. Some other experience may offer you a taste of divine joy, and I invite you to spend a few moments remembering it.

Easter, at its most basic, is a glimpse of heaven. It is our opportunity to encounter the purest, greatest power of God manifest in the natural world. Resurrection challenges our rational mind. Things like this simply cannot happen. Yet, by God's grace, Jesus returned from the grave, releasing humankind from the bondage to fear of death for all time. The incredible act of resurrection changed all the rules. By Jesus' merciful and gracious sacrifice, Christian disciples needed no longer accept anxiety, violence, injustice, cruelty, and oppression as their only reality.

The God who is greater than death is a God greater than terrorism, hatred, bigotry, abuse, or a myriad host of equally heinous evils. No force on earth is greater than God's redemptive power. Salvation no longer exists as a dreamed-of ideal but now is within reach of those who would proclaim Jesus the Christ as Lord.

What a gift! No greater gift has ever been offered; no greater gift may ever be received. Rejoice in this gift, my friends, for it is given to you.

Receive, O Lord, our humble offerings of praise, gratitude, thanksgiving, honor, blessing, and joy. We may never understand the depths of your love but help us share this love with everyone we meet. In the name of Jesus and the Spirit of the Christ. Amen.

Strength in Community

APRIL 13–19, 2009 • TIMOTHY B. WARNER

MONDAY, APRIL 13 ~ *Read Acts 4:32-35*

Everything they owned was held in common.

We live in a world of individuals—individual thinking, individual living, individual issues, individual possessions, *and* individual problems! Like a single piece of driftwood on the ocean, we have no way to go against the tide. When the waves are rough, so are our lives. When the current picks up speed, we scramble to keep up. And when the sea is still, we find it strange and uncomfortable.

Thank God, Jesus had another plan for us. God knows that the only chance we have to be the church in this world is through the life and death of Jesus. When we are unified in Jesus, our hearts and souls become one; and our witness becomes stronger. The Holy Spirit of the living God leads us to live and work together in new ways, ways that the world sometimes doesn't understand. Together, the early church had more than enough of everything because none of them had anything of their own.

If we want to know the power of the early church, we must live less for ourselves and more for our community in Jesus. This is the way to strengthen our witness in the world.

Lord, make us a strong community, and strengthen our witness in the world. We ask this in Jesus' name. Amen.

Pastor of St. Mark's United Methodist Church in Boyds, Maryland, since 2003; also serving in the Montgomery County Executive's Office of Community Partnerships

There was not one needy person among them.

When I was young, we often sang this hymn in church: "Jesus paid it all, All to Him I owe." We know the words, but I wonder whether we realize that Jesus expects the enormity of his gift to us to transform our way of giving. In these times of individualistic stinginess, it is hard for us to understand that Jesus gave the gift—his very own life—that keeps on giving. But we must work to understand this because his gift keeps on giving *through* us.

The new disciples got it right. They didn't give God a tip or even a tithe for that matter. They understood that God's lavish grace had been heaped upon them and that they had a responsibility to be like Christ! They knew they had the responsibility to give not just some of what God had given them but *all* of what they had. They decided together to give to others. They didn't want to build a bigger building or to have a better program. They wanted everyone to have enough, so that none among them would be in need. They realized that God's aim for humankind was to be in community with God, as well as to be in community with one another.

God has provided everything we need as a community. But our problems arise when we refuse to give as Christ gave. The kingdom of God comes in our world when we adopt Christ's new standard of giving.

Lord, we beseech you in your generous nature to guide us toward a new way of giving. Forgive us for not trusting you enough to give to you and to others as you gave yourself for us. Help us to envision a new standard of giving for the sake of your kingdom. In Jesus' name. Amen.

How good and pleasant it is when kindred live together in unity!

Those who have ever lived in the chaos of a contentious, divided community can testify as to how very good it is for brothers and sisters to live in unity! How much time and energy are wasted when we are working against each other instead of living in the unity that God has given us?

Since God first moved among us, unity has been ours to treasure—or to lose. Unity is not some goal we must achieve; it is a vision we must live.

My great-grandmother made stew the way I think the Holy Spirit makes unity. She would imagine what needed to go in to make it taste just right for all of us who were hungry. She would add the right vegetables to the pot in the right order at just the right time, so that when it was done, the stew satisfied each and every one of us.

In a similar way, God takes who we are—as different as we all are from each other—and enables us not just to live together but to blend together in a way that makes our witness nourishment for the world. This is the work of God's power through us. It is like pouring holy anointing oil on the world's head and watching it drip like a blessing down over all the world's people. God's power in the world rests in large part in our unity!

Precious God, you made us to be together in you. May we be less for ourselves that we can become more for you, together. Pour us out as a blessing for the world. Amen.

We are writing these things so that our joy may be complete.

Christians long to share their faith with others and have good reason to do so. Once we have heard God's word; been touched by the witness of Jesus' life, and come to know the Holy Spirit, the only thing we can do is share our relationship with others. Something about a personal relationship with Jesus Christ makes us want to tell people about it.

First John describes in vivid terms what motivates us to speak about our relationship with God: God is the light that brings us out of darkness. God brings us from *darkness* into *light!* This is the amazing news we must share. First John says God does this not once or twice—*but as many times as we need.* We are believers, members of the fellowship of believers, who live in the light; still we sometimes fall away from God into sin and darkness. But each time that happens, we have a strong advocate in Jesus who, if we confess our sins, is faithful and just, who forgives us and brings us back into the light.

We share because we are blessed to be part of this strong fellowship with God in Christ. We share to fulfill our joy. God's heart glows when we live out our witness to the light in ways that touch those around us. God's light and forgiveness—given to the whole world—makes our hearts glow too.

O God, whose heart glows with love for humankind, remind us of your joy at the beauty of our transformed hearts. Help us live in the light so that we may daily witness to your love. We ask it for Christ's sake. Amen.

The doors of the house where the disciples had met were locked . . . and Jesus came and stood among them and said, "Peace be with you."

Imagine being captivated by the power of Jesus' witness on earth, accompanying him as he preached and taught, as he made the lame walk and the blind see. Then imagine Jesus being captured, tortured, and put to death. See yourself hiding away with the disciples in fear of what the world might do because you had associated yourself with him. Picture yourself in a small room, behind a locked door. See yourself sitting there in despair—when suddenly Jesus appears in the middle of that room and says, "Peace be with you." Imagine being there, sequestered behind a locked door. And then imagine Jesus suddenly appearing right in the middle of that locked room, saying, "Peace be with you." What a wonderful and frightening surprise that would be!

Has Jesus ever surprised you this way? Remember a time when you were struggling with a difficult situation, worrying your way into a frenzy, when suddenly, unexpectedly, Jesus just shows up out of nowhere and says, "Peace be with you."

Thankfully, Jesus does come through the locked doors of fear, despair, and sin in our lives—but not to condemn us. He comes to give us the peace the world can't give, the world can't take away.

God of open doors, show up and surprise us right where we are in our lives! Help us to know the peace you give so graciously and freely. In Jesus' name. Amen.

A week later his disciples were again in the house, and Thomas was with them. Although the doors were shut, Jesus came and stood among them and said, "Peace be with you." Then he said to Thomas, "Put your finger here and see my hands. Reach out your hand and put it in my side. Do not doubt but believe."

There is no worse feeling than to have experienced what it means to have found peace with Christ, to live in the grip of God's grace that will never let you go, and yet to have loved ones who, for whatever reason, choose not to make their own peace with God through Christ. We live between the ecstasy of salvation and the agony of not having the ones we care most about share it with us. Many Christians live in this reality every day.

But there is hope. Jesus had the same problem with one of his own loved ones. Thomas lived under the paralyzing indecision of doubt; he would not believe until he had visible, tangible proof. Jesus didn't worry about him. Jesus didn't beat him over the head with a Bible. Jesus, above all, didn't condemn him. Instead, Jesus chose simply to be present with him.

We would do well simply to offer to our doubt-filled loved ones our hands, which have been wounded and now are healed by the blood of Jesus. Just as it was for Thomas, so it may be for our loved ones. They may only be able to escape their doubt through touching our testimony. Perhaps, like Thomas, they will simply believe.

Lord, we thank you for salvation that is full and free and available to everyone. Anoint us afresh with the Holy Spirit, power to carry the word of your testimony in us, that our loved ones and others may come to know you for themselves. Amen.

Now Jesus did many other signs in the presence of his disciples, which are not written in this book. But these are written so that you may come to believe that Jesus is the Messiah, the Son of God, and that through believing you may have life in his name.

If the story of the passion of Christ on Calvary and his seven last words didn't get your attention, there is more. If the story of the women who went to the tomb and found the stone rolled away did not surprise you, there is more. If the angel's proclamation of the resurrected Christ didn't completely convince you that something miraculous had just happened, there is more.

The writer of John pushes Jesus' death and resurrection even further, to Christ's revealing himself to the disciples in the upper room. This, on top of everything else that had happened, is nothing short of amazing.

The writer's point, though, is not simply to amaze us with the story. The point of these things having been written down at all is so that we may come to believe that Jesus is Lord; that he is God's son, our savior, one of a kind in all eternity. Jesus was the only one capable of taking on a death sentence that belonged not to him but to us. These things are written because God wants us to know as surely as we know our own names that Jesus is the way back to eternal fellowship with God.

Don't just be amazed at what Jesus *does*; be faithful to who he *is*.

God of amazing love, draw us closer to you in faith through your word. Speak to us. Get our attention and then teach us how to lead lives of faith so that others might come to you through Christ. In the name of Jesus. Amen.

Peace with God, Peace through God

APRIL 20–26, 2009 • TWILA M. BELK

MONDAY, APRIL 20 ~ *Read Psalm 4*

A requisitioned artist struggled to paint a picture portraying peace. After a few unsuccessful attempts, he captured the idea. The artist painted a turbulent sea with storm clouds overhead. A fierce wind blew, yet a mama bird and her babies nestled in the cleft of a rocky mountainside.

That's a picture of today's scripture. The psalmist cried out to God in a time of great distress. He faced grave danger and wrestled with inner turmoil. He could no longer trust his family and friends.

But the psalmist knew something his enemies didn't. Because of his intimate relationship with God, he knew he was safe in divine protective care. He could trust God to hear his cries and to respond out of love. He was able to "rest in his nest" in the midst of distress.

Our situations may differ, but we all face adversity. We struggle with family issues and problems with friends. Harsh circumstances, often beyond our control, cause emotional duress and keep us awake at night. Stormy winds of criticism rage against us and dark clouds of doubt linger over us. But it is possible to find safety and a haven of rest in the cleft of the Rock.

The same peace that David felt is there for us through the God who hears when we call. Peace comes from trusting—maybe even knowing—that God is there for us. We can call on God directly, with confidence, even when life is hard and we are hurting. We know that God is with us. We are not alone.

My righteous God, give me relief from my distress; be merciful to me and hear my prayer. Amen.

Christian speaker, author, and radio personality, sometimes known as the "Gotta Tell Somebody Gal;" serving on the Board of Overseers of the Baptist General Conference and living in Bettendorf, Iowa

When doctors at Mayo Clinic diagnosed my husband with a rare, incurable disease, I cried out to God. When my son almost died from a ruptured appendix, I cried out to God. Through the years I've cried out to God countless times.

I've observed some things from the psalmist's life. As in many of the psalms, Psalm 4 begins with his crying out to God because of the trials he faces. It shifts midway and turns the focus from his troubles to God's goodness. One minute the psalmist begs for relief; the next he's filled with great joy. One minute he cries out in distress; the next he's at peace.

A problem many of us have when we cry out to God and complain about our predicaments is that we don't allow God the opportunity to assure us of God's goodness in our lives. We cry out in desperation but focus on our circumstances without waiting for God's response.

The psalmist was honest toward God about his feelings. He didn't hold back. Instead of spouting off and turning away, he stayed in God's presence with his attention directed toward God. As he focused on God's goodness, he saw things from a different perspective. He realized that God was bigger than his enemies and his problems.

Like the psalmist, I've learned that when I have nowhere to turn but to God, God is all I need. When I turn my focus from my problems to my Lord, I discover the same things that David did: The joy of God is incomparable. God's peace is unexplainable. God's love is incomprehensible.

It is possible to experience joy in the midst of distress. It's possible to sleep in peace when facing trials. It's made possible by focusing on God and by revisiting God's goodness often.

Loving God, your goodness is unlimited. May I know the joy and peace that come only from you. Amen.

Jesus died a tortuous death. Three days later he appeared to some of his followers. After his resurrection, Jesus appeared to five hundred people. Those amazed people quickly spread the word.

At Jesus' command, disciples assembled in Jerusalem. While they discussed the reports of his appearances, Jesus stood among them. He could have made a grand entrance and said, "Hey, here I am. Look! It's me—Jesus!" Instead, he chose to greet those gathered with a simple statement: "Peace be with you."

Why were those Jesus' first words? Perhaps he knew this is what the disciples needed most. Jesus knew they were startled, frightened, and troubled. He knew they had doubts. He knew what they were going through. So Jesus offered them peace.

To calm their fears and to let them know that the Prince of Peace was already in their midst, Jesus showed them his hands and feet. He told them to touch him. Jesus asked for food and ate it in front of them. He assured the disciples of his presence, and they received his peace.

Today we can't physically see Jesus or touch him, but we can know he's alive and at work in our lives. Daily he offers peace. Daily we see God's miracles of timing, wisdom, and provision. Daily he assures us of his presence. Our personal experiences with Jesus prove the truth of God's word. Jesus is who he says he is—the Prince of Peace.

Jesus, thank you for your presence and your peace in my life. Thank you for knowing what I need most and taking care of it for me. Amen.

When Jesus reminded the disciples of the things he told them before his death, they felt great excitement. He opened their minds so they could understand him even more deeply. Jesus spoke again with the disciples about the scriptures that said he would suffer and rise from the dead on the third day. It had to be true because Jesus stood there before them.

Jesus told them they were to preach repentance and forgiveness of sins to all nations, beginning in Jerusalem. (See also Acts 1:8.) They were already gathered in Jerusalem. I wonder if that was the moment the disciples realized they had a job to do. They had a story to tell. Since the disciples had witnessed all the things Jesus spoke of and they knew that Jesus was God's son, it was their job to tell the world. All the days they had spent with Jesus made sense. With Jesus' gentle guidance and revelation from the scriptures, the disciples understood that Jesus had been preparing them for this time.

When Jesus returned to God in heaven, he sent the Holy Spirit to empower the disciples to fulfill the commission. Today, as believers, we too have the benefit of the Holy Spirit at work in our lives. Part of the Holy Spirit's purpose is to guide us into truth, remind us what we have forgotten, and reveal to us important insights from God's word. The Holy Spirit helps us understand things that haven't made sense to us. The Holy Spirit is the author of these moments of insight and energy.

Holy Spirit, open my mind so I can understand the scriptures. Reveal to me things I need to know. Use me as a powerful witness to others of your truth. Amen.

A man, crippled from birth, was given new life. His ankles and feet became strong. He jumped. He walked. And he praised God. He was full of joy because he had been refreshed. He was a new man. Should that surprise people? Not if they know the story of Jesus.

In yesterday's reading, Jesus repeated to the disciples what the scriptures had said about him. "The Christ will suffer and rise from the dead on the third day. . . . " (Luke 24:46, NIV) Before Jesus left them, he reminded the disciples that they were witnesses of those events. Jesus told the disciples that repentance and forgiveness of sins would be preached in his name.

Peter reviewed the same message with those who were surprised by the lame man's healing. Peter claimed he witnessed the death and resurrection of Jesus before he preached repentance and forgiveness—just as Jesus had promised.

Peter testified to the power of God, and he made sure the people of Israel knew that the same power that raised Jesus from the dead made the lame man walk. Not only that, but that same power could wipe out sins and bring refreshment if they would repent and turn to God. They could receive spiritual healing and become new people.

These are big ideas for us to think about. Healing power, resurrection power, and forgiveness power can operate in our lives daily through faith in Jesus.

Should we be surprised when we experience it? Not if we know the story of Jesus.

Should we be grateful? Of course.

Should we tell others? Absolutely! If we have witnessed the power of God at work in our lives, the world needs to know.

Lord, thank you for displaying your power in my life. May I be a bold witness for you. Amen.

After my dad died from a brain aneurysm, a woman from church sent me a note that read, "I know you miss him. You could tell you were Daddy's little girl. He loved you." As I read the words, I got a warm, special feeling.

Today's portion of scripture reminded me that I'm my heavenly Father's little girl. The first verse (in the NIV) refers to the great love God has lavished on us. The word *lavish* means rich, generous, and beautiful.

God's love is lavished on us. While we were sinners, Christ died for us and thereby lavished love on us. Our old life of failure, shame and doubt is redeemed. Because of God's lavish love, our new life is filled with confidence and joy. We are God's children—loved, cherished, and valued.

Some of us have had good earthly fathers and some have not. The father you grew up with may not have been a good father. He might have marred—or scarred—your concept of what a true father should be. Your father might have been absent. Or your father may have been a good and loving parent. But regardless of who your imperfect parent was, God has claimed us as God's very own—as beloved and cherished children.

Our God is trustworthy and keeps all promises. Our God's goodness is limitless.

How great is God's love, that we have been made children of God.

God, how great it is to be your child! Thank you for loving me so lavishly. May I learn to trust your love and rest in your care. Amen.

Have you ever noticed that family members sometimes act alike? They might demonstrate similar mannerisms or say things in the same way. Whether this comes from being related or from spending a lot of time together, it happens. Even when people are adopted, they often take on the family traits. The longer our association with someone, the more we imitate them, and their habits and attitudes rub off on us.

After observing my daughter in action, people have told me that the nut didn't fall too far from the tree. Laney shares many of my qualities: she loves to talk; she is creative; she can be downright goofy; she is passionate about God; and she's an encourager. I've also seen her copy a few of my bad traits such as a grumpy attitude or impatience.

Today's passage tells us that Jesus had no sin and that no one who lives in him will keep on sinning. First John 2:6 (NIV) says, "Whoever claims to live in him must walk as Jesus did." Although it's impossible to live a sinless life, we strive daily to become more like him because we're part of his family. If we are children of God, that means we're related to Jesus. We can expect to display Christlike qualities.

Sometimes I'm aware that I don't always manifest my Lord's qualities. Usually that's because I haven't spent enough time with him. The more connected we are to Jesus, the more we "live in him" and know him, the stronger our family resemblance.

Are you living like a child of God?

If a family portrait were taken today, would people see a strong family resemblance between you and Jesus?

God's All-Embracing Care

APRIL 27–MAY 3, 2009 • JUAN BEK

MONDAY, APRIL 27 ～ *Read Acts 4:5-12*

Peter, filled with the Holy Spirit, gives account to the Sanhedrin by what power and in whose name he had healed a crippled beggar the day before. The bystanders noticed that Peter and John were ordinary, unschooled people. So it was not the theological depth of Peter's words that amazed the listeners but the courage, passion, and persistence they received from the Holy Spirit. That is why, at the end of the audience with the Sanhedrin, Peter challenged the rulers, the teachers, and elders of the law who wanted to silence them, saying, "We cannot help speaking about what we have seen and heard" (Acts 4:19, NIV).

That is what happens with the Spirit in our ordinary Christian life. Once we are "possessed" by the Holy Spirit, there is no turning back. Acts describes the force, the power, the strength, the passion, and sometimes the violence of the Spirit's transforming task in the early church. According to Genesis, the Spirit of God was at work when God created the heavens and the earth. In the same way God is at work in the creation of the new human being in the new community we call the church.

With the same persistence and courage, with the same passion and emotions of Peter and the other apostles, we have to give testimony of being re-created by the cross of Christ and by the power of the Spirit. We cannot keep quiet about the great thing the Spirit of God has done to us, among us, and within each of us. Nobody can silence our voice.

Lord, open my heart so the Spirit can transform me to be a powerful witness of the cross and resurrection of Jesus Christ. Amen.

Dutch Roman Catholic, retired professor and former dean of the Evangelical Seminary of Puerto Rico, current coordinator of the seminary's Doctor of Ministry program

Once, when I was teaching a course in an indigenous community of a small Central American country, I was surprised to observe that the majority of the women in the village were crippled. When I asked the students why nearly all the women walked bent over, they took me outside the village and showed me a brick factory. The women carried the bricks on their backs and shoulders from the factory to the trucks. If you do this day after day, week after week, year after year, there comes a time when you cannot stand upright. The interesting thing was that none of the women lived in a house built of bricks!

This came to my mind when I was reading Peter's defense of having healed a crippled person. The Sanhedrin wants to know by what name Peter did this. He answers that he did it in the name of Jesus of Nazareth. Jesus healed crippled people too. Think of the miracle in Luke 13. A woman who was unable to stand upright was straightened up by Jesus and given the good news that she was set free. In the kingdom of God she symbolizes the new woman, freed from the weight of male domination. She is also the woman who reveals the meaning of Jesus' name.

Matthew knows the importance of naming Mary's baby Jesus (Matthew 2:22). The name Jesus derives from the Hebrew *Yasha*, which means "to deliver" or "to straighten up." Jesus embodies the meaning of his name when he straightens up the bent-over woman. It is in the name of the one who came to straighten up all of us—in Jesus' name—that Peter healed the crippled beggar.

> *Lord Jesus, take my hand and straighten me up. Heal me in the places where I still need your touch. Amen.*

The text of Psalm 23 is frequently printed on "in memoriam" cards and icons. For a long time I identified the psalm with death, tears, grieving, and funerals. I asked myself many times, *Why do I have to wait until after death to enjoy God's loving presence? Shouldn't I feel that presence during my life, when I am lonely, fearful, or in need?*

I have discovered, little by little, that the psalm is not about my relationship with God after I die. The psalm is a song about the present. It is about life. It invites us to discover God's guidance, God's company, and God's protection in our daily life. We can be aware of God's acts of love and concern in our day-to-day lives.

God's presence is everywhere. We do not have to wait until death to know God's gifts. God is present when somebody takes care of our physical needs, our psychological needs, and our social necessities. Psalm 23 praises God's support, provision, and providence. Through others God provides food for us, prepares the table, and fills our cup until it overflows. Through others God gives us a roof and comforts us. God's love will follow us all the days of our existence. That is what the psalm affirms: "Surely goodness and mercy shall follow me all the days of my life" (NIV).

God is the shepherd who offers help, protection, and care. But sometimes that help, protection, and care come through others. We must prepare our eyes, ears, and heart to be aware of God's presence in every person and situation we encounter. God is here with us now. Because of that, we are called to shepherd other people, to make God's presence real in the lives of others, to love them as shepherds love the sheep.

Lord, guide me to discover your presence in the fullness of life and to communicate it to others. Amen.

The image of the shepherd has a long history in biblical tradition. All the patriarchs were shepherds: Abel, Abraham, Isaac, Esau, and Jacob. Jacob's sons identified themselves before Joseph as shepherds, just like "our ancestors" (Gen. 47:3). Moses was taking care of the sheep of his father-in-law when the Lord called him. The young boy David looked after his father's sheep. Shepherding was part of Israel's DNA.

It is no wonder that one of the most appealing symbols the people used to describe God's relationship with them was that of shepherd. It was God who walked with the people, who took care of them in the past, who looked out for them in the present, and who promised always take care of them. This was the people's faith and conviction.

Little by little the Israelites lost their nomadic lifestyle, settling into cities and towns. Nevertheless, the heritage of being a wandering people remained part of Israel's self-identification. They considered themselves to be a people of strangers and expatriates in this world. We find this in the letters of Paul and Peter. Peter writes to "God's elect, strangers in the world" (1 Pet. 1:1, NIV). "Our citizenship is in heaven," says Paul to the Philippians (Phil. 3:20, NIV). And according to the letter to the Hebrews, Noah, Abraham, and others "admitted that they were aliens and strangers on earth. People who say such things show that they are looking for a country of their own" (Heb. 11:13-14, NIV). And, just as the original readers of these letters, all of us are in a sense strangers in this world. We all need a shepherd. Thank God for the care and protection of Jesus Christ, our good shepherd!

Good shepherd, guide and protect me on my journey to the Promised Land. Give me comfort, care, and mercy that I may dwell in your house forever. Amen.

We all know people who, when they think about their relationship with God, are overwhelmed by uncertainty, doubt, and guilt. In this portion of the letter, the writer addresses precisely those who are looking for reassurance in the presence of God. How can they be bold in God's presence? How can they stand before God with confidence?

It begins, John says, with love—with understanding God's love for us. We can know God's love because Jesus, out of love, laid down his life for us. Jesus' act of love entitles us to be in God's presence—and it demands of us a bold response. We must lay down our lives for one another—not just care for one another, or look out for one another but be willing to lay down our lives.

This kind of love, given by Jesus and expected of us, is not love that acts only when the feeling is right or when the time is convenient. This love is informed by deep compassion; it calls out the best in us. We can be bold to love this way because Jesus has given us the power to do so.

If we see a sister or brother in need and do nothing, John tells us frankly that the love of God is not in us. Acts of love are the response of the faithful. What happens when we don't show this love? What happens when we disobey the command to love one another? Will we be cast away from God and from the community? No, John says. God will continue to love us. God's love is so great that God will never let us go.

This is the love we must show to one another and to those in need.

Let your love stir within me today, God. Strengthen me to love not with words but through acts of faith. Amen.

When I consulted different versions of the parable of the Good Shepherd in John's Gospel, I was surprised by the fact that many of them made explicit references to Ezekiel 34. That chapter of the Bible contains some of the most beautiful words pronounced by God about God's concern for the people. God is the real and only good shepherd. Ezekiel prophesies against the rulers, leaders, and elders who call themselves the shepherds of the people, but are in fact not good shepherds at all.

When Jesus called himself the "good shepherd," his audience understood that he was in part referring to Ezekiel 34. Among this audience were also some of the leaders and rulers of the people, who claimed to be the people's shepherds. But Jesus knew the truth. He called them what they really were: hired workers who run away and don't care about the sheep.

The contrast between hired workers and the good shepherd is stark. Jesus would never leave his flock to the mercy of wolves. Jesus would protect his sheep to the point of laying down his life for them. Jesus knows his sheep, and his sheep know him. These self-serving, fly-by-night hired hands are not shepherds. They endanger the flock. Only the good shepherd can save the sheep from these hired hands.

Being a good shepherd does put Jesus in harm's way. Speaking the truth, he accuses powerful leaders of being false shepherds. These leaders were angry at him, and it would come down to this: Jesus the good shepherd does actually lay down his life for us. He made himself vulnerable so that we could be saved.

Jesus' parable confronts us to consider whom we follow as our shepherd in our daily lives. Reflect on what shepherd you follow and how you shepherd those who under your care.

As a Roman Catholic, my theology and beliefs were formed both before and during Vatican Council II. I witnessed the church move from an attitude of exclusion to a spirit of change and openness. During my teaching career, I taught at an Episcopal seminary for five years and at an evangelical seminary for thirty-one years. At the evangelical seminary, the student body included six Protestant denominations and a number of Pentecostal and independent students.

During this time, I came to believe that we are all sheep of the same shepherd, but the shepherd does not belong to us alone. "I have other sheep that do not belong to this fold," Jesus said. I have seen that to be true in so many ways.

I have come to know, to respect, and to love a variety of worship styles, a range of theologies, a richness of confessional standpoints, and the strengths of different ways of interpreting the Bible. I have come to understand that we complement one another's visions and that we are enriched by the experience and traditions of others.

I see that no one has the last word about God. The mystery of God is too great to be understood by human beings. When Thomas Aquinas finished his beautiful commentary on the Gospel of John, he wrote: *Infinita enim verba hominum non possunt attingere unum Dei verbum.* The translation from the Latin is this: "An infinite number of human words is unable to approach one single word of God." The unity of the flock does not depend on words or formula but on a spirit of modesty, respect, and humility. Arrogance and superiority have no place here.

The good shepherd cares for all the sheep. As those under God's protection, we can do no less.

Good Shepherd, keep me faithful to you. May I treat all who seek you with tenderness and care. Amen.

Abiding in God

MAY 4–10, 2009 • ANN FREEMAN PRICE

MONDAY, MAY 4 ~ *Read 1 John 4:7-21*

There is a wonderful circular statement within this passage from First John: "God is love, and those who abide in love abide in God, and God abides in them." I relish staying with verses until I find ways to work them into my life.

"God is love." I have believed that for a long time, taught it to my children, and sung it in songs. I have heard it in devotions and sermons.

"Those who abide in love abide in God." Now I need to move from belief to action, from words to deeds, from theory to practice. If I am going to abide in love, I must reach out to others and offer them the love God offers me.

"And God abides in them." When God abides I become a new person because God is my center.

I made a Mobius strip as a visual reminder of this circle mystery. On both sides of a long, slim, rectangular strip of paper I wrote: God is love. If I abide in love I abide in God. And God abides in me. I made it into a circle, and when I connected the two ends, I rotated one end 180 degrees and taped the ends together. Suddenly it was a continuous strip—a Mobius strip—repeating over and over this statement of truth: God is love. Abide in love and abide in God. And God abides in you.

I hung it on my doorknob so I could see it as I went out and came in—an ever-present reminder to love and to celebrate God within me.

Abiding God, I welcome you into my heart and life. Help me abide in you each day and feel your love each moment. Amen.

Freelance writer and musician, social activist, member of Sparta United Methodist Church in Sparta, New Jersey

We love because God first loved us. It's a sentence of seven words. And sometimes I can't decide if it's a simple thought or a complicated one.

One Bible study group decided that it was a little bit of both—simple and yet complex. One woman said, "It's hard to believe sometimes that God loves me. I get so jumbled. My life gets so crazy. I lose my patience and in the middle of all that, I think, now really, how could God love me?"

A man in the group said, "Well, I can believe God loves me because I try hard to love other people. I think God expects that of me, and I think God loves me because I try to do it."

Another woman chimed in, "You know, these verses are clear to me—that God first loved us. Loved us before—before we did anything to deserve the love, before we could stack up credits, before we could get ourselves together. And in that act of loving us, God enables us to be able to love others."

It is simple, and it is complicated.

Thich Nhat Hanh, a Buddhist monk, described four elements of love—lovingkindness, compassion, joy, and inclusiveness. We could make our own list of what elements make up love, and we might each come up with different lists—lists with both similarities and with differences.

Sooner or later we come face to face with the reality that even in our jumbled states, even in the midst of the craziness, even when we lose patience, God loves each of us.

And because of that immeasurable love, we too can love. Perhaps, we can even abide in that love.

God who loves and who loved first, open my heart to accept your love and believe that it is for me. Amen.

Psalm 22 moves dramatically from a plea for deliverance to a great call to praise. Here, all persons are swept into the activity of praise.

> Let those who live now—praise!
> Let those who have died—praise!
> Let those yet unborn—praise!

We sing praise in worship services. We raise our voices as we gather for Bible study. We lift our hearts at a church supper, finding time and making the place to praise God. We say a blessing before meals—and praise God. We light a candle and have quiet devotions—and praise God. We run and laugh with children or grandchildren—and praise God.

On November 1, All Saints' Day, we acknowledge those who have gone before us. We talk about a cloud of witnesses. One year, to celebrate the saints, my co-pastor and I read the names the congregation had given us of those they knew and loved who had died. As we read those names, it felt as if our small congregation grew as over two hundred names were called out, and our combined memories crowded the pews as those persons joined us in praise.

This psalm says God will be praised not only by those of us alive now, but also by those yet unborn, those still to come, and those from the distant past. And so the circle of praise grows far beyond even the faith community to include all of creation. This is indeed a mighty chorus of praise. What joy to abide in such wondrous praise!

God of all times, I praise you! I celebrate your presence with me, with those who have come before, and with all who will come after. Lead me deeper into the mystery of praise and thanksgiving. Amen.

We gather in communities around the world and praise. The psalmist calls this a "great congregation." And within that congregation is an acknowledgment that all who seek God will praise God—all families, all nations, all creation.

Whether we have fully experienced being part of this great congregation or whether it comes to us in bits and pieces—this is still a foretaste of a reality to come. It stands as a testimony to those gathering around a table or within a sanctuary, seated in a campground or clustered in homes. In each of those places—and in all places throughout the world—the charge is to praise.

It is with our praise that we say thanks, because God is a great God, because God loves us with a great love.

A year ago as part of my daily devotions I decided to write a journal about the day before—thoughts I had, things I had done, questions I wondered about. At the end of each day's journal entry, I addressed three categories: the day's accomplishments, the day's gratitudes, and my intentions.

The most interesting of those three categories was the gratitude category. I discovered that writing helped me think through in small, specific ways all the things in my life I am thankful for, the things that call me to praise God. Sometimes it was a child or a grandchild. Another day it was "good doctors." The next it was "the fun of bedtime stories." And one day it was even "zingy energy."

Each time I stop to reflect on my day, I am reminded to praise God and to give thanks. When I do this, I join the great congregation and become part of its worldwide chorus of praise.

Praise and thanks. Thanks and praise. For the wonder, for the ordinary. For the simple, for the complicated. Thanks and praise. Praise and thanks! This is my song of gratitude to you, O God. Amen.

The Ethiopian eunuch existed on the edges of the religious people of that day—for one thing he was a foreigner and for the other, he was a eunuch. Both put him on the edges.

And yet the Spirit said to Philip, "Go over to this chariot and join it." From that point on, the Ethiopian eunuch was included in Philip's witness and in the faith.

One of the important and exciting parts of the Christian life is studying scripture and exploring your own theology—your own system of belief. Through the years I have done this in a variety of ways—through individual study, by reading books, in quiet reflection. But I prefer another way. I like to gather regularly with a group to study, to discuss ideas, to examine the opinions of others.

There is a lightness in my current study group. It is a place for humor and deep questions. There is laughter and serious sharing. There is time for mystery and certainty. There is time to apply scripture to life.

You never know when a chariot will appear, and the Spirit will say, "Go join it." When this happens, our study and reflection quickly become the basis of our witness, and we are called to speak our faith to a stranger or a friend—to someone who is living on the edges and needs to hear our witness to love, inclusion, and abundant life.

It is important to be ready for this day. But it is also important to remember that there is another dimension to our witness. No matter what we've studied, no matter how we have prepared, it is the Spirit that enlivens our witness. It is the Spirit that does the life-changing work of the Lord. In truth, it is the Spirit that, from the beginning, prepares us to witness.

On this day, O God, may I ready myself ready to answer the call to go join the chariot. Amen.

I am not a gardener and never have been. But I appreciate those who are good at gardening because I love its beauty.

I have recently moved and have new surroundings, new plants and flowers. Outside of my window is a lamppost, which until last weekend was totally covered with a vine. My son-in-law climbed the ladder beside the lamppost and started trimming. In just a few minutes, I could begin to see the light that was at the top of the post that had been underneath the vine. It made me think of this passage where Jesus says, "I am the vine, you are the branches."

I took a course at my church in voluntary simplicity and then another in sustainable living. We talked of clearing so we could stay focused. We discussed setting priorities so we could keep balanced. We spoke of the earth and how we could honor and respect creation in our living. During each of these courses I felt the Gardener pruning and urging me to prune some more. I felt a call to prune my possessions, my overextended time commitments, and my busyness. I felt a call to prune until there was new balance in my life.

And with the pruning, I found time and space to breathe and to be more fruitful. With the pruning, suddenly I could see the light at the top of the lamppost.

The John 15 passage ends with an exhortation to bear more fruit and become true disciples. With God's pruning, with our own pruning, it does happen. We begin to bear more fruit, and we become more committed disciples.

This pruning brings a movement toward God, an evolving joy, and a wonderful grace.

Dear God, help me hold still long enough for you to prune, so my fruitfulness can increase. Amen.

The woman looked out the window and said thoughtfully, "Some days I lose my direction and feel like a branch that has torn loose from the vine. I drift in the wind."

She sat still for a minute and silence surrounded her before she spoke again, "And other days I feel I'm a healthy branch on the vine. I feel I can bear fruit and that God is within me. In my clear times, it does feel that with God, I can do so much. But in those drifting times it feels as though without God, I can do nothing."

The verses come full circle. "I am the vine, you are the branches. Those who abide in me and I in them bear much fruit."

My Mobius strip still hangs on the doorknob. It still says, God is love. If I abide in love I abide in God. And God abides in me. It touches my fingers as I go out, and I hear the rustle that says, "Abide."

I think of making another strip and on it writing all the words of the week: *love, abide in God, include those on the edges, give praise and thanks, be pruned, bear fruit, become a disciple.* I wonder if I can transfer the Mobius strip to my heart and to my life?

God's directions this week sometimes seem impossible. Other times, they seem like something I can do, with God's help. Give thanks, prune, become a disciple, and celebrate those God loves—these are daunting tasks. Yet, all this is possible because, the Gospel of John tells us, abiding in Christ is two-sided: we abide in Christ, and Christ abides in us. This is the grace we are given, the grace that is sufficient. This is the grace in which we abide.

God who prunes the branches to make room for the Light, abide in me this day. Amen.

Love as a Verb

MAY 11–17, 2009 • ELAINE PUCKETT

MONDAY, MAY 11 ～ *Read John 15:12-17*

Love one another. On the surface it sounds simple, but it is difficult to do. We know how to be in love. We know about the deep feelings of love that connect us to family and special friends. We even know the pain of losing a love. But when love becomes a verb, a command requiring action, the challenging aspects of loving one another come sharply into focus.

What does it mean to respond to God's human family in ways that bear witness to God's love for us? John suggests it has something to do with dying. And in John's Gospel this is the model. Jesus demonstrates his love for the world by offering his life. His response leaves us with a task to accomplish and a question to ponder, "How shall I love my neighbor when love cannot be limited even by death?"

Life is so much more than simply drawing breath. It's the way we spend our time, use our resources, measure our words, do our work, and tend our relationships. Like the branches on the vine, our lives are intimately connected to Christ and delicately entwined with one another. And every day is filled with opportunities to have a positive impact on someone we meet along the way.

When we think about laying down a life for another we usually think in terms of a singular event. But it is possible for us to lay down our lives over the course of a lifetime, minute by minute and day by day. And it is the work of the Spirit to empower us as we seek to lose ourselves in acts of lovingkindness and sacrificial living.

What are some concrete ways in which I can set myself aside in order to love another this week?

An ordained elder in the North Georgia Conference of the United Methodist Church, adjunct faculty at Candler School of Theology in Atlanta, Georgia

In the ordinary course of living, Peter and Cornelius might never have met—much less shared a baptism, a roof, or a meal together. One was Jewish and one was Gentile, and according to the former, the latter was "unclean." One was a leader in the early Christian movement and the other an officer in the Roman army. They were separated by geography, ethnicity, and religious conviction—but the distance between them was no match for the Holy Spirit of God.

Our reading begins at the end of the story: a manifestation of the Spirit's power, a recapitulation of the day of Pentecost and baptismal water flowing freely across lines that had formerly served to divide. But we can't fully appreciate the majesty of the moment apart from the events that had gone before. In Caesarea the Spirit comes in a vision, acknowledging Cornelius' devotion to a God he cannot call by name. And in Joppa, that same Spirit prepares Peter's heart to receive the very one he has long been taught to reject. Each man is turned in a new direction as they begin their journey into faith, into each other's arms. But the Spirit of God is holding them both, long before they find each other.

In my Wesleyan tradition we use the language of conversion to describe this experience of turning from one reality to face another. We know that this kind of saving work is always accomplished by the power of the Spirit. We may cooperate, but we are never the engine that drives the train. Life is really a series of conversions, shaping us and forming us into the fullness of the image of God. And, just as with Cornelius and Peter, the Spirit is already holding us, preparing us for new relationships that lie just beyond the horizon.

Come, Spirit, prepare my heart to embrace the one who stands outside the gate. Amen.

How easy it is to believe we already know the thoughts and plans contained in the mind of God. After all, those of us in the believing community have some clear advantages in this area. We're familiar with the words, or at least some of the words of scripture. We've had ample opportunity to hear inspired preaching and teaching. We've learned the hymns and liturgies of the faith. And we're the beneficiaries of a long history of Christian doctrine and church practice. It makes sense for us to think that we have certain knowledge about what God might or might not be up to in this world. So we're not unlike the "circumcised believers" who made the journey from Joppa to Caesarea with Peter.

Insiders always come to the table with a set of expectations. Past experience helps us to predict present outcomes. And it's difficult, if not impossible for us to suspend our assumptions. The circumcised believers of Peter's day expected that the preaching of the gospel would result in a conversion to Judaism along with a decision to follow Christ. After all, Jesus was clearly Jewish. Adherence to commands of Torah and a willingness to embrace the traditions of the faith were essential to the life of this newly emerging community. This was the mind-set of the people and they believed it to be indistinguishable from the mindset of God.

And then the world is turned on its head. Uncircumcised Gentiles are speaking the language of the Spirit and praising God, just as the Jews had done on the day of Pentecost. And the certainty with which these insiders knew and understood the mind of God is relegated to the past. In an instant the window is thrown open and the fresh wind of the Spirit begins to blow with wild abandon.

What old assumptions might the Spirit be calling me to suspend?

As I write these springtime meditations, it's winter, and I'm anxiously awaiting the birth of my granddaughter, Ella, who is due on December 25. She's been expected for months now. Ultrasounds has even given us glimpses of what she looks like. Preparations have long been underway. Her mother and her father love her already. And her older sister Caroline can talk of little else.

The writer of First John uses familial images to interpret what it means to love God by loving one another. God is like a parent, who loves us from our very conception. Jesus is the Son whose saving acts make that love visible among us. We are the children who love God by loving Christ. And because we are born into faith by the power of the Spirit, we are charged with loving others. Our obedience to the One who first loved us is the evidence of our willingness to participate in this never-ending circle of love.

When Ella is still an infant, her parents and her church family will make a baptismal promise to surround her in love and strengthen her in the faith. As she grows to maturity she will have ample opportunity to choose whether to reflect the values of her "families" of origin or to go her own way. And so it is with those who are born of God. We have an opportunity to live into the heritage that is ours; we also have the freedom to turn aside.

Our text reminds us the commandments of God are never burdensome to those who love Jesus and trust the mystery of faith: "Christ has died, Christ has risen, Christ will come again." It's the testimony of the Spirit assuring us of God's love that enables our obedient response.

How are you living into your baptismal promises of love and obedience?

In my kitchen there's a long thin picture, a Christmas gift from my good friend Melinda who was living almost a continent away. Its lines are simple: an orb, a mountain, a lake. The colors are varying shades of sepia. But in the foreground there are two large yellow daffodils in full bloom. The artist calls it "Celebration of Spring." I've always loved that picture, especially in the wintertime. But it became especially important to me during the season of my treatment for cancer. Surgery, five long weeks of radiation therapy, anxiety about outcomes, prayers for healing and wholeness—and through it all those two yellow daffodils invited me to trust God. What a relief it was to arrive at the moment when my soul was free and ready to sing again.

Salvation is a marvelous thing. The words of the psalmist echo all that I remember about my feelings of uncontainable joy when the doctors declared that my body's invading enemy had been vanquished. In the aftermath it was simply amazing to feel my own breathing, a delight to spend time with family and friends, a privilege to get up in the morning and find blessed sleep at night. The world around me was a new song waiting to be sung. And I was forever changed.

Life-changing experiences have a way of sorting out what really matters. New songs don't have room for extraneous measures and the chaff of life is simply inadequate to evoke a symphony of roaring seas and singing hills. Instead, every note is a simple doxology.

At the end of the day the psalmist puts it all in perspective. Deep and abiding joy is found in the steadfast love and presence of the Lord. O sing to the Lord a new song.

What new songs of life are waiting to be sung in your life this week?

For many of us the freedom to make choices is a natural part of what it means to be human. We arrive at adulthood having exercised a myriad of options: what school to attend, what vocation to pursue, which friends to spend time with, whether to marry or have children. And along the way we begin to discover the extent to which our early choices affect the options we have later. None of us likes to be without choices, but the freedom to choose always brings with it a corresponding responsibility to choose wisely and well.

In John's Gospel we read, "You did not choose me but I chose you." It's Jesus' way of reminding the disciples that a relationship with God begins with divine action. Our options as human beings are limited. We cannot initiate the relationship ourselves. But the boundless love that God has for all of creation means that each of us is chosen. And each of us is free to decide whether or how we'll respond.

Saying yes to God is one of the options we're free to exercise. But there's also a responsibility involved. Jesus says that we are "appointed to go and bear fruit that will last." John's choice of verbs here is the same as in verse 13, where Jesus speaks of the willingness to lay down one's life for the sake of others. This, then, is our vocation: to love others with the same love that Christ offers to us.

In the end, there's nothing we can do to undo Jesus' love for us. God's love is not ours to control. But whether we respond is strictly up to us. We have options. And the measure of our response is the way we love others.

Focus today on the ways in which your yes to God's love is embodied in your response to others.

"Joy to the world, the Lord is come!" We sing it with gusto when Christmas rolls around. But the words seem a little odd, maybe even out of place in a meditation for the Easter season. Yet, when we take time to reflect, we realize that our Christmas celebration makes little sense apart from the resurrection faith of Easter. It's the latter that gives meaning to the former.

In today's reading the psalmist invites us to join in a hymn of joy that celebrates God's saving action among the people of Israel. It's a song of blest assurance reminding God's chosen ones that they have been neither abandoned nor forgotten. Voices rise; trumpets and horns sound forth. The seas roar. Hills shout for joy. In the end, the whole world joins in the chorus of praise. God has indeed done marvelous things. And then there it is, right at the end of the psalm, an announcement that is worthy of such universal celebration: God is "coming to judge the world with righteousness, and the peoples with equity."

In the history of the world there have been many mighty warriors, many magnificent kings, and many tiny infants born to parents like Mary and Joseph. But not every king is interested in equity for all people and not every mighty warrior is an advocate for justice and righteousness. This is what makes Israel's God worthy of universal praise.

Why does an ancient psalm point us in the direction of a Christmas hymn even as the season of Easter draws to a close? It's because the world finds joy when justice and righteousness reign. And Jesus' resurrection is the guarantee that such a world will surely come.

Give thanks for what God is doing in your life and in the life of the world right now. Give thanks for the joy that comes when justice and righteousness reign.

The Spirit of God in Our Lives

MAY 18–24, 2009 • AKIIKI DAISY KABAGARAMA

MONDAY, MAY 18 ~ *Read Acts 1:15-17, 21-26*

After I read this scripture several times, two issues caught my attention: how the apostles conduct their election and how they treat a newcomer. The apostles prayed before electing someone to replace Judas. When electing leaders, religious and secular, do we invite God to be with us in the process? Before election times, we need to pray, to seek God's direction.

When Matthias was elected to join the eleven apostles, he was a newcomer. He had been a follower of Jesus from the beginning, but he had not been part of the leadership. Was he made to feel welcome and respected as one with authority, or did he simply occupy a position and remain an outsider?

We live in a diverse world. People from different backgrounds join our congregations, communities, and nations. Do we treat them as brothers and sisters? According to Acts, we should honor them as faithful followers.

God calls us to offer hospitality. God moved people from their places of birth to foreign places so that they could be a blessing to others. Even today, God sends strangers to our communities. We welcome them with respect and love.

God of all creation, remind us to pray before electing leaders. Teach us how to be hospitable to the strangers that you send to us. Help us treat them as faithful brothers and sisters in your loving family. Amen.

Born and raised in Uganda; a professor, writer, and diversity consultant; residing in the United States for the past twenty-four years

The psalm reminds us that there is a reward in standing up for what is right. The writer uses vivid imagery to describe a person who stands strong: he or she is like a tree by the river that brings bring forth fruit, with leaves that do not wither. By contrast, the ungodly are like chaff that the wind blows away.

Increasingly, the world is a place that doesn't value these acts of conscience. False doctrines of greed, hatred, and materialism have permeated our world to such an extent that standing for what is right often looks and sounds outdated. Conflict, violence, and war have replaced the peace that God demands from us.

I lived through Idi Amin's rule in Uganda in the 1970s. Those were tough times indeed. I saw firsthand the meanness and cruelty of human beings. Greed for power and worldly possessions gripped people's souls to the extent that life became a cheap commodity. I witnessed many deaths and destruction of all sorts. As people scrambled for physical survival, it was often difficult to risk doing what was right.

Yet even in the midst of difficulties, I saw people who made stands for their conscience. Alongside war and atrocity, hope was demonstrated by those who chose the path of righteousness. Many prominent leaders, including an archbishop of the church, were murdered; others had to flee into exile.

Interestingly, during Uganda's hard times, churches were filled on Sundays. People's faith in God increased. We experienced many miracles. We offered prayers to God as we searched for peace. Change occurred and many people's lives were spared. In a time when life seemed an insurmountable challenge, God's grace—and the strength to live godly lives—anchored us and kept us.

Merciful God, thank you for the gift of faith. Make us mindful of your love and protection, and help us lead righteous lives, anchored in you. Amen.

In court hearings, eyewitness accounts are much more believable than testimonies that come from witnesses who were not present at the crime scene. The evidence is even stronger when the victim takes a stand in his or her own defense. All those present can feel the emotion and see the nonverbal communication as the story is told. We believe such people because they were there physically, emotionally, intellectually, and spiritually. The events that took place drastically transformed their lives.

This letter reminds us that God's testimony is greater than that of human beings. Because Jesus received God's testimony firsthand, it is real, authentic, and unadulterated. It comes from the source. When we accept the testimony of Jesus Christ, we are given eternal life: "Whoever has the Son has life; whoever does not have the Son of God does not have life."

Believing Jesus' testimony is the foundation of Christianity. Holding our faith loosely causes us to stumble. How many of us, upon finding a treasure, would hold it carelessly? One of my Tooro tribal beliefs is that a treasure is to be held with both hands. Holding something of value with one hand shows lack of care. That is why tribal members are taught to receive gifts and food with both hands.

Our Christian identity is rooted in Jesus Christ. He is the true witness to God's presence among us. From him we receive our inheritance as children of God. He gave to us salvation. We are empowered by the Holy Spirit to share this good news throughout the whole world. We are believable because we are Jesus' representatives.

Loving God, thank you for sending Jesus as your witness to the world. Empower us to share this testimony with others. Amen.

In this text Jesus reveals himself as God's ambassador, with full rights accorded to him by the one who sent him. He took his followers under his wing, considering it a privilege to know them. When the time came for him to leave them, he prayed for them and promised to send the Holy Spirit to continue caring for them

We often hear of ambassadors being sent to other countries as representatives of their own countries. While living in Uganda, I remember the special treatment and honor accorded to ambassadors. They lived in areas with nice homes and were offered extra protection. When they came to speak to us at the university or at my work place, we all dressed up to receive them. There was no doubt that these were special people.

Before being sent to other nations, the earthly ambassadors needed to know what their countries stand for. While on foreign soil, they represent their countries. They have the power to act on behalf of their countries, working to establish peaceful relations between nations.

Despite the respect accorded ambassadors, it can be dangerous work. Jesus knew this. He took on human flesh as God's ambassador on earth. He was often in danger because of his life and his witness.

Through him, we are adopted into the family. Jesus intercedes for us and the Holy Spirit guides us. Knowing this truth can free us from worry. We constantly rejoice, celebrating our relationship with God through Jesus Christ. We have inherited the gift that obliges us to continue Christ's work here on earth.

Thank you, Jesus, for being the ambassador who brings us to the knowledge of God. Enable and empower us to be your ambassadors throughout the earth. Amen.

Have you ever felt restless because you did not have all the details regarding a particular situation? Picture an expectant mother. For nine months, she waits for the arrival of her baby. Even when the doctors give her the estimated time of arrival, she does not fully know the specific day and time. However, when that special day arrives, the signs are clear and the baby finally is born.

In this text, we are reminded of the important lesson in patience. Jesus told his followers to wait in Jerusalem for the power of the Holy Spirit to come to them. Before ascending to heaven, Jesus promised that he would return. These promises meant that Jesus' followers had to wait with a great deal of patience. Although they lacked all the details, they took Jesus at his word.

It is often difficult for us to remain in ambiguous situations. Especially in this age of science and fast-paced life, we are tempted to work ahead of God's plan for our lives. Many people are constantly in a hurry, never stopping to think how their hurriedness might impact their relationship with God. We need always to remember that God's ways are not our ways and God's timing is not the same as ours.

Through faith, we are assured of things unseen. So how do we navigate this exactness-vagueness path? We must approach God with faith and humility, asking for God's will to be done and not our own. Because God created us and loves us dearly, we can trust God's time will be the right time for us. As a popular African American song says: our God "is an on time God."

Precious God, we know you have our best interests at heart. Calm our anxieties over things beyond our control. Help us rejoice and do your will as we anticipate the fulfillment of your promises. Amen.

The resurrected Christ has the rule, authority, and power—both now and forever. As followers of Christ, we inherit this power. Through wisdom and revelation, we get to know the deeper things of our faith. The church, which is under Christ's leadership, must be a strong body.

This passage makes me think of being a member of a sports team. Picture your favorite team. When you see the players at practice or at a game, you know that they are up to something important. They are well-trained and believe that they are winners. They have the power, the knowledge, and the capacity to handle whoever or whatever may come. If they don't have these attributes, they do not know who they are and what they possess. Defeat comes even before they get on the field. Unsure of their position, any little gust of wind makes them fall.

How is the church of Jesus Christ today? Do we know that we have a great inheritance that gives us power to win against the world's dark forces? Through Jesus, God took on human form and came to live among us. He bore our sins when he was crucified on Calvary. But death was not the end. When Jesus rose from the grave, he brought to us salvation power. This is a great inheritance for us, his followers.

We know that we are God's children. We repent of our sins and invite Jesus into our lives. With the power that comes to us through the Holy Spirit, we are able to live victorious lives.

Our Savior Jesus Christ, your death and resurrection gave us eternal life. This is a precious gift. When we go astray, lead us home. Amen.

After the resurrection, Jesus appeared to several of his followers. The women saw the empty tomb. Jesus appeared to Simon and then to Cleopas and his colleague, on the road to Emmaus. When they returned to Jerusalem and joined the other disciples, Jesus appeared to the whole group.

Jesus reminded his followers of what he had told them before his death and what the scriptures had announced prior to his birth. Many had already forgotten what they had been taught. How quickly do we forget the truths that matter!

Even today, God speaks to us in so many ways. How often do we connect the events of our day with what we have learned? God is with us, speaking to us through nature, fellow human beings, scriptures, catastrophes, celebrations, and even through history. We get visited by angels through visions and dreams. God is with us always.

It is interesting to note that Jesus instructed the disciples to remain in Jerusalem so that they could receive power from the Holy Spirit. As they waited for this promise to be fulfilled, the disciples spent their time in ecstatic worship together. Jesus had left them, but they rejoiced in worship and prayer. As they prepared to go out and proclaim God's message, they were renewed and refreshed by worship.

Holy Spirit, you are a wise counselor, teacher, and guide. We honor you in worship and we witness in the world to your redemptive love. Amen.

Voices On Fire

MAY 25–31, 2009 • FRANK RAMIREZ

MONDAY, MAY 25 ~ *Read Acts 2:1-12*

Words matter. Words are powerful. Words can change people. At Pentecost, the evidence of the power of words is dramatic.

Luke demonstrates in his Acts of the Apostles that rhetoric—the art of speaking well—can change lives. In this passage, alive with the Spirit, the disciples of Jesus set out to tell the good news. They spoke in joy and were heard.

This week as we walk toward Pentecost, I want to tell stories about people who were touched by the Spirit. These are people—both in scripture and in history—whose voices were on fire.

In 1708, eight believers gathered at the Eder River in Germany and baptized each other. They had studied scripture together and decided as a group that they were called to attempt to restore the practices of the first Christians in the early church.

These believers did not do this lightly. The brutal Forty Years War waged by Christians against one another in Europe ended with a treaty that decreed people had to worship at whichever of three sanctioned churches their local ruling prince had chosen to worship. Those who broke this law were subject to the penalty that was traditional for believer's baptism—death by drowning.

But this threat did not stop these eight separatists. Founders of my denomination, the Church of the Brethren, they declared "We must publicly profess that which Christ Jesus taught and did without hesitation or fear. . . . We need not be ashamed and must suffer and endure all things with rejoicing. 'Joy! Joy! More Joy!'"

Lord, we proclaim in joy that your Spirit still lives in us, sustaining us in all trials and strengthening us in faithfulness. Amen.

Pastor of the Everett Church of the Brethren in Everett, Pennsylvania

The Spirit of truth speaks through many lives. Certainly one of the most powerful came from a woman who took the name of truth itself—Sojourner Truth. Born into slavery as Isabella Baumfree in 1797, she was one of thirteen children. Sold and resold several times, she endured great hardships including separation from family and friends. But she endured. Sojourner Truth eventually adopted her new name and preached with great passion. She worked with abolitionists and her biography *The Narrative of Sojourner Truth, A Northern Slave*, published in 1850, was extremely influential.

After the Civil War she worked on behalf of the newly freed slaves of the South and continued to preach the gospel throughout her life. She also worked for women's suffrage. These words from one of the "certificates of character" she had to carry with her are a testament to her faith: "We, the undersigned having known Isabella (or Sojourner Truth) for several years, most cheerfully bear testimony to her uniform good character, her untiring industry, kind deportment, unwearied benevolence, and the many social and excellent traits which make her worthy to bear her adopted name."

Her fame has continued to grow since her death in 1883. She remains a shining light that was never quenched, a voice on fire that was never quenched by slavery and oppression. Sojourner Truth refused to accept the limitations of her time against women, against slaves and former slaves, and against all African Americans. Instead she preached boldly on behalf of God's kingdom.

Jesus said, "The Spirit of truth . . . will testify on my behalf." Sojourner Truth's faithfulness, courage, and witness surely were a testimony of the Spirit. Her example encourages us to become a voice on fire too.

O God, I thank you for your Spirit of truth. May it move us to speak out for your people in all times and places. Rest with me now. Amen.

For me, there are times when Paul's letter to the Romans seems like some sort of advanced calculus or a string of verses clapped onto Burma Shave signs along a Roman road that tell us we're all lost, but if we say the right words we'll be saved and have nothing more to worry about.

However, other writers have helped me to understand that viewing Paul's words through "Western grid" is wrong. I must instead read Paul in a framework based on Paul's Hebraic background to see that he considers the righteousness of God as the true state of creation. For him, all things—human and animal, earth and all stars, the creator and the created—are in the joyous state God originally intended. Sin is the state where even our best efforts go awry, but God in Christ Jesus seeks to restore right relationship in Christ.

In this passage Paul tells us in no uncertain terms that the time of redemption is close at hand. With all creation groaning in labor pains, Paul knows that God's time is very near. The witness is powerful; something new is coming.

There are many ways of bearing witness in the world—some don't involve any words. One of my personal heroes is Mary Dadisman, who was a witness to God's redemption until her death in 2005 at the age of ninety-two. From 1941 to 1979 she worked as a missionary and a nurse in Nigeria. She delivered thousands of babies. Her hard work helped to lower dramatically Nigeria's high infant mortality rate. And though she never had children of her own, when she returned to Nigeria at the age of ninety, she discovered that she was included in innumerable family trees!

Great and powerful God, speak through our actions. May our acts speak your word of redemption in the world. Amen.

I live in the north end of the Appalachians, a couple of hours from any large urban centers. When it comes to the radio, my listening choices are few, and even those few stations fade in and out as I drive around the hills. My wife and I decided that investing in satellite radio was not a luxury but a necessity if we were to stay informed about the world. Because of our radio subscription, I was able to hear an hour-long interview with Dr. Clea Koff not once but two times. She talked about her book, *The Bone Woman: A Forensic Anthropologist's Search for Truth in the Mass Graves of Rwanda, Bosnia, Croatia, and Kosovo.*

Dr. Koff had decided as a child that she wanted to be a forensic anthropologist. At age twenty-six, she began the first of several United Nations' missions to exhume the bodies of those murdered in genocide or civil war. Sometimes called "the interpreter of tragedies," she has worked at the site of many mass murders. Though she cannot bring people back to life, she can, by studying bones, restore people's names, tell stories about their lives, their health, the manner of their death, and help to convict their killers.

The psalmist praises God for God's wonderful works and great power, and adds: "When you hide your face, they are dismayed; when you take away their breath, they die and return to their dust." The Bible recognizes that it is God who has the power of life and death. When murderers seek to usurp God and destroy whole populations, we can be thankful for people like Dr. Koff who stand up for the justice that comes from God and restore to our memory those who have been taken from us.

How wonderful are your works, O Lord. We give thanks for those who are dedicated to serving humanity around the world. Amen.

I was researching the life of World War II conscientious objector Harold Lefever for my book *The Meanest Man in Patrick County*, a collection of peace and justice stories for children. One day his widow told me she had found his notes from an important speech he had made.

Lefever had a deferment from military service to work at Westinghouse in Pittsburgh, but once he realized the top-secret project was a device to trigger a nuclear weapon, he resigned from his job. Because of his refusal to work on the project, he was arrested.

Lefever struggled and gave careful thought to what he would say to the judge at his sentencing hearing. Today's passage might have come to him: "The Spirit helps us in our weakness; for we do not know how to pray as we ought." In the face of war hysteria that branded an act of protest as the act of a traitor, Lefever said this: "War is a great evil . . . since it tries to convert a people by . . . killing them off in sufficient numbers to 'reform' them."

Lefever continued: "The way of suffering love for enemies has been demonstrated to be the only effective way to reconciliation. This was the way used by Jesus Christ in his day and to which his life is the greatest testimony."

Lefever was sentenced to two years in the federal penitentiary at Leavenworth. His work on the electrical system there was so valuable that he was allowed some freedom. He served the last of his sentence in a medical hospital. He paid a price for his witness, but his faith would not let him do otherwise.

Are we willing not only to count the cost of radical discipleship to Jesus Christ but also to pay that price?

God of clarity, when we struggle to express ourselves, speak for us and through us. Amen.

Catharine Hummer lived in a part of colonial Pennsylvania where German was spoken more frequently than English. She was one of the Dunkers, a group of plain people who separate themselves from the world by simple living and dress. Her father was the first minister of the White Oak congregation.

In 1762 Catharine claimed that she was visited by angels who told her that love had grown cold among the brethren. Her father, moved by her vision, invited her to preach, a rarity for a woman in that era. Her preaching was so effective that people came as far as sixty miles to hear her. Many claimed that when she spoke they could hear angels singing.

Needless to say, Catharine experienced opposition from her own people and from others. Nevertheless, her message was one of joy consistent with the words of the psalmist: "I will sing to the LORD as long as I live; I will sing praise to my God while I have being." Catharine said she sang with an angel: "How well I feel, how well I feel . . . so that within I leap and jump for joy."

At one point, in answer to her critics Catharine wrote, "The winter of persecution is here. But I comfort myself with the dear Savior." And she prayed for her enemies: "May the Lord have mercy on us and our enemies and let none perish."

Catharine's prayers and songs of praise are in the great tradition of the Psalter. God, the psalmist says and Catharine echoes, is so great that we must rejoice, sing, and praise God with joy.

Does the joy that Catharine had permeate our own lives as Christians?

This prayer is adapted from a letter by Catharine Hummer: God, fill all our hearts with your Holy Spirit so that we might pray from our whole hearts for divine peace. Amen.

PENTECOST SUNDAY

The experience of being transformed by the Spirit is sometimes so overwhelming that the only conclusion some people draw is that those who believe that Jesus is Lord are either drunk or crazy.

When Peter was accused of drinking too much, he responded with words from the prophet Joel: "In the last days it will be, God declares, that I will pour out my Spirit upon all flesh, and your sons and your daughters shall prophesy."

In all times and places, when God's Spirit falls on women and men, believers are still accused of being crazy when they're being faithful. Dorothy Day (1897–1980) was a journalist and an activist on behalf of the poor. When she came to believe in Jesus and to believe the words of Jesus mattered, she was not content to return quietly to church for Sunday duties. Instead, she worked even harder on behalf of the poor—this time in the name of Jesus.

Day worked with the poorest of the poor in the worst of neighborhoods. She founded the *Catholic Worker* newspaper in 1933 to spread the word of Jesus' concern for society. She was jailed several times for many causes: for women's right to vote, against war, for civil rights, and for farm workers. There were those who thought of her as crazy. But she countered, saying, "If I have achieved anything in my life, it is because I have not been embarrassed to talk about God."

Dorothy Day set the bar of discipleship high. Her life made it clear that we have no real option except to follow the Spirit's leading. God's Spirit is poured out upon all flesh—and this most definitely includes us. Be prepared to receive God's Spirit—and to go forth in that Spirit.

Pray these words from a Church of the Brethren hymn by Ken Morse: Move in our midst, thou Spirit of God.

God in Three Persons

JUNE 1–7, 2009 • EMILY M. AKIN

MONDAY, JUNE 1 ~ *Read Isaiah 6:1-3*

"Holy, Holy, Holy." These are words from a hymn that we sang often in my home church as I was growing up. Still one of my favorites, it is the first thing that comes to my mind when I read this passage in Isaiah. Back then, I was fascinated with the hymn's images of saints "casting down their golden crowns around the glassy sea." Cherubim and seraphim sounded like mighty creatures, yet, in the hymn and in this scripture passage, they fall prostrate before God. At first, I had no idea what some of those words meant, but the music helped me understand that we were praising a wonderful, majestic, and powerful God. I knew instinctively that God's power and glory were beyond my ability to describe them.

Later, I learned about the hymn's symbolism of the Trinity and of its references to scripture. The hymn motivated me to study the Bible and to learn more about God, Jesus Christ, and the Holy Spirit. My experience confirms John and Charles Wesley's idea that hymns could be teaching tools.

When we sing our songs of praise, we glorify the Creator who made the world and everything in it. And since we are made in God's image, all of us share in God's creation, seeking each day to make a difference in the world. When we come together to worship, we praise God for the transforming power of God's mighty presence.

Reflect on the meaning of the word holy. *What images come to mind? How can we lead holy lives to honor God in whose image we were created?*

Freelance writer and church musician living in Union City, Tennessee

In the ancient world, people thought if they saw the face of God, they would die. Pagan gods were considered powerful and vengeful, often requiring sacrifices to fend off their anger or earn their favor. However, the Hebrew God Yahweh was different. This God sought a relationship with the chosen people. Still, this Yahweh was known to punish the people when they did not follow the law. Imagine yourself as Isaiah, a sinner in God's presence, wondering what awful judgment would come down on you. Would your knees be shaking?

In the Jewish religion, the people had to be "clean" according to Mosaic law before participating in worship. In the Christian tradition, we have the need to cleanse our souls by confessing our sins to God. Often, we find it hard to confess, fearing perhaps that we deserve to be punished rather than forgiven. Isaiah knew he was not "clean," but the hot coals purified him so that he could be in God's presence, hear God's words, and carry that word to the people.

When God asked for volunteers, Isaiah spoke up. How many of us would have been brave enough to speak in the presence of God? To be in God's presence can be terrifying—but it also can be cleansing and powerful. Isaiah felt inadequate to speak God's word to the people—until he was cleansed by the application of the live coal to his lips.

It is the act of being cleansed that frees us both to hear God clearly and to respond in faith. When we go forth, we go with the clarity of God's words on our tongues and in our hearts.

Lord, we fall short in our efforts to hear you clearly and to serve you. Forgive us and strengthen us for the work you have for us. Amen.

The psalmist attempts to describe God's power and glory by naming all the things that God can destroy just by speaking. God breaks the cedars, flashes fire, and shakes the ground with the same voice that created the universe. The psalmist's God is more powerful than any natural disaster he can imagine. He prays for God to share that power and to give the people peace.

I once visited the chapel on the campus of Duke University late on a warm summer day, near sunset. Standing at the bottom of the two-hundred-foot bell tower, I marveled at the beauty and grandeur of the structure. Inside, it was cool and a little dark, totally different from the atmosphere of the busy campus outside. The glow from the windows magnified the beauty of the waning sunlight. An *a cappella* choir was rehearsing, their music magnifying the moment's holiness and grandeur.

The people with me seemed to be awed by the beauty of the sanctuary too. A sign warned us not to talk lest we disturb the choir's rehearsal. But no one wanted to speak—we simply basked in the beauty of the place. It was peaceful, a welcome change from our day of meetings and lectures.

In the building of that chapel, the creators had attempted to represent God's power and glory in tangible form. For me, the outer structure of the stone chapel represented God's strength, but the inside portrayed God's peace. Like the psalmist, we regularly ask God for strength. God does give us strength, and along with it, God gives us peace.

Mighty Lord, give me strength. Give me peace. Let me, along with all the world, praise you today. Amen.

Nicodemus, a member of the prestigious Sanhedrin, was taking a risk being seen with Jesus, a known radical, a man who was outside the religious establishment, held in suspicion by political and religious authorities alike. Perhaps it was out of caution that Nicodemus came to Jesus under cover of darkness. A teacher of the law, Nicodemus certainly knew the law and tried to keep it. Jesus said that the law was not enough. To please God truly, one must be "born from above." Nicodemus did not understand.

What does it mean to be born from above, or to be born again, as the King James Version says? Jerome Hines, a famous opera singer, had a conversion experience that led him to witness to people in the world of opera. When he signed his autograph on programs, he usually included a Bible reference. After a performance at my college in the late 1960s, he signed my recital program with "Jerome Hines, John 3:16."

In the world of professional musicians, Hines was a star, but he was also criticized for his evangelical activities. That's not surprising: John's Gospel is clear that coming to know Christ is radical and reorienting. God's revelation of Christ to Hines had touched him; he was radically changed. That Bible reference on my program told me that he was a follower of Christ. He didn't tell me personally that he was a Christian, and it wasn't necessary for him to preach to me.

Hines was "born from above" in a dramatic way. Some of us find faith as Hines did. Others grow into it in a more gradual manner. To be "born from above" is to accept God's generous gift of new life in Christ. It means that we now follow a new path—the path of Jesus Christ.

Lord, help me to be a better follower of the way you have set before me. Show me, as you showed Nicodemus, the way of life eternal. Amen.

In the Jewish culture, a man with many sons would consider himself blessed for the abundance of heirs. However, the oldest son was the one who would receive the largest inheritance. If a man had only one son, imagine how he would treasure the one and only heir. Jesus was God's only son. Think how hard it would be for you to know that your only child would suffer and die.

Recent natural disasters have spotlighted people who rescue others from mine cave-ins, floods, tidal waves, or hurricanes. Imagine sending your only child out to rescue storm victims or coal miners trapped underground. We know that people in danger must be rescued, but it takes real fortitude and a willingness to sacrifice to send our own children into such a dangerous environment. Today's scripture tells us plainly that God sent Jesus as a person just like us to rescue us from the consequences of our sin.

People needing rescue don't always react rationally. Drowning victims often panic and grab the rescuer with such force that the rescuer's life is in danger too. Someone stuck on the second floor of a burning house sometimes fears jumping to a waiting firefighter so much that he or she waits until it is almost too late. Crawling from a sinking ship into a lifeboat can be paralyzing. It's hard to give up control and stop the struggle, futile though it is.

Jesus struggled with God's plan for his life, just as we do. But, when we remember that God did not send Jesus to condemn us but to save us, we realize that he can rescue us from the flood of doubt, fear, or turmoil that exists in our lives. We don't have to struggle anymore. We can let our Rescuer take over and guide us from that point on.

Thank you, God, for the gift of eternal life through Jesus Christ. Help me to remember that I need your guidance always. Amen.

Paul says that God has adopted us as God's own children, "joint heirs" with Christ. We are not debtors or slaves. Instead, we are freed from this "spirit of slavery" to a new relationship with God. As God's children, we know that God stands very near at hand. We can speak with God on intimate terms and express our needs to God without fear. As our parent, God will respond to us in love.

When Paul wrote this letter, the custom in the Jewish culture was for the firstborn to receive the largest inheritance. Younger brothers had a smaller claim—but women with brothers had no rights at all. If we are joint heirs with Christ, we become equal recipients of God's love. Led by the Spirit, we join the family of God as equal inheritors of eternal life through Christ.

When God adopts us and brings us into the family, we come to realize just what our standing as inheritors of God's kingdom means. Normally, to be an heir carries some power, some freedom, some expectation of a gift with it. To be an heir of God, however, turns all this on its ear. In becoming a child of God, an heir, we inherit the glory of God that comes only by sharing in all that Christ is—beginning with his suffering. We have the inheritance of eternal life. Paul reminds us that Christ's suffering—and our joining in Christ's suffering as heirs—is the way to the kingdom of God.

Spirit of God, lead me today and every day, so that I may become a willing heir of the family of God. Amen.

On this Trinity Sunday, we praise God as Creator, Christ as Savior, and the Holy Spirit as Guide and Comforter. Theologians have struggled for centuries to explain the concept of the Triune God, yet none has truly succeeded in "proving" how God exists and functions as Three-in-One. Saint Patrick of Ireland was thought to have used the native Irish plant, the three-leafed shamrock, to teach the concept. Some have described the Trinity as a three-legged stool, all three legs being required for the stool to function. Saint Elizabeth of the Trinity, a Carmelite nun in France, believed it was the mystery of the Trinity that enabled her to experience God's mysterious grace in her everyday life.

Methodism's founder, John Wesley, in his sermon on the Trinity, stated that because the term is not mentioned in the Bible, he hesitated to use the word *Trinity*. He went on to say that we don't have to understand fully how something works in order to believe that it exists.

We come to today's text with many different ideas of what God as Trinity means, and the Trinity remains a mystery that still eludes us. But some things are, through the eyes of faith, apparent to us. The Spirit of God is uncontrollable; its power reorients our lives. The presence of Jesus Christ in the world is life-changing; it brings redemption to all. And the God who created us loves and sustains us every day; this love is the bedrock of our existence.

God of the past, the present, and the future, help us to be aware of your presence in our lives. Help us to be holy—set apart for the work of your kingdom. We pray in the name of the Triune God. Amen.

Seeds of Faith

JUNE 8-14, 2009 • MARILYN DICKSON

MONDAY, JUNE 8 ~ *Read 1 Samuel 15:34-35*

Samuel, who had anointed Saul king of Israel, was sorely disappointed and distraught when Saul was exiled for disobeying God. Samuel openly grieved. He grieved over what could have been. He grieved for the man he had watched grow from childhood. He grieved for himself and for Saul.

When those we love disappoint us, we grieve for them and for ourselves. We grieve the loss of a dream, and both the losses and the mourning are difficult. But God gives us resources to help us cope with our grief. Grieving—intentionally acknowledging our loss and our disappointment—is God's way helping see us through these tough situations in our lives. God knows we need to deal with pain and loss, so we are given minds to think about what is going on and feelings to experience the separation. Memory's gift reminds us that no matter what has happened we receive joy and strength from one another.

It takes time to grieve, to use all the resources God gives us to cope. Grief can't be rushed. Participating in our own grief helps us move forward, but it can be slow work. How do we grieve when our dreams implode? How do we get through grief to the other side? How do we come to understand, with both our heart and our mind, that God is with us in our grief? What does it mean to trust our grieving to God's care?

Imagine yourself in a favorite place; sit and reflect. Who or what are you grieving today? Invite God to be with you. Tell God of your grief, and listen to hear what God might be saying to you. Imagine being held in God's holy embrace.

Ordained Disciples of Christ minister, spiritual director, and part-time associate pastor at First United Methodist Church in Richardson, Texas

"Honey, we're moving to Texas!" Thirty years ago when my husband announced that possibility, I was less than enthusiastic. We'd lived in Australia for ten years, having accepted a work contract that had moved us from our home in Canada and sent us to live on one of the world's largest islands. I was tired of packing up and moving, and I felt overwhelmed by the daunting task of moving from one continent to another. I did not want to leave cherished friends and the way of life I had come to love. Texas was foreign territory. This might be a good move for our family, but I was resistant.

The story of God's people all through scripture is that of resisting change, overcoming fear, and moving into the unknown. When we believe God is with us as we enter the unknown, we are able to venture out. When we remain reluctant to make changes, we get stuck. We stagnate, and it is harder to experience what God has ahead for us.

Samuel, still grieving Saul's departure, was afraid when the Lord asked him asked to find and anoint the next king of Israel. But Samuel overcame his fear. He obeyed God's call, and in Bethlehem he found David, the young shepherd, the eighth and youngest of Jesse's sons. David was anointed by Samuel and went on to become Israel's greatest king.

Overcoming the fear of change and recognizing new possibilities is often hard. Samuel knew what God wanted him to do, and his desire to do God's will finally overcame his fear. I moved to Texas and found this new place to be a source of many blessings. In the past thirty years, we have been gifted with an abundance of friends, adventures, and new discoveries that I could never have anticipated.

Thank you, Lord, for the challenge of changes in our lives. Your steady grace and your presence with us on the journey help us overcome our fears and move ahead. Keep us always in your way. Amen.

The great sound of God's people celebrating is recounted in joyous words in this communal royal psalm. The people sing responsively, chanting back and forth, their many voices raised in a mighty cascade of sound. Close your eyes; imagine the scene; hear the celebratory song.

We lift our voices in song today, as the Israelites did in their time, because of our faith. We repeat responsive liturgies, and our souls leap within when we give thanks to God. It is magnificent when we together seek God's favor, relying on what has happened in the past to embrace what will happen in the future.

But frequently our songs of praise to God are muted, shallow, or silenced. Psalm 20:7 sums up the problem succinctly: we may put our trust in the "chariots" and "horses" of this world, or we may trust "in the name of the LORD our God." The psalmist tells us that the choice is ours; but if we choose the power of this world over the power of God, our faith will weaken. Those who choose God will "rise and stand upright." Those who choose the power of the world will "collapse and fall." The choice may not always be easy, but it is clearly drawn.

What has utmost importance for you? Do you care most about what God can do and is doing in your life? Do you take pride in the name of the Lord, or does your pride sometimes lie with the success-minded and materialism-oriented world?

It is difficult to focus on God and God's ways when the false promises of the world's chariots and horses beckon so strongly. What matters is the name of God, the source of our strength. We must examine our priorities closely. It is so easy to replace passion for God with a timid spirit that has been tamed by the world.

God, your name is great. Keep my trust focused on you. Let me join in songs of joy with all those who love and trust you. Amen.

Some people touch our lives in such significant ways that we are never quite the same. They show us a truth that reveals a newer, fresher dimension of life and faith.

Dan was a church elder, Stephen Minister, Bible teacher, friend and father. But Dan's three failed marriages made him question the kind of a role model he could be for others. What legacy of faith would he leave behind?

When Dan entered the hospital the day before he died, it became obvious that this question was very much on his mind. We talked about his illness and about his impending death, about what was next. We joined in sacred prayer. "Is there anything special you want me to pray about?," I asked. Eyes brimming with tears he said, "Please pray that in my dying, I will please God . . . that I will please God." We prayed, we wept, we rejoiced together. But Dan's request took my breath away. In that moment, as Dan was joining the great cloud of witnesses, I heard a witness to the faith so genuine and authentic that it stunned me. With that one simple request, Dan gave himself fully into God's care. Since then, I have often wondered if I will be open enough, strong enough, vulnerable enough to walk with such a faith-filled heart into my own death.

Paul writes that we walk by faith, not by sight. When I witnessed Dan's final prayer, I saw firsthand what it means to walk not by sight but by faith. God, through Dan's faith, gave new life to others in the faith community even as Dan was dying and entering God's eternal embrace. May we too discover that deep desire to please God. And may we evoke that desire in others as we journey toward God into the unseen realm of eternity.

Lord, bless those whose lives and faith have shaped our own faith journey. Grant us the deep desire to please you and honor you in all that we do and are. Amen.

Falling away from God is not a new problem. We have all done or said things that were neither loving nor helpful. All of us have strayed into behavior that took us far away from who God intends us to be. We experience regret and sometimes shame over things we have done or how we have treated people. How do we return to God? How do start over? Where do we begin?

People who know the pain and separation of divorce know all too well the challenge of rebuilding their lives and starting over again with family and friends. People who have gotten caught up in the world's false values know what it means to try to reclaim their life and rediscover whose they really are.

Paul tells us in this text that even after we have sinned and fallen short, we can start over and walk with assurance toward the light of hope offered by God. We can do this again and again and again. Does God love us? Yes! Does God desire good for us? Yes! Are we, in spite of our actions, loveable? You bet! Are small steps toward a new start possible? Absolutely!

We have the assurance that God desires the best for us even in the midst of unwanted, harmful, or difficult situations. God is good. Our challenge lies in accepting God's grace and choosing this new beginning with God as our guide. Others who have gone before us give witness to God's power to restore and make life new. May we all find hope and assurance during our times of confusion and fear. Let us trust in God and accept God's invitation to go back to the beginning and start anew.

Great and loving God, you offer us grace and forgiveness. Your love for us is endless, and your care for us is true. When we walk away from you, reach us and move us forward to a new beginning. In the name of Christ we pray. Amen.

How is faith sustained when the storms of life challenge us? How do we keep our sometimes tenuous grip on faith when it is threatened? Fragile faith falters, but deeply rooted faith withstands the stresses of everyday life even in the dark times of doubt, worry, and uncertainty.

Jesus used parables to make us question, to stretch our minds, and to lead us into new understandings of the mysteries of faith. Jesus challenges us to weave mind, heart, and experience together to realize our faith more deeply. How does the unseen Holy Spirit work this slow and miraculous nurturing of our souls? How do we grow into increasing clarity and discernment to know God's will in our lives?

Like a tiny seed planted in the soil, faith grows into a slender stalk of grain until it is ripe for harvest. The miracle of growth happens within us. Some mysterious rhythm works to water the tendrils of our tender faith. Bad choices and poor decisions, like bad weather, can slow the growth of our faith. But faith survives these bad times, and God continues to tend the roots of our faith, keeping it alive.

The paradox of the parable is that God's work in us is ongoing. Even when we do not feel or see it, something holy is happening. We may sometimes slow the process; at times we don't understand what is happening to our faith, but our understanding of God's vision for us keeps growing. We are constantly guided into a new understanding of the wonders of faith in our lives, whether or not we are aware of God's sometimes subtle work in our lives.

Who has planted seeds of faith in your life? How and when did this happen? Have there been times when you didn't really notice God's work in your life until suddenly one day you realized your faith had changed and deepened? Spend some time in prayer thanking God for nurturing the miracle of faith in you.

One afternoon more than twenty-five years ago, a professor in my seminary class asked what images came to us when we thought of the God as the Trinity. He wanted us to be able to claim for ourselves with clarity what we believed so we could build a deeply rooted faith, one that would be viable in all life circumstances for our ministry and for us as individuals.

Like Jacob, I wrestled long with this question. What images came to me when I thought about Jesus the Son, God the Creator, and the Holy Spirit? How did those images build upon the truth that would sustain my faith?

Our vision of God's kingdom and our work as God's people depend upon a clear vision of the faith: what we are doing, why we are doing it, and with whom we work in this world.

Jesus' parable says that the mustard seed, that tiniest of all seeds, grows into a formidable and strong bush. This image of faith as a mustard seed proclaims an important mystery: insignificant beginnings can lead to vast and powerful conclusions. Faith may start out looking like a small thing, but God's vision for the world will eventually accomplish great things—things beyond all our imagining. From this tiny seed God establishes the kingdom that changes the entire world.

Becoming Christlike starts with small, everyday acts of faith. Then, like the mustard seed, God helps our faith grow into something mighty and strong until it reaches fullness in us. The process of becoming one with Christ in mind and spirit feeds our soul and moves us into the future with hope.

God, you have placed within me the small seed of faith. Nurture me so that my faith may grow. Challenge me so that my faith will be made strong. Give me hope so I may move with confidence into the future with my faith. Amen.

God's Pursuit . . . Our Response

JUNE 15–21, 2009 • LAURA FLIPPEN TENZEL

MONDAY, JUNE 15 ~ *Read Psalm 9:9-16*

The loss of a job, a sudden death of a loved one, news of a serious illness—these are all difficult situations, and we find ourselves in dire need of God. These first verses of Psalm 9 are a doxology of sorts. They praise the God who is a stronghold for the oppressed, for those in trouble, and for the afflicted. In hard times, it is our human nature to turn more often to God and to pray more earnestly. Ironically, sometimes our prayer life is richer when we face trying times.

We live in a complicated, demanding culture that conflicts with our call to live the simple life of faith. It is easy to abandon our reliance on God and become self-centered and self-absorbed. Political parties, competition, athletics, computer technology, and food are only a few of the areas where we find ourselves seduced and forgetful of God.

This psalm reminds us that it is the Lord who pursues us. It is God who stands ready to rescue us. And it is God who does not forget the needy. God is the one who moves with power to rescue the vulnerable and the weak.

Surely we, who are so strongly pursued by God, are called to join God in the work of caring for others in the world.

We sing your praises, O God. You are the helper of the weak and the afflicted. May we hear the call to justice; and, when we do, may we know that it is your call. Help us to respond. Renew our faith and remind us to be grateful for your care. Amen.

Communications coordinator for military and institutional chaplains in the General Board of Higher Education and Ministry of the United Methodist Church and an active member of Blakemore United Methodist Church in Nashville, Tennessee

Because God cares for the world, we are called in our personal prayers to remember the nation and the world. We belong to the nation and the world. Because of God's promised help to the vulnerable, we can be glad, rejoice, sing praises, and ask for God's mercy. The poor and the needy have hope.

Sometimes we think that we ourselves can change the world. But the psalmist is clear that the nations are "only human." These words from the psalm actually are a reminder that human efforts are always futile. We may intend to do the right thing, but we realize that relying on human effort alone is a dead end.

Dedicated persons at Blakemore United Methodist Church in Nashville, Tennessee, heard a call to provide affordable housing to low-income families and individuals. People put time, effort, and energy into the project, and the Blakemore Housing Trust was established. But it would be two years and three attempted building sites later that construction finally began.

Relying only on human effort, the Trust would never have been realized. And there were times when human effort faltered. But because the faithful persevered in their knowledge that God was involved in the work and because they stopped and listened to God at every turn, their vision became a reality. When they share their knowledge with other congregations, the chair of the Trust begins with a straightforward truth about their experience: "Blind alleys were ours; the path was God's."

May we, along with the Blakemore church, remember that God meets our "only human" efforts and carries us forward as we work to make the world more safe and just. The psalmist is right: "The needy shall not always be forgotten, nor the hope of the poor perish forever."

How is God calling you to join in the work of healing and saving the world?

The Philistines challenge Israel to a fight, and the stakes are high. The winners would take the losers as slaves. Goliath, the warrior chosen by the Philistines, stood nine feet and nine inches tall. Most armor was made of iron but his was made of bronze, and it protected his body down to his knees. He was a terrifying sight. Saul, the king who was to be Israel's deliverer, and all his army were immobilized by fear. Scripture says they were dismayed and greatly afraid.

David had been sent by his father Jesse on an errand to deliver loaves and cheese to his brothers in Saul's army, When he reached the army's encampment, he heard Goliath's dreadful challenge. It quickly became clear to David that Saul and his army were afraid, but David also realized that Israel's cause—not that of the Philistines—was just. Perhaps this is what David realized when he weighed Goliath's threatening words.

In our own lives, giants call us out too. Financial trouble, addictions, tormented relationships—all these and more are fearful challenges to our faith. We know, as the Israelites did, that God is more powerful than these "giants."

While fear is sometimes our response to the big troubles in our lives, David knows (and First Samuel assures us) that God is more powerful than any of our troubles, more powerful than our fears. As difficult as it can be when life is tough and fearsome, God's power and right can carry us through. David did not face Goliath alone, and we do not face our giants alone. God is with us. It is important to remember this, especially in our darkest times.

Gracious God, in the face of fear and trouble, remind us of your great power. Amen.

David and Goliath is a story for all ages. Giants are powerful, bigger than life. In David's time they were the embodiment of evil. In this story, the underdog defeats the giant—not with power and might—but with God. David rejects the offer of armor and says, "The LORD . . . will save me from the hand of this Philistine." Saul, on hearing this, says, "Go, and may the LORD be with you!" David goes into battle knowing it is God, and not he, who will overpower Goliath and save Israel. The worthless gods of the Philistines are no match for Yahweh, the God of Israel.

There is no real struggle once the battle begins. Goliath is defeated before he can strike his first blow. The future King David rescues the land from the chaotic threat of the Philistines. This is a strong affirmation that David will be a powerful ruler, able to defend Israel against all threats.

It may be difficult, but when you find yourself in a trying time, when you are weak, marginalized, or powerless, remember David. Remember his steady faith in God. Trust the Lord the way David did. David believed God—and not David himself—would protect him and Israel against this Philistine giant. He knew that human power does not ultimately save and that God would never let injustice prevail for long. In our lives, there will be times when we know fear. In these fearful times, a space opens in us that allows God to pursue us and to draw close to us. Thanks be to God!

O Holy One, have mercy on us. We know there are giants in this world. Help us today to walk in your way, so that we may know your strong protection. In the name of Jesus, our Lord and Savior, we pray. Amen.

Beginning with 2 Corinthians 5 Paul speaks of the ministry of reconciliation. This reconciliation points to a restored relationship with God and a reconciliation of the people to one another.

In a continuing education course I took, a member of the class stated that he did not understand why countries of the Middle East could not simply sit at the table and talk. The instructor answered his question with a question, "And how does that work in your family?" Without hesitating, the student answered, "I understand perfectly."

When we understand that Christ died for all people, we value everyone and respect everyone. Because we are loved, our love in Christ enables us to love in turn. This way of life has its challenges. Paul knows many of these hardships, and he lists some of them for us. He writes of tough afflictions, hard labors, physical hunger, and sleepless nights. Paul also gives us an account of some of the weapons of righteousness that are ours: genuine love, kindness, truthful speech.

Challenging times and situations (you can name many for yourself) become opportunities to experience God's reconciling pursuit of us. Trying times also give us the chance to respond to God in trust and to know God provides. The words of Second Corinthians bring the message home: "At an acceptable time I have listened to you, and on a day of salvation I have helped you." Given this, Paul says, "Open wide your hearts" to God's great gift of reconciliation.

O Holy One, help us to remember we are reconciled to one another in Christ. May we remember all who have hardships this day and pray they know their relationship with Christ. In the name of the one who calls us. Amen.

I was eight years old, on vacation with my family. We were going to the upper peninsula of Michigan, traveling in our 1954 Ford. Somewhere in Wisconsin, we saw the sky turn a bright lime green, a color I had never seen in the sky before. When we came to a fork in the road, my father went right. It was raining, and the wind got stronger and stronger and stronger. He pulled off the road. Immediately, the wind became so strong it rocked the car from the left two wheels to the right two wheels. We were afraid.

After the storm passed, we drove along on our way. A short distance down the road we saw that an entire community had been devastated by the tornado that had just passed through. Even as an eight-year-old, I was aware of how close we had been to the destruction.

In Mark's story, Jesus, the disciples, and others were going across the Sea of Galilee at night. The trip was not the disciples' idea—Jesus had suggested it, and the disciples had followed his lead.

While they were in the boat, a great storm arose. The boat was in distress; water was filling the boat. And Jesus slept. The disciples were very frightened. They woke Jesus. He heard their fear and, scripture says, he rebuked the wind. With one command he stilled the sea and restored its calm. Can you imagine such power? The disciples certainly were amazed.

Jesus calmed the seas that night for his disciples. He can do that for us too. When our lives are in chaos, when the storms come, and they will, remember Jesus' words, "Peace, be still." Breathe in that peace. Know that God is near.

When storms rage, Jesus, be with me. Remind me of your power, your peace, and your love. Amen.

The disciples were terrified in their tossed-about little boat when the storm suddenly stopped—there was calm. They had a mighty God moment. The boat is one of the earliest symbols of the Christian church; the storm is a metaphor for risk, chaos, and calamity. All the disciples were amazed and, even after the time they had spent with him, wondered who their teacher was. Who was this one that the wind and the sea obeyed?

Jesus demonstrated authority over the watery chaos, an authority usually associated with God. The disciples did not understand it. They lacked faith even though they saw Jesus' power to still the storm and even though they reached the other side of the sea safely.

We hear the stories of Jesus; we see miracles; and sometimes we experience a mighty God moment—a moment when we know our life has been saved. When we are in a storm, Jesus is there. Jesus not only shares our chaotic predicament, he has the power to do something about it. And this is true not only for our lives; it is also true for the life of the church. When the church is in chaos and facing troubling times, Jesus has the power to still the church's storms and give us peace.

God pursues us every moment. Jesus is with us in the storm. May the grace of God fill us with awe so we may know God's love and power.

God of grace and mercy, we long to be safe. Protect us in the storms of life and make our faith strong so that we may witness your love every day and show compassion for all your creation. Amen.

Trust in Times of Trial

JUNE 22–28, 2009 • JACOB DHARMARAJ

MONDAY, JUNE 22 ~ *Read 2 Samuel 1:1, 17-24*

David mourns the death of two important people in his life, both lost in fierce battle: one a beloved friend, the other a dangerous enemy. Jonathan and David were lifelong friends; Saul and David were longtime enemies. Jonathan and David had shared life's joys and sorrows; David had suffered much at the hands of the jealous Saul.

Saul was a charismatic man, a gutsy warrior with a volatile temperament. As the people's admiration for David grew, Saul became increasingly jealous. He was driven by an unreasonable anger and eventually David had fled his wrath. David had three opportunities to kill Saul, but he abstained from laying his hand upon "the LORD's anointed." Now that Saul is dead, David laments, "How the mighty have fallen!" This is not the lament we sometimes use to gloat over a rival's misfortune. It is a deep and true lament: though Saul has been his enemy, David is full of grief at Saul's death in war.

How we respond in the most desperate situations, particularly in the face of jealousy and hatred, reveals our true inner qualities. David admires Saul and grieves for him, though they have been enemies. And, on a broader scale, David is saddened by the casualties of war. When Saul fell, David says, so did the virtues of loyalty and courage. The lament is not only for Saul but also for war itself.

David's grief over his friend Jonathan's death is understandable and expected. But his unexpected grief over the death of Saul, his enemy, is also deep and heartfelt.

O God, the price of war is overwhelming. Help me learn to grieve for both enemies and friends. Amen.

Pastor in the New York Conference of the United Methodist Church; formerly of the Bombay Conference in India

The friendship between Jonathan and David is one of the greatest recorded in the Bible. At Jonathan's death, David fasts and weeps. David expresses his grief in poetry and song. His friendship with Jonathan, David says, is deeper than any between a man and a woman, stronger than a brother's.

David and Jonathan's friendship cannot be forced to fit into some simple category. Theirs was a covenantal relationship with a deep sense of commitment and care. It was a friendship that lasted a lifetime, ending only with Jonathan's death in battle.

A toddler who loved his family pets was busy learning new words. *Cat*, *dog*, and *bird* were his favorites. He had just learned the word *tiger* after visiting the zoo. The next day a neighbor came by and brought along his dog named Tiger. The toddler was absolutely confused. He had mastered some categories of things and the words to go with them. But now he faced a more complex situation! For a long time, he refused to pet the dog or to call the dog by its name. He finally adjusted and accepted this new arrival—a dog named Tiger.

Sometimes we fall prey to our preconceived and outdated categories, and we try to force them to fit. Just as there are many forms of love, there are many levels of friendship. Jesus called his disciples "friends." And, when he was betrayed by Judas, Jesus still called him by the name "friend."

I have witnessed Christian friends who are closer to one another than they sometimes are with their family members. David's friend Jonathan was irreplaceable. It is the loss of this friendship David mourns so eloquently. His grief is a moving tribute to a relationship born of faith and friendship.

O Lord, we thank you for our loyal friends. We give special thanks for Jesus, our true friend and companion. Amen.

Today's passage is one of the early accounts of ministry in a cross-cultural context. The parent church in Jerusalem was in need of relief. The believers in Corinth, who are Gentiles, are taking an offering to help the believers in Jerusalem, who are Jews.

The gospel had taken roots in the Corinthian soil, grown with its particular understanding of the gospel, and gained the momentum to cross boundaries. Corinthian believers were willing to share the pain of other believers living far away because they understood themselves as members of one body. This gift from the Corinthian church to the church in Jerusalem was a "thank you" offering for the gift of the gospel the believers in Jerusalem had given to the Corinthians.

There was no compulsion to give, just a simple reminder of Christ's own self-giving example. Such an act demonstrates that mission does not belong only to one particular community of believers. Christian mission is "from everywhere to everywhere," and it is a "back-and-forth" movement.

In *The Prophet of Zongo Street*, Mohammed Naseehu Ali writes about an African musician and an Armenian cabbie who competitively compare their countries' tragic histories on a ride from Manhattan to Brooklyn. As the ride ends, the cabbie catches his passenger off guard by declining to take money for the ride, saying: "In Armenia, when we greet each other, we say, *Savat tanem.* . . . You know what that means, *Savat tanem*? . . . It means 'I'll take your pain.'" Totally surprised and with one foot already on the street, the passenger responds, with deep respect, "I'll take your pain too."

A sense of connectedness and generosity between believers can be achieved only when we share each other's pain! It is this act of faith that makes our gifts to one another effective and good.

God of generosity, teach us to give and share with all sorts of believers, for the sake of the world and your church. Amen.

From the beginning of his ministry in Corinth, Paul's concern is not about maintenance and management inside the church but about common goals and shared values, unifying compassion and common vision.

In this nonlinear, circular, and ever-moving missional context, one of the best ways the church engages in mission is through the spirit of mutuality and creative, cooperative opportunities. Mutuality becomes witness when the stronger partners and the weaker partners willingly yoke together their God-given resources for the sake of the gospel and for the unity of the body of Christ. Neither group hesitates to acknowledge the need for the other.

The apostle Paul nurtured and encouraged the Corinthian partners to rise above regionalism and parochialism. He took them to the ever-expanding, concentric circles of established Christian fellowships.

Mutuality openly acknowledges our need for one another and our readiness to be with and work with the other for the long haul. An African adage goes, "When there is a thorn in the foot, the whole body stoops to pull it out." That is what Christian sharing is all about.

During a trip to India on a British airlines jet, I heard the flight attendant, a Briton, announce, "Ladies and gentlemen, we are landing in Chennai. For those of you who are coming to India for the first time, have an enjoyable visit. And for those of you who are returning after being abroad, welcome home!" It was striking to me: a British flight attendant welcoming natives of India back to their homeland! *That's it*, I thought. *That is what the messengers of the gospel have been doing since apostolic times. That is what mutuality is all about.*

O God, make us humble enough to acknowledge our need for one another and keep us ready to be with one another for the long haul. Amen.

The psalmist cries from the lowest point in his life, "My soul waits for the LORD, more than those who watch for the morning."

Waiting! It feels so passive; it makes us feel powerless. How we hate it! Our culture constantly lures us into the urgency of *carpe diem* almost as though that means "sieze the moment." A comedian observed, "In my father's time when people missed a train or bus, they just waited for the next one. And now when we miss the first section of the revolving door, our whole day is shot!'"

Waiting is a spiritual discipline. It is a necessity for us as humans. It is a precondition for hope. To live in hope is to live in the power of the future without yet realizing it. Deep inside, the psalmist knew that God would answer him, so he waited expectantly for God's redemption.

A retired dentist, living in the same building in New York City where my wife, Glory, lived for a while, told me this story one afternoon. Growing up in the Bronx, Fred's family did not have money to spare. His mother walked everywhere and spoke little English. One day, when Fred was six years old, his mother stopped him in front of a shoe repairer's shop. His mother asked Fred to read the sign in front of the shop. He read it haltingly, "Shine Inside." She asked him to read it again, and he did. Then, Fred recalled, she said to him, "Shine inside, son. Always shine inside."

In a startling way, this is the message of the psalm. No matter what we are waiting for, no matter what we are hoping, we can "shine inside" because we know God has redeemed us, hears us, and is with us.

God who dwells in light, shine your light on our path, so we may live today, sure of your faithfulness. Amen.

Sir Jonathan Sacks, chief rabbi of the United Hebrew Congregations of the Commonwealth (the United Kingdom), says, "The supreme religious challenge today is to see God's image in one who is not in our image." His words are apt for today's meditation.

Mark writes of a woman who was marginalized and left to fend for herself because of a physical ailment. She was poor, considered unclean, denied entry into the Temple, and ostracized by society—all because she had been bleeding for twelve years. Every attempt she had made to find help from other healers had failed. She was now both desperate and destitute.

Hearing about Jesus, she sought him out, hoping to touch the garment of this holy person, hoping that it might have the power that would heal her. When she did touch Jesus' garment, she was instantly healed. Jesus realized that something unusual had happened to him too. Looking around at the crowd, he asked who had touched him. The woman identified herself, but she did so in great fear.

Jesus extended his compassion and called her "daughter." At last, she regained her identity. She was no longer a nameless woman; she was a daughter of God.

At the physical level, her hemorrhage was gone. She was cured and healed at once. But at the deeper level—at the spiritual level—she was restored as a child of God, claimed by Jesus in front of the entire crowd.

Jesus, who was hurrying on his way to tend the daughter of a prominent religious leader, stopped to heal this nameless, ostracized woman. Once again, we are reminded in a powerful way that the poor and marginalized have a very conspicuous place in God's kingdom.

God of healing, we stretch out our hands, seeking your healing for us and for your world. Amen.

Jairus, a well-respected and well-educated leader of the synagogue, was close to hysteria with fear when he threw himself at the feet of Jesus. His twelve-year-old daughter was at the point of death, and he pleaded with Jesus, "Lay your hands on her, so she may be made well, and live." Soon after this plea, he learned that his daughter was dead.

Jesus said to Jairus, "Do not fear, only believe." Jairus, terrified for his daughter, does not say anything. He just follows Jesus to his home. There, Jesus takes the child's hand and heals her. She was dead, but when Jesus spoke to her she got up and started walking.

How agonizing to watch your child suffer and even die. I vividly remember when the father of a dying girl asked me at a hospital, "What am I, an old man, doing here when my baby is dying?" I didn't have an answer then. I don't have an answer now. I simply said, "I don't know. My wife and I also lost a child. Perhaps someday we may know."

The belief of which Jesus speaks in this passage is not what Jairus, a leader in the synagogue, is accustomed to in his faith life. The belief Jesus calls Jairus to is a larger orientation to commitment and trust. Belief implies risk. It involves movement and memory, honesty and hope. Most of all it is the willingness to trust Christ's power over the death of this little girl and over Jairus's own life.

When Jesus said, "Do not fear, only believe," I often wonder about the tenor of Jesus' voice and the mood of Jairus's personality. What went through Jairus's mind when the mourning at the house gave way to derision and laughter when Jesus arrived—*too late* they thought—and said the girl was not dead?

The time between the promise and the fulfillment is most difficult of all. Yet we find God's comfort and divine encouragement only by trusting Jesus' soothing words, "Do not fear. . . . Believe!"

In times of trial, O God, help our unbelief. Amen.

Steadfast Presence, Sufficient Grace

JUNE 29–JULY 5, 2009 • BARBARA J. LINDGREN

MONDAY, JUNE 29 ∼ *Read Psalm 48:9-14*

The city of Zion, Jerusalem, the city destroyed but never erased. It is a city that changes the lives of pilgrims who journey to it. Psalm 48 focuses on Jerusalem, the city that exudes God's greatness. The psalmist encourages pilgrims to walk around Zion, count its towers, observe its citadels and ramparts, and know that God's presence and steadfast love reside there.

I made pilgrimage to the Holy Land with a group of people who wanted to experience some of the sites that give life to our Christian heritage. Most often, churches were built over the site of a particular event. But to see the two-thousand-year-old olive tree in the Garden of Gethsemane and to walk by the Sea of Galilee, the same sea that the disciples fished and whose stormy waves Jesus calmed—these moved me deeply.

Our knowledgeable guide noted, however, that nothing is inherently holy about the Holy Land. The area has become holy through the stories of our ancestors in faith that have given it its spiritual shape, bringing it to life. For hundreds of years pilgrims have come to meet the God who endures forever, to pray; and they are changed. Journeying through the Holy land increased my faith and made it complete. Being there and walking the ground enlivened my faith and renewed my resolve to "tell the next generation that this is God, our God forever and ever."

Think of a place that holds significance for you and that you would call holy ground. Reflect on what makes it holy. How do you come away changed?

United Methodist clergywoman, freelance writer, mother of two daughters, with two sons-in-law and two grandchildren, living in Long Prairie, Minnesota

David was only thirty when he was anointed king over Israel and began what was to be a forty-year reign. He captured the Jebusite city Jerusalem and claimed it as his own: the city of David. And God was with him, says the text. Jerusalem becomes a holy place, alive with God's presence and hopeful vision for peace.

There is rarely a more challenging time in the life of a congregation than when it decides to build a new building. Often it takes more than one attempt and several years before enough people are on board with the vision to make it a healthy and life-giving process.

From the outset, as soon as the words *new building* start seasoning the conversation, the attachments to the old building surface. The more history people have with a particular church building, the more cherished memories they hold of generations of weddings, baptisms, and funerals; Sunday school Christmas programs; choirs, youth groups, and bazaars. Soon the line becomes very thin between worshiping a building and worshiping God in a building.

Jerusalem became David's city, a symbol of David's newly formed kingdom, and is a holy place now to three world religions. But as with church buildings that become beautiful with the signs and symbols of our faith in Jesus Christ, those signs and symbols do not contain the presence of God. God was present with David and with the people, who were both faithful and successful. Even so, God is with us, as we strive not only to worship in Christ's church but also to be Christ's church in the world.

Make me aware, O God, of your presence that lives in me and through others. Help me to worship you with a thankful heart. Amen.

We know quite a lot about Paul. Much of his character comes out in his letters to the churches he founded and truly loved. He's been called bold, courageous, and even arrogant. One word we don't often hear in relation to Paul is *humble*. But if we look at this passage closely, we'll see it.

We know much about the sufferings he endured: the beatings, imprisonment, shipwrecks, and his sometimes troubled relationships with people. Yet always, he was concerned about the churches. In Corinth, Paul ran into trouble. His authority had been questioned because while others in the community were boasting about their spiritual accomplishments, Paul refused to do so. Instead, he tells the Corinthians of his experience of being caught up in a vision of paradise—but he tells the story in the third person. This person, Paul says, heard things so sacred mortals couldn't repeat them.

A close reading of the scripture makes one thing clear: the person Paul speaks of (himself) is a person in Christ. He wanted others to see in him the living spirit of Christ. Boasting about his own abilities would only get in the way of others' seeing the power of God working through his weaknesses.

Celebrating our strengths must always grow out of being willing to acknowledge our weaknesses. But we cannot work with our weaknesses until we name them. Sometimes others help us to identify them. And other times circumstances surprise us and reveal a weakness deep within us that catches us unaware.

Working to accept weakness is humbling. But it is in our weakness that we find God—the God who gives us strength and courage for the journey.

God of love, be with me today in the challenges and opportunities before me. Help to know of your blessing in the midst of them. Amen.

Paul accepted all the suffering he endured and still remained joyful. But he wasn't above asking God to remove the thorn in his flesh. Three times he pleaded with the Lord to remove what Paul believed was a messenger from Satan sent to torment him and keep him from being too elated.

He tells the Corinthians that the Lord's response was to say, "My grace is sufficient for you, for power is made perfect in weakness." Strength in weakness is a strong theme running through Paul's writings. Because he so completely knew the spirit and strength of Christ, he was content to endure the hardships that threatened him. He learned the lesson of strength in weakness over and over again.

I have had my share of strength-in-weakness lessons, coming after illnesses and emotional shipwrecks. In the midst of each situation I wonder where God is. Sometimes I even have trouble praying. When this happens, I need to remember to rest in the prayers of others. I need to pay attention to the signs of grace, however small, that are all around—from the listening ear of a friend to an understanding smile, to the simple pleasure of preparing a nourishing meal. As the situation eases I realize that God's grace is indeed sufficient; God's strength finds a home in me.

We have all suffered. We have all experienced thorns of one kind or another and probably have had a shipwreck or two in our lives. When I walk into a new day of resurrection, I am on my knees in humility before God. And when I can learn the lessons suffering has to teach I realize that gratitude is the only response. Grace is sufficient—and it is God's greatest gift.

Help me to look for signs of your grace even in the midst of shipwrecks, O God. Remind me that your love is steadfast and your grace is sufficient. Amen.

The first of two distinctive stories in this passage from Mark's Gospel tells of the disappointing reaction Jesus faced upon returning to his hometown. In Nazareth he might have spent some time catching up with family and friends. Things changed on the sabbath, however, when he began teaching in the synagogue. Many who heard him were astounded, Mark says, but not from a belief that the power of God was at work in this man they knew so well.

Familiarity with this man got in the way of seeing who he really was. Other than healing a few sick people, Jesus could not accomplish anything; he was rejected. But rather than feel rejected, he stood in amazement at the people's unbelief.

We have all experienced rejection of some sort. Asking someone to the prom and being rejected, interviewing for a job that feels very promising only to have it be offered to someone else, receiving rejection notices from publishers—the list goes on and on.

It seems that pastors are especially susceptible to criticism that feels like rejection. Part of the job is to listen to feedback and criticism and to evaluate ministry in terms of living out the call. But in one church I served, evaluation erupted into a major conflict, and I was asked to move. The hurt went deep. After a voluntary leave of absence I heard God calling me back to parish ministry. When I could reclaim my sense of who and whose I was—a child of God, loved unconditionally and even delighted in—I felt whole once again.

Jesus refused to let rejection determine his faith. He quickly moved on. We can choose to feel rejected or we can remember who we are and move on.

God of grace, in those times when I feel rejected, help me remember that I am yours and that you delight in me. Amen.

SATURDAY, JULY 4 ~ *Read Psalm 48:1-8*

Today is Independence Day, a day of celebrating the anniversary of the birth of the United States of America, a time for celebrating the freedoms won, albeit some won by way of war. People in the United States celebrate well, with parades and picnics, fireworks and the goose bumps on our arms when the band plays *Stars and Stripes Forever*.

Psalm 48 celebrates the city of Jerusalem, the city of God, as greatly to be praised, The psalm describes Jerusalem as "the joy of all the earth." Throughout the psalm, however, the writer sometimes comes close to confusing God's providence with the city.

I have walked around many sanctuaries, noting the symbols of the Christian faith that clearly identify the building as a church of Jesus Christ. Sometimes an American flag appears in the sanctuary, sometimes not.

One church I served had a small chancel area. The American flag, along with the Christian flag, flanked a picture of Jesus on the wall behind the altar. In contrast, another church placed its sanctuary cross on a pole on the end of a pew in the middle of the congregation. The visual reminder symbolized Christ's presence *among* us, not separate from us watching from a distance. No American flag was on display in this church.

The flag is symbolic of values Americans hold dear. Those who gave their lives to protect our freedom need to be remembered and honored. But, as this psalm reminds us, the unwavering focus of our worship is on the God who saves us through relationship with Jesus Christ, the God who loves us unconditionally and frees us from ourselves for service to others.

Walk around your sanctuary, noting the symbols of the faith. Reflect on the thoughts and feelings that arise. Give thanks for God's presence through sign and symbol.

Jesus has been traveling around Galilee with his disciples, preaching, teaching, and healing. Now he sends them out two by two to evangelize and to do Jesus' work. They are to travel lightly and rely on local hospitality when and if it is offered. Their mission focuses on the message not the messengers. And if their message isn't received, they are to shake the dust from their feet and move on.

It is a great challenge for followers of Jesus today to understand themselves as disciples. In the present culture Christianity has long since lost its place at the center of daily life. It is no longer the way of life that it once was for some people. The message and the meaning of the good news of God's grace gets lost amongst media, technology, and the resulting loss of human interaction. A "Sunday morning faith" that is left to gather dust on the pews could be a big reason for declining membership among the mainline denominations.

As the church faces this loss of power and status, Jesus' words give us some guidance. Just as the disciples were to "take nothing for the journey," so we are called to go forth unencumbered, ready to face the reality of rejection.

The gospel message is simple, yet not everyone is ready to hear it. It cannot be forced into hard hearts. But we are to continue offering that message. (In fact, to shake the dust off one's feet was in biblical times one last way to show people the significance of the message they were rejecting, thereby giving them one more chance to hear it.) Even if our message seems not to be heard, we can move on, praying that we have left a seed of the good news that will one day sprout into a transformed life.

Gracious God, be with me as I set out to live another day as a disciple of Christ. Grant me the courage to live as you would have me live and love as you would have me love, all in the name of Jesus. Amen.

Claimed by God

JULY 6–12, 2009 • MELODY PORTER

MONDAY, JULY 6 ~ *Read 2 Samuel 6:1-5, 12b-19*

David's celebration with the ark follows an epic story, as he leads his people in struggle and at last claims kingship of Israel. The path to Hebron and Jerusalem is tense and bloody, and as his people win one victory after another, they feel the special "chosenness" of God. They are the people God wants in Jerusalem, and David is the man that God has handpicked to be their leader.

Have you ever felt like you were in just the right place, handpicked to do what you're doing? Maybe it's taken you some time to get there; perhaps you haven't been sure it would work out. But then you finally arrive, and it's as if you and God are in the groove together, set to do great things in the name of God who has led you.

It's quite a cause for celebration, and David and his men can't contain themselves. As they carry the ark into Jerusalem, they dance because they are where God has led them and because they see God's fingerprints in the life of their community. In gratitude they continue into Jerusalem with dancing, shouting, and music.

As Christians, we struggle with the sense of being "chosen" as a nation over another nation; we hear Peter's voice echoing in our ears that "God shows no partiality" (Acts 10:34). Still, we know that at times grace and faithfulness work together to put us just where we should be. The Spirit once again works through flawed people and hard situations to bring joy and dancing.

God, who carries us, help us to carry you in our plans, our travels, and our hopes. As we seek to follow you, bring our feet to dancing and set our lives to the rhythm of your Spirit. Amen.

Director of the student volunteer program at Emory University in Atlanta and ordained deacon in the Eastern Pennsylvania Conference of the United Methodist Church

When I was in third grade and feeling particularly inspired by a good day at vacation Bible school, I sat down with my Bible, opened it to Genesis 1:1, and began reading. My goal at the time was to read the Bible straight through, and I figured it would take about a week. As you can imagine, that enthusiasm lasted for three chapters. I didn't complete that cover-to-cover quest that week, but if I had, I might have noticed something: there's a lot in the Bible that we never hear in church.

Today's reading proves to us how much scripture we miss by just focusing on the lectionary. We are taken from dancing, a huge party, music and celebration to Uzzah, who reached out to steady the ark as it teetered on its perch. "God struck him there because he reached out his hand to the ark; and he died there beside the ark of God" (2 Samuel 6:7).

It's a scary, confusing story that scared and angered even David when it happened. It is hard for us to see the God of love as the same God who in this story is so concerned with propriety and boundaries.

Still, it's wise for us to keep reading between the lines of the lectionary—even when what we find is troubling—because doing so can bring us closer to God. Uzzah's story speaks to a reverence for God's power, even if it does so out a mind-set that we today cannot understand. But the story does bring us into deeper conversation, beyond celebration to struggle. And like Jacob in his struggle with the angel, we are blessed in authentic struggle with God by coming closer and engaging with this holy story.

Holy God, we don't always understand how you have moved in the lives of your faithful, but we know that you are present with us in our struggles to understand. Grant us faithfulness as we seek to draw nearer to you. Amen.

All is claimed by God. All belongs to God. From the very beginning of the earth, all that was in it was founded by God as belonging to God.

Still, even while all is claimed by God, the psalmist is clear: Those who wish to enter the sanctuary must be pure and moral, having "clean hands and pure hearts." Today, we might read it this way: to draw close to God, we must have our hearts in the right place. We must be who we truly *are* before God, without pretense. "Who shall ascend the hill of the Lord?...[Those] who do not lift up their souls to what is false."

It can be tempting to try to fake it before God. We can get into patterns of going to church, praying the prayers, reading the Bible without really reading. We may avoid the struggles of the soul that make us ashamed or scared. We may even count on God to come through for us when we're not giving our full energy and attention to growing with God.

In times like these, when we'd rather skate along than dig in, the psalmist reminds us that we already belong to God. Because we already belong to God, we must stand before God with honesty, and as exactly as we are. In doing so, we are freed and empowered once again to seek holiness—in ourselves, in our relationships, in our care for the world, and before God. We seek holiness in our work in the world (clean hands) and in our lives before God (pure hearts). Only then can we "stand in this holy place," our whole lives belonging to God.

God, who claims us as your own, help us to be our true selves with you, so we might grow closer to who you are forming us to be. Amen.

Psalm 24 teaches us that we must be holy to seek God and to approach God's presence in the sanctuary. Our clean hands and pure hearts show our readiness to grow closer to God. In a sense, purity is our way of welcoming God. As we continue reading, though, we get a little surprise: the welcome mat is turned around. Even as God claims us and calls us near, God also prepares to enter our daily lives. The psalmist shows us how preparing to enter the presence of God brings us to a place where God visits us right back. "Lift up your heads, O gates!...that the King of glory may come in."

This quick reversal of imagery is the sung version of a truth that unfolds throughout the Bible. We need God; we love God; we seek God—and God does the same for us. God pursues us relentlessly, finding us in our caves, showing up at the door of our tents, and walking alongside us on the road. This is love on a two-way street. Even as we love God with all our heart, soul, mind, and strength, we discover that God too would stop at nothing to love us.

How do we "lift up [the] heads" of our gates today? How do we prepare our world to be a welcoming place for God and make a way for God to approach us where we are? We can start by making our whole world one where hands are clean and hearts are pure. We make the world a home for God by pursuing justice, where work is honest and wages are fair, where the earth is revered, and relationships are loving and compassionate. We make our world one where heads are lifted up in love and justice to greet the King of glory.

God of glory, give us strong hands and pure hearts to make your beloved world a welcoming place for you. Amen.

What have you been destined for? Prophets were made to speak the truth; amazing performers were "born to sing," and great leaders ascend to positions of serious responsibility. We like to think that each of us has a destiny to fulfill, a calling that lines up with particular gifts, skills, and qualities that we're born with and foster through learning, hard work, and growth.

In Ephesians, we learn that we all share a destiny—to belong to God. We are destined for adoption. God "chose us in Christ before the foundation of the world to be holy and blameless before [God] in love." Even with all the other things God has formed in us to make us uniquely who we are, we are first and most fundamentally made to be children of God.

And as children, we have an inheritance from God, to "live for the praise of his glory." When we think of inheritance, we think of money that will enable us to be financially stable, build up the 429 plan for the kids to go to college, or make that exotic vacation trip. For some, an inheritance is a right—so much that we joke about how parents should live frugally so as not to spend their children's inheritance.

As Christians, our inheritance is not financial stability or wealth. Our inheritance is a responsibility: amidst the deep security of knowing we belong to God, we are called to respond by *praising God enthusiastically*. Amidst the joyful security of knowing who we are and to whom we belong, our inheritance is energetic praise. As we live out our inheritance of praise, it is clear that we know what we live for. As Christians and children of God, our inheritance is much more than a back-up financial strategy—it is our strong and joyful identity.

Loving parent, form us to live our lives in praise to you, knowing that we belong to you and are yours. Amen.

When I was taking Spanish classes in an immersion program in Guatemala, I lived with a family in Antigua. A family from the US was staying there too: a mom, dad, their biological daughter, and the son whom they'd adopted from Guatemala six years earlier. It was their first visit back to Guatemala. They wanted him to reconnect to his home country and its beauty and customs.

As the parents spoke about their process of adoption, they talked about their search for children who needed a home. After a lot of research, they discovered the orphanage in Guatemala and saw how much the children there needed a loving family. In the process of adopting their son, they soon learned that he was adopting them too. He brought them lightness, humor and curiosity. Their adoption worked both ways—they opened their hearts to take him in, and, in turn, he opened up their lives to the fullness they were meant to have.

Ephesians reminds us that through adoption, God adopts us as children. By adopting us as God's own, God shows us more than pity or magnanimity and gives us a deeper connection than that between friends or even between worshiper and the One who is worshiped. God makes us family.

In fact, God's hope for creation is to make this family larger and wider than we can imagine. "In the fullness of time," God will adopt the entire world. All will be drawn into God. We will all be gathered to share the name of God in grace, forgiveness, and redemption. We will discover that world-wide family into which we have been adopted.

Draw us together, God. Draw us to know you as our loving parent, and gather us into your family so we may share with others your grace and love. Amen.

As this difficult story unfolds, this Gospel shows how the dynamics of power, fear and jealousy affect Herod, Herodias, and John the Baptist. Close up, it is not uplifting, warm, or fuzzy. But within its larger context, we can see that God's merciful Spirit is at work in our world and our lives, even in the midst of tragedy.

Looking closely at this text, we see a story about the nature of power. For Herod, Jesus' power is overwhelming and hard to understand—so he attributes the works of the disciples to this difficult character of John the Baptist. Herod uses his power to get his wishes, rewarding Herodias's daughter for pleasing him with her dancing. Then Herodias uses her power for revenge, paying back John the Baptist for condemning her marriage to Herod. Throughout, we see how power, when mixed with fear and lacking love, leads to tragic destruction.

Let's zoom back from our close-up to see this story in its context through a wider-angle lens. Here, we can see a larger truth and a glimpse of the gospel. Mark lets this story unfold right after the disciples are sent out to heal and cast out demons. They're not promised a safe journey, but they are given authority and direction. Right after this story, we read about the miracle of the loaves and fishes, a witness to the surprising abundance of God. Sandwiched between these themes of courage and abundance, this tragic story is a witness to the way God brings life out of death.

On our journeys as disciples in our time, we are not promised ease. John the Baptist and the disciples knew this. Still, they also knew that somehow their faithfulness to Christ would eventually lead to abundance even in the midst of suffering and, through the Spirit, miracles would still unfold.

God of mercy, help us to see the ways your Spirit brings life and abundance out of the most painful and tragic events of our lives. Amen.

The Blessing of Identity

MONDAY, JULY 13 ~ *Read 2 Samuel 7:1-14a*

Attempting faithfulness, we sometimes try to put God in a box. Put so bluntly, it seems absurd. However, marshalling our efforts toward concisely defining God can, momentarily, give us a feeling of control. It is that very feeling of control that we must abandon if we are to allow ourselves to be defined by God.

King David desired not only to bring the ark of God—a sacred container holding the Law given to Moses and other sacred writings—into Jerusalem. He wanted to "house" it in a temple that would add further cache to the holy city. But word comes to the prophet Nathan that God is the one who will be doing the housing, making for David "a great name, like the name of the great ones of the earth."

By *naming* David, God is blessing him with the identity and the skills he needs to lead the faithful. This moment of consecration trumps the royal-but-too-human plans of David.

In our spiritual strivings, we sometimes invite God's blessing of our human systems, empires, and activities. This sort of invocation promotes a religious glossing-over. It's asking God to bestow glory on what we would have done anyway.

As with David, the word comes to us that "the LORD will make *you* a house" and only then will you "build a house for *my* name" (italics added). When we are open to God's naming us, we find sustenance and wholeness far greater than anything we could achieve ourselves.

> *Life-giving Creator, forgive our attempts to limit you. Open us to be named by you. Who would you have us to be? Amen.*

Writer and activist in East Lansing, Michigan

This song of David's anointment not only as God's son and victor over enemies but as "the firstborn, the highest of the kings of the earth" underscores God's commitment to David that comes through Nathan. It affirms David's identity in covenant with God and the people of the Davidic kingdom. The song expresses radical opposition to the many gods of the day.

To gain clarity concerning who we are as individuals and as a covenant community alternately brings us blessed assurance and frightening insecurity. Meanwhile, detours abound. While working out who we are in deeper and eternal ways—"working out our salvation," it has been called—we are constantly offered seemingly strong and comfortable handles for self-definition. While searching for selfhood rooted and grounded in the sacred, we can unknowingly become over-identified with entities most iconic in our time— popular culture superstars, financial institutions, "insurance" promises, and sports affiliations, for starters.

Can we fall into many categories, even camps, and still let our allegiance to God and God's world-transforming love provide a basis for distinctive individuality and integrity? Perhaps, but only if we gain clarity in the discernment of the sacred such that we can put other interests and involvements in their place.

God's "faithfulness and steadfast love shall be with" us, both individually and corporately as a church. I am able to know who I am as I work out who I am *with God* and who I am *with you*. A psalm that helps me realize who I am inspires me to sing along.

God of legacies and leaders, communities and individuals, help us loosen our grip on temporal loyalties. Help us take your hand and the hands of one another. Amen.

The song remains the same: the Holy One of Israel will remain faithful, loving, and honest with David, the people of faith, and the covenant they share. The relationship will survive. The connections will hold. Blessed be the tie that binds.

The covenant that formed the identity of the people of Israel was a promise and an oath witnessed and celebrated liturgically generation after generation. In good times, Israel's allegiance to God overshadowed all else. For modern and postmodern people, laws, treaties, and even church polity have replaced ancient covenants in much of our social organization. Centuries of a culture governed by God have given way to a stridently secular world.

At their best, the covenants of baptism, church membership, ordination, and marriage carry on the heart of the ancient covenant. Taken seriously, these covenants wed promise, religion, and law in life-sustaining and relationship-ordering ways. At their worst, they celebrate cuteness and consumerism, bowing before the whims of popular culture and secular powers and principalities.

Do we still experience—or even, with vibrant imagination, picture—the sacred promise made to David being made to us that "my covenant with him will stand firm . . . forever. . . . I will not remove from him my steadfast love?" Do we hear this holy voice? Do we feel the presence of God daily in our covenants? Does God's love define our movements and decisions? Do we honestly see ourselves as characters in this ongoing sacred story?

As we intentionally participate as New Testament people who acknowledge their roots in Hebrew scripture, the promise goes on. The singer still sings; the song remains the same. God is faithful.

Substitute your name for David's in the following scripture. Read it aloud several times. Hear God's promise speak to you.

"Once and for all I have sworn by my holiness; I will not lie to David" (Psalm 89:35).

God, in Christ, seeks harmony and unity. The divisions between Jews and non-Jews is one dramatic example of the kind of split that stands in the way. In the twenty-first century, we tend to speak of conservatives and liberals, undocumented aliens and citizens, the young and the old, black and white, and on it goes. These words simplify humanity into categories, but also speak to very real divisions.

The other day as I sat at a shared lunch table, a young graduate student attempted a joke in reference to a historic personage the student's friend speculated might have sunk some famous ships. Remembering the person's picture, the student announced, "It can't be him. He doesn't even *look* Muslim!" Stunned, my mind raced: Is he saying all terrorists are Muslims? All Muslims are terrorists? All Muslims look alike? I was only able to mutter under my breath, "I can't believe you just said that."

God, in Christ, steps into those places where we say and do inhumane things that only deepen divisions. We might envision the Christ entering each chasm to create "one new humanity in place of the two, thus making peace."

In this context, these words to the church at Ephesus of Christ about abolishing laws and ordinances make sense. For laws, even religious laws, often serve to deepen fissures and calcify our differences. The holy work of creating one new humanity demands that we loosen our grip on our prejudiced certainties and begin to embrace a deeper understanding of unity and diversity.

Somewhere at a lunch table in the Middle East, a young graduate student referring to someone shooting civilians might be blurting out an attempted joke: "He doesn't even *look* Christian." The peace of Christ, overcoming tears in the fabric of humanity, be with us all.

O Prince of Peace, grant us healing and reconciliation from Brooklyn to Baghdad, from Toledo to Tehran, and from Georgia to the Gaza strip. Amen.

The most insidious form of identity theft may take place long before a credit card is stolen. However, that colorful card might offer clues. It could suggest something about who or what took off with a person's broader, even sacred, identity. Created in the image of God, he or she has stumbled into Credit Card Land. In the disorienting swirl of mall stores and picture phones and high definition televisions, a fourteen-year-old or a fifty-four-year-old can experience media overload that dulls vital memories, holy and personality-forming memories. Amidst a quicksand of stuff and worries about stuff, can we forget from whence we've come?

Can we actually lose a conscious mindfulness that we are "citizens with the saints and also members of the household of God?"

That this letter was read by a variety of churches in Asia Minor and not only by the Ephesians, might be instructive for individuals and churches as we try to remember who we are in our travels through a world of sensory overload. This passage paints a clear picture of a community identity that is both broadly inclusive (peace for those far off—and for those nearby) and solidly founded on the saints, the apostles, the prophets and, as cornerstone, Christ Jesus.

Participating intentionally and regularly as members of the household of God, we can better isolate and acknowledge the ephemeral and identity-stealing claims on our lives. And this may mean even the mighty credit card. Financial advisors recommend that significantly indebted folks cut their cards in half. A spiritual director might suggest the same action as preparation for prayer or a call to worship. In God's household, membership has its privileges too.

Next to your Bible, lay your credit card or checkbook. Reflect on times when your spending conflicted with your biblical values. Envision future opportunities to put your checks or charges in the service of the household of God and its service to the world. Pray earnestly for guidance.

Christian theologian John S. Dunne of Notre Dame writes of the power of "passing over," caring for others and all of life so profoundly that one comes to understand deeply the life experience of another person. He describes the extraordinary transformation that then happens as one "comes back" to one's own journey, now full of the understanding of another.

Dunne writes that "the sympathetic understanding into which [one] must enter in order to pass over to another [person's] life is itself compassion, for it involves a sharing of feelings and images as well as insight into the images and feelings."

Entering into the disciples' experience, Jesus sees and feels their fatigue even as he begins to sense his own. So he offers rest. Crossing the water and going ashore, Jesus moves into a crowd and has compassion for them, for they are "like sheep without a shepherd." He begins to teach.

One might assume Jesus would always know what an individual, community, or crowd would need before he gets to them. Instead, he *passes over*, with love and compassion, into their reality. Avoiding a one-size-fits-all approach, Jesus demonstrates how those of us who would follow him are to minister to others, each of sacred worth.

How easy it is to prejudge what others need or desire. What looks like anger at a distance might really be exhaustion. What first appears to be hedonistic conformity from afar might prove to be an unhappy search for meaning in life. If we can see that another's struggle is truly his or her own and not about us, opportunities might come for us to be compassionately present and, God willing, helpful in a healthy way.

Can you remember someone who *passed over* into your journey? Where do you see others willing to live Christ's presence by "passing over" into someone else's life?

Gracious God, make me an instrument of your love. Amen.

Here is a worthy question: Who am I *today*? There are variations: Who am I *in this place*, at this time? Who am I with *these* people in *this* setting? How am I different from who I was five years ago? What kind of a person do I want to be—or, does the Creator want me to be—going forward?

Mark's Gospel is lush with the particular things of a specific time and place, redolent with local foliage and nearby waters. Commentators refer to his writing as the "Galilean Gospel." When Jesus gets out of a boat at Gennesaret, the sick are brought to him. They come to him as who they are—people suffering illness. They touch him. He touches them. They are healed.

Just as surely as Jesus blesses the people with healing, he first blesses them simply by being with them. He is where they are. He eats the food they eat and breathes the air they breathe, amidst all the sounds and smells of Galilee.

Who am I today, right now? Who am I when I am lonely or ill? Who am I in my hometown or in a new city? What wounds and memories and past successes inform who I am today?

Through all the changes in our lives, we need acceptance of who we are *today*. How easy it is to turn someone away for past transgressions. How difficult it can be to accept someone who is angry or unhappy. Yet there is no greater blessing to a person's self-worth than to be loved unconditionally. It is a time of healing. Jesus has come ashore.

Hymn singing is a powerful form of spiritual formation. Reflect on these words from the nineteenth-century hymn "Just As I Am." Reflect on why it still moves you today.

> *Just as I am, thou wilt receive,*
> *wilt welcome, pardon, cleanse, relieve;*
> *because thy promise I believe,*
> *O Lamb of God, I come, I come!*

Imagine That

JULY 20–26, 2009 • MARY DONOVAN TURNER

MONDAY, JULY 20 ~ *Read 2 Samuel 11:1-15*

It is a story embroiled in violation, adultery, misplaced loyalties, arrogance, deception, and murder. It is a stark, understated account of a king who abuses power, whose moral fabric is beginning to unravel. And it is a story about a woman who becomes a victim of the king's abusive power. We know little about her, only her name and that she is beautiful. We do not know what she thinks or feels; she says nothing.

There is another in this story, Uriah the Hittite, the husband of Bathsheba. He is the foil, the sharp contrast to all that dismays us about the great King David. In contrast to David who stays home when he should be with others on the battlefield, Uriah goes out to save his community. He lives out his commitment, fully and wholly, by denying himself nourishment and pleasure, his identification with other soldiers so complete. He is honest, faithful, trusting, courageous. (The king himself depends on one with these values to keep his kingdom and power intact!) But in the end, Uriah's integrity does not guarantee his safety or shield him from danger. He is the one who loses his life. He seems to have been powerless in contrast to the great King David. Or maybe not.

Perhaps this story is God's way of challenging us to imagine that commitment and compassion are not weakness and that the ability to command and oppress is not strength.

> *God of true strength and wisdom, lend me your vulnerability and compassion. Amen.*

Vice President for Academic Affairs, Dean of the Faculty, and Carl Patton Professor of Preaching at Pacific School of Religion, Berkeley, California; ordained minister in the Christian Church (Disciples of Christ)

Psalm 14 is not, as are many psalms, a prayer; the psalmist does not speak to God but for God. These are words of lament and distress about the world's condition; the psalmist imagines the world as God sees it and as we frequently experience it.

God is looking for the wise ones, for those who seek God. God finds none. "No, not one" who knows and lives as if there is a God. The matter of intellectual assent to the idea of God is less important here than how we alter our lives because of it. We betray or honor God by how we choose to live.

When the foolish one says there is no God, the vacancy in that one is filled with self. The person becomes ultimate wisdom. The thinking of the foolish one cannot detect self-deception, making that one vulnerable to error and self-righteousness. Self-deception cannot see beyond its own limits and needs. It is stifled. It suffocates. It is limited. It lives in a closed circle of certainty—a denial of community.

We can easily distinguish between wisdom and folly when we read Psalm 14 but find them difficult to discern in our own lives. When are we misguided? When do our self-sufficiencies blind us to the needs and desires of those in the world around us? When are we living as if we do not believe in God? What does God really require?

If this psalm (and Psalm 53, which is virtually identical to it) is not a prayer, how did the Israelites use it in worship? Perhaps it functioned as a call to confession for the Israelites just as it does to us. It calls us to confess the many ways in which we deny God's presence. And to repent. So that when God looks upon the world in search of wise ones, God will not be disappointed.

Dear God, open our eyes, our ears, our hearts, our hands to the world around us. Amen.

The Hebrew Scriptures repeatedly call the community to a care and concern for those less fortunate and less powerful and more vulnerable than themselves. When one gathers wheat from the field, she is to leave grain for the alien, the widow, and the orphan who have none. And when gathering grapes off the vine, one is to leave fruit for those who have none. How one shows concern is a part, a crucial part, of living up to one's covenantal commitment with Yahweh.

In Psalm 14, how the foolish deal with the poor graphically demonstrates the stark contrast between the foolish and the wise ones. Those who do not seek God, who have gone astray, who are perverse, who do not do good, are those who devour the poor just as casually as they eat a loaf of bread.

These are the same ones who would "confound the plans" of the poor, making life even more difficult in a world that already oppresses, ignores, alienates, and denies them. The foolish ones imagine that the poor are defenseless in the world because no God stands with them.

Those who seek after God know that to oppress another child of God is the most egregious offense to Yahweh. How can we honor a parent by destroying the child? To be wise we must take account in our religious practice and in our politics of the most vulnerable ones among us. Dare we imagine a world where the spiritual, physical, and emotional needs of these are filled?

Dear God, help me imagine myself with unlimited compassion and concern for others. Amen.

While appearing in the middle of the book of Ephesians, this text has the quality of benediction and blessing about it. These intercessions are filled with gratitude. The author bends his knees, not in submission or defeat but in awe of this God who gives every family its name. Every family, then, is part of a great web of being, each related to the other.

The prayer asks that those in the community be strengthened, rooted, grounded in love, empowered, and filled with all the fullness of God, becoming a tapestry of unimagined beauty. The language of the prayer, while abstract, is strong; it is powerful. Its greatness, its loftiness, only serves to reinforce what the writer of the prayer has known. The community needs to be wrested from its small understandings, its reduced expectations, its diminished theologies to understand the breadth, the length, the width, and the depth of God's mystery and power.

The prayer does not tell us how this wresting comes about, but it does fill our imaginations with the sights and sounds, thoughts and feelings of God's wonder stirring in our lives. When have we known the strength of God's power within us? How do we remain rooted and grounded in the love of God so amazing we cannot possibly understand it? How do we empower others, the community, for faithful service. When will all be filled with the fullness of God?

The prayer stirs within us a great longing that this "benediction" written for others some two thousand years ago might fall gently upon us to renew and restore and to stir our dormant imaginations.

Dear God, what does it mean to live in your fullness? I long to know. Amen.

Somewhere along the way, as lessons from life take their toll, we lose it. We lose the ability we had as children to be playful, to rearrange the world according to our imaginations, to make believe. We lose our capacity to travel to distant places, solve problems, create alternative worlds, and think our way into new ways of being.

The Old Testament prophets tried to call people to newness. They called people to imagine an alternative way to live—a way grounded in justice and righteousness: a stretching of horizon, a widening of peripheral vision, an expansion of compassion that would both see and include those on the margins.

According to Luke, the Magnificat of Mary imagines a world where structures, paradigms, oppressions as we know them are no longer with us. Jesus helps us imagine such a world when he tells simple parables. He helps the disciples and all who hover about him to imagine a different way of seeing life.

Imagination becomes our "bridge." It shows us how to span the gap, the empty space between the actual and the ideal, the yet and the not yet, between being and becoming. And so the writer of Ephesians prays that somehow the community of the faithful will begin to imagine what God can imagine.

Stir my imagination, God, to see the world as you would have me see it. Unsettle me. Amen.

The time of year is the Passover, a springtime festival that commemorates God's great intervention and protection of the Israelite people in Egypt. Year after year the story of deliverance is told so that the generations can remember how God was present with their earliest ancestors as they began their journey from slavery to freedom.

As John 6 begins, the Passover is approaching. Jesus will spend this festival day in Galilee. The crowds gather around him, aware that there is something extraordinary about his power. He heals, touches, teaches. He comforts. They press in around him from all sides to see, to touch, to hear.

Those in the crowds become hungry. The disciples cannot begin to imagine how the people will be fed, but Jesus knows that he will perform another "sign," another miracle for them. With only the lunch of a small boy, the pressing crowd of 5,000 is fed. The people become even more convinced that Jesus should be king; and in an effort to avoid them, Jesus withdraws to the mountain.

It is a strange story. Jesus performs a "sign" but doesn't want the crowds to be impressed by it. Somehow he wants them to see beyond, to see something different, something more important, something longer lasting. The crowds are easily impressed with bread. But Jesus wants them to know he is Bread, the Bread of Life. And they, as we, have a difficult time understanding this one who is more than we can imagine.

Help us understand, God, this Jesus who was so strong, so weak, so unlike us and so like us. Amen.

In the stories of the Exodus, God demonstrates God's remarkable sustaining presence by parting and calming the Red Sea so the Israelites can safely cross over. God also provides food in the wilderness—manna and bread—to sustain the people in their long and grueling wilderness adventures.

The Gospels of Matthew, Mark, and John remember these manifestations of God's presence by pairing the stories of the miraculous feeding of the 5,000 with the calming of the storm-tossed sea. After Jesus withdraws from the multitudes, the disciples, their stomachs filled with fish and bread, board a boat to cross the Sea of Galilee. Jesus has left them, and they are fearful, for it is night. They panic because the storm renders them unsafe on the wave-ridden waters.

Then out of the chaos and on the horizon of their fear, Jesus appears as a sign of hope. He comes to them, walking upon the water. And he says to them, "Do not be afraid."

Do not be afraid. From the mouths of the prophets and angels these words constitute the constant refrain from God to God's people: *Do not be afraid. I am with you.*

The words pale oft times when we hear them in light of the excruciating, painful, fear-driven circumstances within which many people of the world must live. *Do not be afraid.* How do the world's people know that God is there? Perhaps they know through our constant care and attention to their need. Perhaps our vocation, our mission, is to wade into the waters of the world and stand by those who may be swept away. We take their hands and, by our very presence, help them imagine a God who has not forsaken them.

God, give me the courage to wade into the deep waters. Amen.

True Sorrow Brings
Forgiveness and New Life

JULY 27–AUGUST 2, 2009 • LEONA ELLIS

MONDAY, JULY 27 ~ *Read 2 Samuel 11:26-12:13a*

It must have been a frightening moment and a stark conversation. It certainly was a conversation that could have cost Nathan his life. But God told Nathan to go to King David and tell him the truth of David's sins against Uriah, Bathsheba—and God. So he went.

The story Nathan told of the rich man, the poor man, and the sheep was shocking. It moved David to anger. But it didn't stir recognition in David, so Nathan had to come right out and say it, "You are the man!"

David was brought up short, but as he listened to the rest of Nathan's words, as he listened to the consequences of his sin, David came to a painful realization, "I have sinned against the LORD."

This passage is considered by some to be one of the greatest in the Bible: it speaks the truth starkly and shows us as we really are. Not even the powerful can break the laws of God with impunity.

God, through the Holy Spirit, is our constant companion. God leads us away from sin and guides us into truth. But God never violates our freedom of choice; we, like David, make our own choices. But David's response to Nathan shows us that godly sorrow is the best response to sin in our life. When the Holy Spirit convicts us of sin, we must confess to God and say, "I have sinned against the LORD." Then God brings us back to wholeness. Restored, we can again be used by God to bring glory.

God, empower us to confess our sin and trust you to forgive. Amen.

Director of children's ministry at Windsor Village United Methodist Church in Houston, Texas

David wrote Psalm 51 as he struggled with his sin of adultery with Bathsheba and the scheme to murder her husband, Uriah. David responded to his sin by crying out to God for mercy; he knew God's mercy and God's lovingkindness could restore him.

As Christians in human bodies we are mindful of how easy it is to sin and yet how difficult it can be for us to face the consequences of our sin. Sin brings torment, restlessness, and dis-ease. When we come before God to confession, we bring our transgressions and iniquity to our confession. God, however, meets us with steadfast love and mercy.

This psalm is a heartfelt confession of guilt—but it is clearly not focused only on guilt. There is one more thing. David's psalm expresses the confidence and the courage with which we can approach God in repentance. The psalm reminds us that God gives us endless possibilities for pardon, for another chance, for new life. We need not be preoccupied with guilt—we only need to repent, seek forgiveness, and trust in God's power to change our lives.

All the sinners (and all the saints) throughout our history have struggled to be faithful. They were sorrowful when they sinned. They came to God in repentant prayer. And they were restored— time and again—to live as the faithful followers God intended them to be. We, as present-day Christians, join David and all the others who have come before us in this gracious litany of confession, repentance, and restoration to the life of faith. With confidence and courage, we can start again. God's grace and steadfast love surround us now and forever.

Being a Christian means making daily choices between good and bad, between obedience and sin. Today, be aware of God's presence in the strength of the Holy Spirit to guide you.

David's words in this psalm are strong and heartfelt. Aware of his sinfulness, he asks God to purge and cleanse him. To those of us who live in a world that prefers denial to honesty, this psalm is audacious and bold. David does not dissemble. He doesn't try to put himself in a better light. He is a sinner who confesses and asks for God's mercy.

Then David asks God to do something quite remarkable: "Hide your face from my sins." Only a sinner with great confidence in God can approach God with this petition. David is sure of God's mercy and lovingkindness. His request of God is this: "Create in me a clean heart, O God, and put a new and right spirit within me."

This psalm can be a guide for us. David did not get stuck in his guilt. Neither should we. He knew that his sin was great. We too know the severity of our sin. As he recovers from his folly, he sets about reorienting his life toward God. We, along with David, can turn ourselves toward these changes.

David focuses on what he most needs: a restored life, a new relationship with God and the community, and the companionship of the Holy Spirit. That must be the focus of our prayers too.

When we confess our sins, when we ask God to forgive us, we receive the great gift of a new heart and a right spirit. God creates a clean heart in us and sustains a right spirit within us. The God who can do this for us is a powerful and gracious God.

God, thank you for always loving us. We sin and still you reach out to us. You forgive us and restore us. Amen.

The miracles and works of Jesus always drew a crowd. People traveled wherever Jesus went to receive healing and to hear his teachings. Jesus knew that people sought him, many times for the wrong reasons. He spoke often with them about the deeper spiritual truths of their experiences with him. In the first verses of John 6, Jesus miraculously fed a multitude of people with five loaves of bread and two fish. The people responded to this miracle by wanting to make Jesus a king.

So Jesus went "to the other side of the sea." But the people followed him there. He knew the crowd was seeking him because he had fed them, and he told them so. He told them they should instead seek the bread that gives eternal life.

Even today, we often seek to be with Jesus for the wrong reasons. We must always check our hearts, our motives. Do we seek Jesus for healing and miracles or are we seeking eternal life? All Jesus' words and commands provide us with the truth that leads to eternal life. And it is all right to seek Jesus for healing and for wholeness—because we know that salvation brings with it healing and wholeness.

But salvation—eternal life—is more than earthly healing and heavenly life after death. Eternal life—salvation—is abundant living that starts here, now, on this earth. Like the kingdom of God, our salvation is not in some faraway place. Salvation, eternal life, God's kingdom—all these are gifts we are given now to live into the future and beyond as children of God. This is the bread of life—we eat it and are never hungry again.

God, we thank you for the gift of Jesus, the bread of life. May we hunger and thirst only for him today. Amen.

Questions! Questions! Jesus was asked all kinds of questions by all kinds of people every day. Some questions came from those who wanted to destroy him. But some questions reflected someone's genuine concern to understand God's will. The people in this passage seem genuine: "What must we do to perform the works of God?"

Jesus told them that the work of God is belief—what they must do is believe. Struggling to believe, they asked Jesus for a sign. Their ancestors, they said, had received the sign of manna. Jesus reminded them that the manna came not from Moses but from God. He told them that, beyond sending manna, God had sent them the true bread from heaven.

Hearing this, they asked Jesus to give them this bread. In response he said, "Whoever comes to me will never be hungry and whoever believes in me will never be thirsty."

Today, in the midst of our own questions about the world we live in and the God we serve, Jesus comes to us again as the bread of life. We ask Jesus many questions. His answer to us is the same one he gave to those around him at the time of the disciples: "I am the bread of life." He sets before us the opportunity to hear his call and to believe in him. With belief and obedience, we find peace and power in the midst of our questions. God loves us. Out of this great love God has given us the bread of life, the bread of heaven. In Jesus, we can experience daily the fulfillment and joy of belief. We can know the bread of life, the gift of heaven.

God, we thank you for the gift of Jesus, our bread of life. May we always hunger and thirst only for him. Make us strong witnesses to your love and power. Amen.

God calls all believers to a life of unity in the midst of differences. The way to unity is to walk worthy of our calling through humility, gentleness, and long-suffering. This disciplined walk brings us together and keeps us in the peace of the Holy Spirit. When we live in unity, we bear witness to the world of the power of God—as one body, one Spirit, one faith, and one Lord.

When we try to obey this call to unity, we find ourselves immediately challenged. Some believers have personalities and temperaments that are hard to handle. Others hold beliefs and ideas we find at odds with our own. Sometimes it may be that we ourselves are the ones standing on the outside, excluded by the faith community. We bond easily with some believers; others seem to rub us the wrong way without even trying.

More importantly, there are differences that keep us from worshiping together, that cause us to reject some believers and bar them from our church, that stand in the way of our common ministry. These differences—real and imagined—give lie to the ideal of our unity as Christians and cause God deep sorrow. Divided, we are a poor witness to the world. Yet in spite of our failures, Ephesian's passionate vision of unity for the church is still strong.

As we try yet again, as we make new efforts to listen to one another, let us remember our greatest resources in this struggle: prayer, love, and being in the mind of Christ. Without unity our witness in the world is divided and weak. With God, through Christ, we can come to wholeness. If this is not yet a reality for us today, we know unity remains God's vision for us all.

Lord, strengthen our hearts and minds so that we live and work together in oneness to reflect your love for the world. Amen.

For a body to be healthy, all the individual parts must work together in harmony. Proper nourishment, daily exercise, and adequate rest are required to maintain a healthy body. When the body is healthy, we can run, play, and work. When the body does not have all of its needs met or has parts that don't work right, the body breaks down in disease and dysfunction.

This passage from Ephesians explains how the body of Christ grows healthy. Each believer is a member of the body of Christ. To keep the body of Christ healthy, God has given us apostles, prophets, evangelists, pastors, and teachers. The body of Christ is healthy when each member works together in harmony and love to fulfill the ministry of the gospel. As each member speaks the truth in love and grows up in the fullness of Christ, the body of Christ is edified in love.

This love reveals to the world that we are disciples of Jesus Christ. If the body of Christ is tossed about by different doctrines, opinions, power plays, or deceitful plots, the body becomes divided. An unhealthy body of Christ is not able to equip the saints for the work of ministry. The divided body of Christ is a scandal. If the body of Christ is divided, its witness is weakened. There has been strong witness by a unified Christian church at various times throughout history. But with our church today still so divided, to speak of the unity of our faith is to speak not of what is but what we hope some-day can be. As Christians, we are called to live toward this vision— to pray and love and work toward unity in the body of Christ.

God of hope and wholeness, grant that I may be a witness to the power of your vision for the world today. Amen.

In the Thickets by the Jordan

AUGUST 3-9, 2009 • AUSTIN B. TUCKER

MONDAY, AUGUST 3 ~ *Read 2 Samuel 18:5-9*

The forest claimed more lives that day than the sword.

We do not always have a choice in selecting our field of combat. The Alaskan National Guard for half a century rendered extraordinary service defending the frozen frontier of America's remotest northwest. Then in 2006 this Guard was called to go halfway around the world into the desert of Iraq. It must have seemed bizarre to leave the cold land of the midnight sun and deploy to the blistering sand. They left their homes on the tundra to fight in Iraq, and some of them did not make it back alive.

Perhaps Absalom intended his deployment in the thickets by the Jordan to be a strategic advantage. If so, it was a fatal mistake. His army paid the price, and so did he himself. Perhaps Absalom's battle plan did not properly take into account the forest of Ephraim. But Joab's plan did. The casualties were great that day, and more than ten thousand of them were victims of the terrain.

In our spiritual warfare we want to take our defensive position on the moral high ground. When we need to defend ourselves against our spiritual foes, we want to do so from a position of spiritual strength. Who will battle political corruption? Who will fight poverty, disease, and hunger? Who will confront moral issues like pornography, gambling, and illegal drugs? These are our battles to fight wherever threat is found.

Lord of Hosts, grant us wisdom for our spiritual struggles. Protect us from peril, and lead us to greater glory. We pray in the name of Jesus, the master of our salvation. Amen.

Teacher, preacher, writer, and member of Summer Grove Baptist Church in Shreveport, Louisiana

O my son Absalom! My son, my son Absalom! If only I had died instead of you. O Absalom, my son, my son!"

When Absalom was born in Hebron, they gave him the name that means "the father is of peace." As he grew, all Israel praised him for his beauty. He was famous for hair so heavy that it was weighed at the occasional cuttings. The beginning of his misery came when Tamar, his beautiful sister, was violated by their half-brother Amnon. Rage smoldered for years and finally exploded in Absalom's murder of the rapist.

After the murder, Absalom hurried across the Jordan to three years of self-imposed exile. Tender in his care for his sister, reckless in his assassination of his brother, Absalom was also ambitious and impatient to replace David as king on the throne.

Years passed before David allowed his son's return. Absalom wasted no time in organizing a campaign to steal away the hearts of the people of Israel from their king. When the plot matured into a coup, David abandoned the royal city rather than fight his son. Absalom took the City of David without a fight. Eventually, though, the battle came. Absalom died, his head caught in an oak in the wild thicket by the Jordan. Three arrows of Joab pierced his heart.

King David would gladly have given his own life for Absalom's, but that was not possible. The tragedy brought on by David's sin with Bathsheba and Uriah was multiplied dramatically by Absalom's own sin. Absalom paid with this death. David paid with a lifetime of grief, an old man suffering the death of a beloved son. Surely we today can empathize with the pain and grief in this text; surely we can lay alongside it our own grief and pain.

God, keep us focused on you that we may pass safely through the thickets of sin and glorify you with our lives. Amen.

I wait for the LORD, my soul waits, and in his word I hope." Imagine yourself singing this song with other pilgrims in a caravan traveling from the Galilee through the Jordan valley on the way to Jerusalem. You are on your way to a festival, perhaps Passover. In the time since you last saw Jerusalem, your life has been marked by death and grief. So, as you begin your journey, you sing this psalm to pour out your grief to God, just as King David poured out his grief before God at Absalom's death.

Evening comes early as the sun disappears over the Judean hills. The Jordan valley will soon be wrapped in darkness; it is time to camp. The scrubby underbrush in the thickets by the Jordan provides plenty of fuel for a campfire. Some among your pilgrim band will need to take turns staying awake to guard against bandits and wild beasts.

When dawn finally comes, it seems to come all at once. A red streak drives the darkness from the hills of Moab. Someone in the camp beings to sing the next words of the psalm: "My soul waits for the Lord more than those who watch for the morning." The river road is soon flooded with light. You know that even as your day begins, the morning sacrifice is being offered for your sins in the temple at Jerusalem.

There are still many miles to go to Jerusalem and the temple. After a breakfast of cheese and bread, your band of pilgrims continues the southward trek. You begin to sing again, the part of the psalm that celebrates the Lord's generous and gracious mercy toward you: "But there is forgiveness with you, so that you may be revered." And you find peace; soon you will be singing with the Levites in the temple.

Gracious God, let your ear be attentive to my cry for mercy. With you there is forgiveness through the life and death of Jesus Christ, your son. Amen.

But there is forgiveness with you, so that you may be revered.

This psalm celebrates God's unfailing love and redeeming grace. God's mercy and forgiveness stir our hearts to reverence and worship. The King James Version of the Bible translates reverence of the Lord as "fear of the LORD." For the Israelites, to fear God is to love God absolutely, to love God exclusively. For them, true love—true reverence—created fear and anguish at the thought that they might sin or compromise their faith.

Constant worship and strict attention to honoring God in their daily lives was the Israelites' response to God's love and forgiveness. Of course, they were not always successful in their attempts to be faithful. They did sin, they did stray from God's ways—and each time God forgave them.

This is the truth of Psalm 130: God loves us, forgives us, and calls us to faithfulness. And when life brings us grief and death, Psalm 130 shows us that we can go to God, cry out to God in prayer, and know that God hears us. This grace is what prompts us to worship such a loving God. God's compassion, clemency, and unfailing love—this is what stirs our hearts to worship. This is why we can approach God with our whole selves, just as we are—content or grieving, giddy with happiness or wracked with grief. This is the love that calls us to worship and to faithfulness.

David knew this. So did Jonah and Job, Mary and John, Martin Luther and Mother Teresa. Fear of the Lord—reverence for the Lord—sustained each of them, even as it sustains us now.

O God of great forgiving grace, hear our cry. You love us with an unfailing love. You alone are our hope. Amen.

No one can come to me unless drawn by the Father who sent me.

A great crowd, attracted by his miracles, followed Jesus up from the Sea of Galilee. With the twelve, the Lord left the crowds and climbed into the hills. Yet a new crowd soon gathered, perhaps a band of pilgrims going up to Jerusalem for Passover. This crowd soon grew to five thousand, and Jesus fed them all miraculously. Surely this must be the beginning of the bountiful age of the kingdom. A clamor arose to make Jesus king.

Again, the Lord withdrew, now higher into the hills beyond the lake. But the buzz about miracles and the Messiah persisted. That is when Jesus spoke these startling words, "No one can come to me unless drawn by the Father who sent me."

Jesus meant that it was not simply by his teaching but also by the power of a divine force that people are pulled to God. He meant that neither he nor God would let the resistance of those who didn't believe go unchallenged. He meant that it was this divine pull, this care even for those most stubborn in their disbelief that would be the source of salvation and everlasting life.

Jesus also knows exactly where this divine concern for all of us will take him. "I am the living bread that came down from heaven," Jesus says. He knows well the sacrifice that lies ahead of him, the sacrifice he will make so that others may live.

Lord Jesus! You are indeed the living bread. We come to you, drawn to you by God. Fill us with gratitude for your sacrifice. Amen.

Be angry but do not sin.

Ephesians is quoting a line from the Greek translation of Psalm 4, "In your anger do not sin." Twice more in today's scripture reading the writer uses the same root word for anger. He tells us not to let sundown catch us still stewing in our anger, and he tells us anger is one of the things we are to banish along with anger's close cousins: bitterness, wrath, wrangling, and slander.

This passage is an attempt to answer an urgent question from new believers. They have just learned that, because of God's love for them through Christ, they have been made new creatures, called to live new lives. This is good news, but it raises a big question for them: Since we are now members of the household of God, how will we know if we are living the new life God intends?

It's a heartfelt question, and one that Ephesians addresses straight on. Put your anger away. Give up thievery. Do not tear down the community by talking evil; build the community up by speaking instead with grace. Be tenderhearted and forgive one another.

Then Ephesians delivers the most amazing part of the answer to their question. In their new life, they are to be imitators of Christ, and imitators not only of him but also imitators also of God. God's love for us in the sacrifice of Jesus demands this, and it can seem to us an impossible command. But along with this command come the gifts of the Holy Spirit's seal upon us and the love of Jesus Christ. These, alongside God's forgiving love for us makes it possible for us to become imitators of God.

Put away anger. Speak with grace. Live in love.

Help me, God, to live as one who tries to imitate your love and grace today. Amen.

Therefore be imitators of God . . . and live in love.

Samuel Taylor Coleridge called the letter to the Ephesians "the divinest composition of man." It sparkles with all the themes we most appreciate: salvation by grace through faith, the doctrine of the Holy Spirit, the mystery of the church and its unity, and especially the theme of love.

In *love* God predestined us for adoption as God's children (Ephesians 1:5). The Ephesians enjoyed a reputation for *loving* all God's people (1:15). It is God's great love for us that prompts God's mercy toward us (2: 4). And we, rooted and established in love are able to grasp how wide and long and high and deep is the *love* of Christ which is beyond knowing (3:17-19). Paul urged them and us to be tolerant of each other in *love* (4:2). We are to live out the truth in love and see the body of Christ build itself up in *love* (4:15-16). So we live a life of love (4:2).

And then comes Paul's benediction: "Peace be to the whole community, and *love* with faith. Grace to all who love our Lord Jesus Christ with undying *love*" (6:23-24).

In our time of increasing trouble, we find stability in God's love for us and our love for God and one another. As Jeremiah writes, "If you have raced with foot-runners and they have wearied you, how will you compete with horses? And if in a safe land you fall down, how will you fare in the thickets by the Jordan? (Jeremiah 12:5)

We will manage, even in the thickets, because God's great compassion gives us strength. We rely on Christ and on the Holy Spirit to guide us and to give us courage.

Thank you, Lord, for that love that infuses us with strength for whatever today demands. Amen.

Wisdom

AUGUST 10–16, 2009 • JANET CASTERLINE

MONDAY, AUGUST 10 ~ *Read 1 Kings 2:10-12*

Which headline would have run in the *Bethlehem Times* if you had been the editor at the time of David's death?

GIANT KILLER LAID TO REST

ADULTERER MEETS HIS FINAL JUDGE

KING SAUL'S PROTÉGÉ IS DEAD

David's life story was not so far removed from the lives of leaders today. Personal failures make headlines. A public figure may be remembered as "the man who slept with another man's wife" or as "the woman who lied to the press." Often we do not consider that the prayer of that person's heart may be as deep as David's was when he prayed, "Cast me not away from thy presence; and take not thy holy spirit from me" (Ps. 51:11, KJV). We know that in spite of his moral failures, David wanted to be close to God and to experience God's forgiveness.

Political leaders are not the only ones who experience this kind of judgment by others. What about friends, family, and acquaintances who have had failures in their lives? There is an old saying that churches are not havens for saints but hospitals for sinners. As we observe these sins in ourselves and in others, do we focus on the sin or on the sinner?

When we are the ones who sin, we want forgiveness and support from others and from God. Can we do any less—for those we know or those about whom we read in the news—than pray for these people and support them in their search for forgiveness?

Gracious Lord, fill our hearts with love and with desire for forgiveness for ourselves and for others. Amen.

Retired teacher who has found a ministry of music with older adults; member of First United Methodist Church in Anderson, Indiana

F*ather Knows Best* was a popular television show when I was growing up. Mr. Anderson was the loving father of three, successful in work, devoted husband. The assumption, played out week by week, was that no matter what problems came along in life, he could provide solutions.

As years went on, television shows changed. Fathers were portrayed as bumbling men who needed to be rescued from everyday challenges. They seemed to stumble through life, providing no leadership in the home and no inspiration to their families. Wisdom was lacking in these characters.

Some of us had wise fathers, kind fathers, good fathers. Some fathers were funny and made us laugh. Other fathers were serious and taught us how to think and how to figure things out. For some of us, our father was neglectful or cruel and mean. Some of us had no father in our lives at all.

Solomon was fortunate. He had a good father. We know David was not perfect; his sins were well known and scandalous. However, Solomon's tribute to David in this prayer focuses on his father's faith. He pays homage to David, calling him righteous and upright in heart. Solomon gives his father credit for influencing his own walk with the Lord.

Our relationships with our father are unique. A father can be as close to us as God was to Jesus. A father can also be as damaging or as absent as anyone could ever imagine. Some of us come to God because of our fathers. Some of us come to God in spite of our fathers. But God is there for us always—keeping us close, no matter what kind of father we have.

God, thank you for those who are wise and loving. Protect and heal those who have been hurt by those who should be closest to them. May they know your kind tenderness. Amen.

Indiana is often struck by tornadoes. News about impending storms interrupts regular television programming, warning what to do to stay safe. On Palm Sunday in 1965, eleven tornadoes touched down in central and northern Indiana, leaving incredible devastation in their paths. At one point, my family and I stood in our front yard and watched a tornado tear across the horizon. When things became too threatening and the lights had gone out, we went to the basement for safety with our three children. We huddled there in the dark when our youngest son said, "I know what! Let's turn on the lights!" In his young life, the lights had always come on with the press of a button. Not this time.

Sometimes in our lives, the light doesn't seem very bright. We live in fear, not knowing what to do next. Solomon felt unsure too as he succeeded David to the throne. God told Solomon to pray for whatever he wanted. He could have asked God for money to hire enough political and spiritual advisors to meet his needs. He could have hired people to run the country while he enjoyed all the things wealth could bring him. Instead, he confessed to the Lord that he was like a child needing wisdom and discernment. He recognized the power of David's rule and knew he did not have the abilities it would take to walk in his footsteps. So he humbled himself, asking for what he needed . . . wisdom and discernment.

God was pleased Solomon had asked for wisdom. God honored his prayer, giving him not only wisdom and discernment but wealth and long life as well.

Gracious Lord, grant that I may see my inadequacies and confess them to you. Grant me wisdom and discernment. Turn on the lights; guide me in your way. Amen.

Our daughter became critically ill on her fifteenth birthday. She had a then little-known illness called Reye's syndrome. The doctor looked at us and said, "Most of them die." Our beautiful, intelligent daughter, so full of life and promise, was at death's door. We were confused and terrified. Was God there? Did God understand the cries of our breaking hearts?

There are times in my life—this was one of them—when God seems far away. God's promises are remote. God's voice is silent. I reach out, but I do not feel God's hand there to accept mine. My heart swells with abandonment and powerlessness. In these times, that come completely from deep and frightening feelings, I try to think with my head as well as with my heart. I try to remind myself of the reality of God. That reality cannot always come through if I simply wait for my feelings to change. I have to refocus.

In many psalms, we read of the psalmist's feelings of helplessness and loneliness. We hear the cries of those who need to be rescued from the pits of despair. We know that these psalms come from hearts that are desperate and alone. The feelings are real, but they are not the final word.

In Psalm 111, we get a reality check. Not only is God present; God is ready to meet all our needs. This is a psalm to read over and over again, especially when we are in trouble, to remind us that God is actually present and in control, though our feelings at this moment don't reflect that. This psalm helps us to *know*, not just to *feel*, that God is omnipresent and omnipotent. This knowledge provides fertile ground for wisdom to come to us and to grow our hearts.

Gracious Lord, grant that we may always know your presence, your love, and your power, even when we do not feel it. Amen.

I have been acquainted with many intelligent people during my lifetime. Some of them were even in the genius category. These were people who could solve problems in cases where I couldn't even understand the questions. In each case they had a lot of knowledge in their heads, but that didn't assure that they also had wisdom. For example, one of these was an extremely intelligent fifth-grader in my classroom. He looked drowsy while I was teaching one day. I said, "Bobby, am I keeping you awake?" He replied, "Just barely!"

An honest answer, I am sure, but not a very wise one. Some of these people have been blessed with both intelligence and wisdom, but those two qualities are not always present in the same person. Wisdom is a precious commodity indeed. There is a great difference between living wisely and living unwisely. To discern the difference and to follow God's wisdom is not so much about acquired intellectual knowledge as it is about turning ourselves to God's values. This is a search not for our wisdom but for God's will.

Time after time the Bible admonishs us to pray for wisdom and discernment. In this passage in Ephesians, we are instructed to learn wisdom by understanding what the Lord's will is and being filled with the Spirit. We need to watch our steps so that we make the most of every opportunity that God gives us. That means being careful, not just stepping out impulsively, in our words and in our actions. Learning God's will comes from studying the scriptures, searching for the Source of wisdom, and seeking the indwelling of the Holy Spirit.

Gracious Lord, set my heart toward wisdom and discernment. Give me the vision to seek your will, the desire to understand your word, and a prayer life that draws me closer to you. Amen.

Music is a vital part of my life. I always have music floating around in my head. As a teenager, I sat at the piano for hours trying to match the keys on the piano with the chords in my head.

Recently I was able to fulfill a longtime dream. When we went out to dinner I often said to my husband that my idea of a dream job would be to play beautiful music on the piano while people dined in a nice restaurant. I am doing that now, in a way I hadn't ever envisioned. I am playing the piano, and people are dining—however, my listeners are older people and they are in a retirement center. It's a bit of a different setting, but it is still my dream come true.

This scripture passage speaks strongly to me of a particular time in my life—a time when the music went away. In the course of only five years, my husband and I learned four different times that one or the other of us had cancer. It was a diagnosis that we never believed would happen once in our family—much less four times. My outward attitude, according to those around me, was positive. However, I noticed gradually that the desire to do anything musical had simply disappeared. I didn't even want to sing in church. I could not follow the scriptural admonition to "make music in my heart." Even though I was able still to give thanks to the Lord, there was a hole in my heart where the music used to be.

It was a terrible time, but we came through it. I thank God that in addition to bringing physical healing to me, God has "reinstalled" the music in my heart. I feel like a whole person again.

Gracious Lord, grant us music and thanksgiving no matter what is going on around us. Amen.

We had a wonderful experience on our visit to Israel. I hadn't been eager to make the trip, but it was more spiritually fulfilling than I ever thought it could be. It brought a reality to scripture that I had never experienced before. I could picture Jesus on the hillside, on the Sea of Galilee, on the dusty roads, and on Golgotha. I could see him rising from the tomb and appearing to the disciples. I developed a hunger for actually being there with him, being fed by him on a daily basis. I craved having him at my side, filling my heart and my mind so deeply that my heart would be full and running over.

I came to have a new understanding of what it would have been like to be with Jesus every day, walking the roads of Galilee and Judea, talking with him, asking questions. I felt deeply moved.

How well our Lord understood our human needs when here in John he gives us the "bread of life that came down from heaven" so that we can be fed and filled with him again and again. How precious are the bread and the wine he blesses for us. Painfully aware of our human weaknesses and needs, we can fill ourselves with Jesus' very presence. Jesus' love assures us that he is with us always. The bread and wine enable us not only to be his witnesses but also to be the extension of his love in the world.

Gracious Lord, fill us with your love and presence. As we take the cup and the bread, may we grow strong and faithful. Amen.

Strength Amid Changes

AUGUST 17–23, 2009 • MARVIN D. ARNPRIESTER

MONDAY, AUGUST 17 ~ *Read 1 Kings 8:1,6, 10-11, 22-30, 41-43*

As I visit with persons and listen to their stories, the word *then* often plays a big role in the conversation. The word *then* indicates a shift is happening. Movement is taking place. Life is changing.

The transitions in the story of the dedication of the Temple by King Solomon are critical. *Then* Solomon assembled the elders and priests. *Then* the priests brought the ark of the covenant, *Then* the glory of the Lord filled the place. *Then* Solomon prayed.

Transitions are markers in our life experiences. I work with a group that guides in people examining a call to ordained ministry. We ask persons to share the story of how they came to this point in their lives. Some people's awareness of their call came early on, but they were unable or unwilling to act on it. But in most every case, some *then* of life opens their eyes and changes their hearts. They tell of moving from the way it was to the awareness of God's call and claim on their lives. *Then* as they respond, the glory of the Lord becomes clear and focused.

For Solomon and Israel, the transition of the ark into the Temple was momentous. They knew that while this building could never contain God, they were sure that God was present with them in this time and place.

God is with us too during our times of transition. Change can be difficult, but it may well be that in these moments God's glory is revealed and life takes on new meaning and beauty.

Think about the then **moments in your life. How has God been present with you in these transitions?**

_____

Senior pastor of Broadway United Methodist Church in Council Bluffs, Iowa

Solomon asks the question many people still ask today: Where is God? "But will God dwell on the earth?" He wants to know the nature of this God for whom he has built this Temple. He makes a bold affirmation of faith, "I know that God cannot be confined anywhere, even in this house I have built."

Then Solomon makes a humble, yet bold, request. He can make any number of requests—remember me, help me, don't forget me, grant me. But he asks for forgiveness. Why forgiveness? Why now? He has just built this Temple and is dedicating it to God!

I believe he asks for forgiveness because standing in the presence of God and seeing the beauty and holiness of God, he experiences a keen awareness of the gap between what is holy and his own sinfulness. Note the progression of the prayer Solomon prays:

> —hear the prayer of your servant Solomon,
> —hear the prayer of your people Israel,
> —hear the prayer of those from distant lands.

The prayer moves from an individual petition to a prayer for a nation and then to prayers for all the people of the earth. Solomon's prayer, the most extended prayer in any Old Testament story, progresses from himself to others around him to the whole world.

We cannot honestly and fervently pray for long without becoming aware of all God's children, whatever their native land or religious persuasion. In the prayer Jesus gave his disciples, he begins, "*Our* Father..." He did not say "*my* Father." His focus was on all of us. We cannot be all God intends us to be until we claim all people as part of God's family.

God, there is nothing big enough to contain you. Remind me today that all the world and all its people are claimed and loved by you. Amen.

This beautiful psalm echoes the prayer of Solomon at the dedication of the Temple. It is a wonderful song of praise to God. It sings the joy and pleasure of deep communion with God.

The first time I read this psalm, I was a teen participant in a youth leadership event at Mount Sequoyah, Arkansas. Psalm 84 was the devotional scripture one morning. I went off alone on that mountain. I looked out over the beauty of the surrounding countryside with birds flying high in the sky that early summer morning. I saw a mother bird fly to feed her young nestled in the safely of their nest. That scene is in my mind's eye to this day as I marvel at the wonder and beauty of God's creation.

The image of the sparrow finding a home and the swallow a nest for herself at the altars of the courts of the Lord reminds us of an eternal truth. God's house is not just for some select group of us; it is a place for everyone. In John Wesley's time, the Church of England sold or rented pews in their churches. This helped support the church financially, and it also kept a social order in place. But in Wesley's Methodist Societies, pews were never sold or rented. Any and all persons were welcome to worship God.

Because even the least and the lost have a place in the courts of the Lord the author of Psalm 84 can soar to such heights of poetic beauty in words and images that sing praise to God. Psalm 84 invites us to ponder when and how we collude in excluding or keeping others out of the house of the Lord. It invites us to be more welcoming and more inclusive. Worship, deep communion with God, is the one true thing for which we all yearn.

God, you take the entire world into your arms. Help us to embrace all we meet with your love. Amen.

This letter reminds the Ephesians about what it means to live as faithful disciples of Jesus Christ. The writer (Paul, perhaps) gives them a template for the new life they have been called to in Jesus Christ. They are to renounce their past sinful ways and live in righteousness. Paul is most explicit and detailed in his instructions to them. He intersperses his letter with the prayer that they might live out their faith in Jesus Christ as he has taught them.

Then comes a declarative word, where Paul tells his readers something important has gone before that is now to be summed up and reinforced. The word *finally* signals us and the Ephesians to pay special attention to what is coming. These seven verses are Paul's summation. He urges them to be as intentional in their walk with Christ as a Roman soldier is in preparing for battle.

This passage makes some interesting observations about strength. First, our strength doesn't come all at once; becoming strong is a gradual process. Second, we don't make ourselves strong—God does. Third, since most of our armor consists of defensive weapons, clearly we are to *defend* ourselves, but God fights the battle.

Paul concludes by reminding us to undergird our lives with prayer at all times. He urges us to stay awake and be sensitive to the Spirit. We have a source of strength, guidance and courage in our connection to God through prayer.

The harder I try and the more effort I make to do the "right thing," the less I wait on the Lord in prayer and meditation. Paul admonishes us to pray. Prayer is the source of living boldly in proclaiming the gospel.

God, let me know your strength today so that I may be a faithful disciple and witness to your power. Amen.

In January 1992, I joined my friend, Bishop Arthur Kulah, in Liberia, for the Liberian United Methodist Church's annual conference. Because of the country's tragic civil war, checkpoints were everywhere. I found not knowing for certain what would happen frightening.

The group of church members I was traveling with was late leaving Monrovia for River Cess. Bishop Kulah was not with us; he would come later. We passed through checkpoints without trouble until we got to the roads that defined boundaries between rebel factions and peacekeeping forces. We were not allowed through that evening.

The only white person in our group, I was taken away, strip-searched, and left alone in a small room for a long time while the rebels argued over what to do with me. Eventually I was released to rejoin the group. With fear I had never before known, I asked God to help. Suddenly one of the youth began to sing in his native language *What a Friend We Have in Jesus*. I knew the tune. With tears streaming down my checks, I joined with all who sang to counter the forces of darkness and fear. I sensed a presence lifting, holding, and soothing my fear. We sang, prayed, and slept on the ground. I slept as well I as I had ever slept in my life.

To be strong in the Lord is to know that our strength comes not from our own will or desire. It comes from God. It gets inside us, and gives us strength from the peace which passes all understanding.

Those young Liberians lived out Paul's wise counsel: "Pray in the Spirit at all times, in every prayer and supplication." Because of them, my faith was strengthened.

God, source of my strength, keep me praying all day long. Amen.

My church is located in the heart of the city. Every day people from the community and travelers passing through ask for *bread*—food, gas, money. We have an emergency food pantry used continuously by folks in need. The church administers a pastor's fund to help people in need.

Early on in my ministry, I determined that, to the best of my ability, I would pray with those who came for help. I ask them to tell me about themselves and the situation for which they are asking help. After I help them with the resources available, I ask if I can pray with them. The responses are varied. Few say "No." Many have told me it has been a long time since anyone prayed with them. I've even had persons return the check after I pray with them, telling me they were scamming me. Sometimes that prayer has been the beginning of a conversation about personal or spiritual matters.

Recently, a man and woman drove up as I was returning to the church from lunch. The man thrust a paper in my face and told me he needed help for his wife to go to a neurosurgery center for tests to determine what was wrong with her and what could be done. I wrote the check to the center as they requested. He gave me a gruff thank you. I asked if I could pray with him and his wife. After we prayed, she gave me a tearful hug and said, "I needed that prayer more than that check you gave us." In the sacredness of that moment, she was speaking about spiritual bread from God. What she most wanted and needed were words that "are spirit and life."

In this text, Simon Peter testifies to his own need for "spirit and life" when he says to Jesus: "You have the words of eternal life. We have come to believe and know that you are the Holy One of God."

God, guide me when I encounter those who seek the bread of life. When I encounter those who don't believe, make me a good witness. Amen.

There are many poignant questions in life. "Do you love me?" "Don't you care?" "Why did you do that?"

Jesus asks a poignant question: "Do you also wish to go away?" He asked this after "many of his disciples turned back and no longer went about with him." Prior to this Jesus had fed five thousand. He had healed people and taught them. But when a number of his disciples finally understand there is more to the teaching of Jesus than healing and feeding—they pack up their stuff and go home.

I sense in Jesus' question a sense of pain and loss. When Jesus invites would-be disciples to open the door of their minds and stretch their mind-set, to see things from another perspective, many find it too difficult. The invitation to grow in their perspective on life is simply too much for them.

In our day, churches struggle with what it means to be faithful in this time and place. Some dig in their heels and refuse to consider doing things any differently than they have always done. While they are singing, "Give me that old time religion; it's good enough for me," people are leaving. Churches are dying, and new people are not coming.

The words Jesus speaks in this passage are spirit and life for those willing to comprehend, eat, and digest. Thank God for those disciples who join in affirming and living out, "Lord, to whom can we go? You have the words of eternal life. We have come to believe and know that you are the Holy One of God." It is grace that draws us to Jesus, and grace that keeps us on the way.

Jesus, guide me in truth and spirit so that I may stay close to you. Amen.

Love's Many Facets

AUGUST 24–30, 2009 • F. DEAN LUEKING

MONDAY, AUGUST 24 ~ *Read Song of Solomon 2:8-13*

Arise, my love, my fair one, and come away.

The Song of Solomon has a firm place in the Bible as a reminder that the love of men and women for each other is nothing second-rate. When God created humans, the Creator wove into us warm and powerful currents of mutual attraction. Our bodies reflect God's design and gift, a source of pleasure and delight toward each other.

Sin entered in and infected love with lust. But a greater love has come to us—the love of Christ Jesus that reclaims us for God and restores romantic love as a sign of Christ and his bride, the church.

The eight chapters of this lesser-known book of the Bible celebrate that love found both in human attraction of the sexes and in the divine love that draws us to God. We need to recover that kind of love. In our world, too jaded by romantic love that does not last, the deep, exciting, enduring love that resonates through this ancient book needs the embodiment of modern people.

Arise, my love, my fair one, and come away. . . . If it has been too long since you have spoken such beautiful words or recalled the memory of them, this is a time to renew and remember. This facet of love should season, not wither. How? By establishing romantic love on God, who blesses and deepens it. After all, why should the description of romantic love be left to the National Enquirer?

Season our human love, O God, with your eternal love. Amen.

Pastor emeritus of Grace Lutheran Church, River Forest, Illinois

Now the winter is past . . . the time of singing has come, and the voice of the turtledove is heard in our land.

A wisdom and hope underlie this beautiful image of a springtime freshness following on winter doldrums. The wisdom is that human love, fragile and vulnerable, can have its wintry season. Passions subside, and intimacies slacken. Divorce is a bleak time, as all who go through it know.

But the winter of the heart may take the form of slow erosion in marriage, in family, or in friendship ties because one takes the other for granted. So people end up having all they can do to get up in the morning, let alone find the energy to nurture, care, give, communicate, grow.

The hope this passage offers is that winter passes. It does so because a spiritual strength well anchored in the grace of God in Jesus Christ has been like winter borne, continually flowing down under the icy bleakness. It brings back a springtime freshness and thaws frozen hearts. Thawing happens when the community of worship lifts us from our isolation; when truth is spoken in love, and we come upon those surprises of grace that open a door where before a dead end seemed final.

Not long ago I spoke this text to a bride and groom. She is eighty-six; he is eighty-eight. They were high school sweethearts and went to the senior prom together. Their paths parted. Marriage and widowhood followed for both. Then they resumed correspondence, sensed a fresh breeze of love, and chose to marry.

Each time a I hear a turtledove singing, I think of them.

Gracious God, bring the springtime freshness of your grace back to wintry hearts. Amen.

My heart overflows with a goodly theme. . . .
You are the most handsome of men;
>   *grace is poured upon your lips;*
>   *therefore God has blessed you forever.*

What's going on here? It's a royal wedding. The psalm writer is present and effusive in his approval of the young king about to take a bride. We who can remember the splendor of British royal weddings have a link to the grand moment Psalm 45 captures.

But a hint of something deeper and grander by far appears as the psalm continues, "Your throne, O God, endures forever. . . . Your royal scepter is a scepter of equity; you love righteousness and hate wickedness."

Leap through the centuries to great David's greater Son, the Messiah, the Christ, whose realm does indeed endure forever. And keep the spirit of the psalm writer as you transfer this lavish praise to the Son of God who loved us and gave himself for us. Then this psalm invites us to do something we do not do often enough—pour out the best of the heart to the Savior. Being made in God's image and restored to that image by Jesus who came to his kingdom by a cross for us, we respond from the deepest part of us, the soul.

The American television producer Norman Lear once asked the preeminent American theologian and historian Martin Marty what was the essence of worship. "Gratitude," Marty answered, " . . . outpoured from the heart." And the souls of two very different men found common ground where there is room for all, where the heart overflows in grateful praise to the God who has first lavished regal love upon us.

God of grace, fill me to overflowing with your love, that I may give it back to you in loving service. Amen.

THURSDAY, AUGUST 27 ~ *Read James 1:17-21*

He gave us birth by the word of truth. What can a word do? Plenty. A word can crush or inspire, kill or give life. Such a word connects inseparably to events, deed and word needing each other to be powerful, even life-changing.

The New Testament Letter of James was written to counteract an old tendency of talking but not walking the truth of God. "What good is it, my brothers and sisters, if you say you have faith but do not have works?" (2:14) was the problem, and still is. James meets that dilemma by focusing on God, who fulfills promises and gives us birth by the word of truth!

God has packed the power to redeem and renew us into a word, the holy gospel that bears to us the good news of Jesus who loved us and gave himself for us. Not just any news, not just any religious talk. This gospel is life-giving because it is inseparable from the risen Lord who comes among us through the word that points to him. In Christ we find ourselves on speaking terms with God and are called to speak the truth in love to one another.

In a world pelted daily with words beyond number—dumb talk, phony speech, angry words, pointless yakking—God takes an amazing risk. God entrusts the gospel word to the lips of God's people to speak the truth in love, to upbuild one another in faith, to speak good news where there is none. Think of it: We hang on the word of life as we speak Christ to others again today, which makes us midwives in that wondrous mystery that quickens souls and equips lives to be abundant in works of love.

Speak to me, blessed God, that I may speak life to others. Amen.

Be doers of the word, not merely hearers.

James may have been a relative of Jesus who became a leader of the early believers in Jerusalem, a group greatly beset with needs of body and soul alike. No wonder then that this letter is a steady call for deeds as a sure sign of living faith. Hearing but not doing the truth is unthinkable in the new creation Christ Jesus has brought.

I think of my own spiritual journey and consider what puts distance between hearing and doing the word. Procrastination is a common roadblock. I know what needs to be done but postpone it. Distraction also puts distance between hearing and doing—again not willful rejection of the concrete action of faith but giving in to the magnetic pull of busyness or some other excuse. Lethargy, a more serious spiritual malady of inner listlessness, leads to a shrug of indifference rather than arousal to serve.

To all of these excuses and more, the call of God is to be doers of the word. Let the spirit of God do the sanctifying work of carrying the good news of Christ from the ear to the heart—and then to the hands and arms and legs and feet in deeds of loving God and neighbor with all our being.

James calls for specific action, caring for orphans, widows, and all persons in distress. Faithful doing of the word comes from seeing, really seeing, in others with needs of every kind none other than Jesus himself. Jesus told a great story about such seeing (Matt. 25:31-46). Doing because of seeing is blessed beyond words!

Move me, blessed God, to see and do today the deeds that honor you and serve others; and make me glad to do my part. Amen.

They noticed that some of his disciples were eating with defiled hands, that is, without washing them.

Winston Churchill told the story of the man who leaped into a river to save a drowning child only to have the mother, when she held her rescued child in her arms, exclaim, "But you didn't recover his cap!"

That story tests credibility. Could anybody, especially a mother whose child was snatched from death, really be that blind to what counts? Yet I trust Churchill's story because our fallen humanity has an astonishing capacity for blind, stubborn ingratitude that is deeply embedded.

The moment in Jesus' ministry recorded by Mark touches upon what makes one clean before God. Jesus has just fed the five thousand, stilled the storm, and healed the multitudes of the sick and suffering who rush at him as he comes ashore at Capernaum— all signs of the kingdom, signs that cleanse us before God.

Mark carefully notes that some Pharisees and scribes have come all the way from Jerusalem, a ninety-mile journey, to confront Jesus with sharp accusations of undermining everything holy because his disciples ate without washing their hands. Yes, to the Pharisees hand washing moves beyond manners or hygiene; it symbolizes being clean before God. But that's the point; rightness with God does not come by scrupulous keeping of human regulations. Cleansing comes by loving God who first loved us and by translating that received love into the practiced love of neighbor and self. This is the cleansing that counts.

Seeing the forest, not just the individual trees, is an old but relevant principle for this day.

God of grace, help me love others in the fullness of your great-heartedness. Amen.

There is nothing outside a person that by going in can defile, but the things that come out are what defile.

Is our behavior the product of nature or nurture? That debate goes on endlessly, and it is well that it does because the subject is mighty important.

In this brief passage, set in the context of ceremonial cleanness, Jesus speaks a strong word about nature rather than nurture as the key to behavior. Evil of every sort originates deep down within the soul where all our woes begin.

Despite our fallen humanity, we may not adopt the slogan, "The devil made me do it," and evade our own responsibility. Fallen nature is also redeemed nature. We have a Savior who went to the cross to accomplish that for us. All the religious rules in the world will not turn us Godward, which is the context in which Jesus spoke this truth.

Claim that redeeming love again today, and then instead of getting stuck in the nature vs. nurture debate, be an influence of genuine goodness toward others. Of course nurture counts tremendously, especially when it springs from a heart where Christ dwells and the fruits of the Spirit are abundant.

Renew me from the heart, redeemer God, and let it show in my words and deeds again this day. Amen.

Wisdom, Compassion, and Faith

AUGUST 31–SEPTEMBER 6, 2009 • ALBERT ISTEERO

MONDAY, AUGUST 31 ∼ *Read Proverbs 22:1-2*

Making a name for oneself—we usually think of this in terms of working hard and succeeding in one's field. And that is one understanding of the phrase. But it's not the meaning Proverbs takes. In today's text, the author gives preference to a good name that comes from compassion and kindness rather than from riches, to a loving favor rather than silver and gold. God accords approval to those who act selflessly and become involved in the welfare of others.

Proverbs levels the standing of the rich and the poor. Since God is the maker and creator of both, rich and poor are equals and are to be treated equally with compassion. As the creator of every being, God is to be taken into account in all aspects of life. The thought of God is not to be limited to special seasons or sacred places. God is present in our homes, in our businesses, in our work, and in our play. We must fully trust in God.

To fully trust in God is to understand that genuine wealth lies not in riches but in compassion. Hebrews 11 recognizes a large group of the faithful who put their trust in God, lived so as to acquire good names, and are praised as part of the "great cloud of witnesses."

We, as Jesus' followers, are called to be people of integrity. We are to be upright and honest, choosing a good name above riches in a world that is seeking quite the opposite.

Dear Lord, help me to be honest and true, and give me the courage to do what is right in your sight. Amen.

Editor of the Arabic edition of The Upper Room *devotional guide, former general secretary of the Middle East Council of Churches, former president of Cairo Evangelical Seminary, and retired Presbyterian pastor living in Cairo, Egypt*

The wisdom of Solomon is an important element in the religion of Israel. This wisdom, as Proverbs makes evident, is based on two fundamental pillars: the love of God and the love of one's neighbor. The first pillar—love of God—begins with what wisdom calls the fear of the Lord. Knowing God as our Creator, trusting and loving God, and being obedient to God—this is what it means to fear the Lord. This is what brings wisdom.

The second pillar is love of neighbor. Anyone who reads Proverbs is impressed with the high ethical standard of its teaching. Proverbs expresses great concern with how the poor, the weak, and the needy are treated. Most of the world's human affairs come under this kind of critical scrutiny. The contrast in verses 8 and 9 between the conduct of those who treat the poor unjustly and those who deal with the poor justly is stark. Those who abuse the poor, Proverbs says, will watch their authority fail. These people who sow injustice will reap calamity. Those who are generous, who share their bread with the poor, will be blessed.

All through the Old Testament, God insists on proper care of the poor. This is not just a passive admonition. It is an imperative. It is not sufficient to know that the poor are not to be oppressed; it is essential to take active measures to care for the poor and advocate for them.

Where does your life stand in relation to today's text? What kind of relationship do you have with God? With your neighbor? Whose "name" do you carry?

Gracious God, compassion and justice are near to your heart. Search me and know my heart, test me and know my thoughts. See if there is any offensive way in me, and lead me in the way everlasting. Amen.

This psalm is written after the exile of the Jews. Jerusalem, the center of Israel's religion and the land that the Lord allocated to the faithful, is under the dominion of the oppressors. The oppression of the invaders is so cruel that it leaves the righteous suffering and in desperation. Today, we live in a world not unlike that of the Jews after their exile. We are beset by terrorism, religious fanaticism, social injustice, and calamities that make us restless and fearful.

Confronting these calamities, the psalmist responds with this particular psalm. It is one of a large group of psalms known as the "Songs of Ascents." Sometimes seen as a prayer book for those on pilgrimage to Zion, this psalm urges the community to apply justice in its communal life. It is an affirmation of faith and a psalm of trust and comfort. This psalm assures us that God is always present, surrounding us in protection the way the mountains surround and protect Jerusalem. This steadfastness will endure forever and we may be assured, therefore, that no believer will perish either in life or death, in time or in eternity.

The psalmist lists characteristics of the faithful, those who acquire God's promises and enjoy God's protection. They are known as "those who trust in the LORD," "the LORD's people," "the righteous," "those who are upright in heart," and "those who are called Israel."

The psalmist knows that Israel cannot abuse others and still expect good to come to them. It is only by right living, by honoring the values God holds dear, that Israel can be assured of safety and security. When we trust in the Lord, we become *the Lord's people*, just and compassionate.

Help us, O Lord, to trust in you; lead us into justice, peace and safety. Amen.

James, writing for a community of Christian readers, gets right to the point with a question that verges on the sarcastic: "My brothers and sisters, do you with your acts of favoritism really believe in our glorious Lord Jesus Christ?" Two visitors come into the community's meeting. Both are strangers. One is rich and one is poor. The rich man (the one with gold rings and fine clothes) is deemed worthy of a comfortable seat, perhaps a special one. The poor man (the one wearing dirty clothes) is denied a seat; he has to stand or sit on the floor.

James is appalled with this act of favoritism. Such conduct does not befit Christians, who hold the faith of our Lord Jesus Christ. He wants to see their faith—not their prejudices—in action. This is not the faith that the Lord himself exercised.

The antithesis between the godless "rich" and the righteous "poor" is clear in the Old Testament and later Jewish literature. James reminds his readers of this, asking them to refrain from their discriminatory attitude. But then James goes one step farther. Favoritism does conflict with God's teachings and values. But favoritism is also a sin—a violation of the law.

The condemnation hits home for us. We too are guilty of judging people by the world's standards instead of by God's. And if we follow James to the next step, we must ask the deeper question. What about favoritism that goes beyond individuals and runs rampant in the larger world? What is the role of the church in working toward justice in our society? Do we heed God's injunction to do justice, or do we violate the law by violating the poor?

Our loving, merciful God, help us to speak and act in ways that are just and true. Amen.

The Christian life is like a boat that has faith and works as its oars. If the boat has only one oar, it goes around in circles, or it does not go at all. For James, salvation depends on the word received and obeyed. Faith that lacks works is not faith. The practical fruits of Christian life indicate whether faith is hearty or weak.

James gives the illustration of a brother or sister who is without clothes and daily food, who asks for support, and the response to their need is friendly but without action—instead, they get an empty blessing. "What is the good of that?" James asks. Goodwill or a friendly attitude is not enough. Faith without works is dead. James attacks the perversion of Christian teaching that says a confession of faith guarantees salvation regardless of the believer's conduct. The recital of a creed does not make one acceptable to God if one's behavior toward others is not godly.

Faith alone does not address the needs of those around us who suffer hunger or poverty. Works must flow naturally from faith in concrete action on behalf of those in need. What is the significance of church membership if we do not honestly seek to live in accordance with the principles it is founded upon? What is the profit of pious words, such as "Go in peace," if these words are dissociated from merciful conduct? True Christians are known by their fruits. The boat of Christian life can go forward in peace if both oars, faith and works, function in tandem!

O Lord, help me to express my faith through my deeds. Make me both compassionate and responsive to the needs of others. Amen.

Jesus had been among his own people. Many gathered to hear him and believed in him, but there was also opposition to his ministry by Pharisees and scribes. He left his Jewish followers and went into the borders of Tyre and Sidon. This story gives us an idea about his ministry among people outside the Hebrew covenant.

Jesus secretly entered the house where he was to rest, but he could not keep his presence secret. A Gentile woman immediately intruded on his privacy. She fell at his feet, begging Jesus to drive a demon out of her daughter. Jesus' response was both negative and harsh. When he refused to listen to her, she persisted. She came back to Jesus with an ingenious reply, sticking firmly to her request. Her persistence came out of love for her daughter; her tenacity was impressive. Jesus granted her request: "For saying that, you may go—the demon has left your daughter."

Two things come to mind in reading this story. The first focuses on what God might be able to do when Christian parents bring to their prayers for their children the same kind of persistence the Gentile woman had. Many children are taken over by drugs, sex, depression, and fear. If the church and parents persist the way this mother did, what might happen?

The second is how significant it is that Jesus granted the request of a Gentile—a non-Jew. This was the first time Jesus had granted the request of a Gentile. God's mighty works happen to Gentiles as well as to Jews! This expansion of Jesus' ministry was at times challenging even for him. We also find ourselves challenged when God works in ways outside our understanding.

And yet, in both instances—in prayers for our children and in the fact that God's ways are sometimes beyond our understanding—God's power and love are available to all.

God, may we bring our children to you with persistence. Open our eyes when you work in ways we don't understand. Amen.

After healing the daughter of the Syrophoenician woman, Jesus left the immediate neighborhood of Tyre and went through Sidon to the Sea of Galilee. Mark tells us that he came into the Decapolis, so evidently Jesus remained in Gentile territory. Mark tells the story of some people who bring a deaf man to Jesus and beg him to heal him. What made these people bring a deaf man who could hardly speak to Jesus and beg him to place his hand upon him? It was *faith!* Not faith as a theoretical conviction, not faith as a creed recited but faith in a person—faith in Jesus' compassion and ability.

Jesus healed the man. His hearing was restored, and he was cured of a speech impediment. Jesus' elaborate steps to heal this man affirm that God has power over human infirmities and diseases. It is clear God is at work in Jesus; the one who could not speak plainly now hears and speaks.

But Christ can also restore spiritual hearing and cure spiritual deafness. He makes our minds and hearts more sensitive to the voices of God and of the world. He cures our speech impediments. We are set free to praise God with new voices and new energies.

Jesus brings us into a place of blessing. Persistent faith is powerful.

Jesus works in unexpected places with unexpected people. As disciples of Christ, let us also be persistent in our faith. Let us look for faith in unexpected places and not shun places like Tyre and Sidon because "there are only Gentiles there." God gives us a freshness of faith that is waiting around every turn to surprise us. We must only trust in God, persist in faith, and venture into unknown territory.

Lord, increase our faith! Make us persistent. Open our ears, minds, and hearts to hear what you are saying today. Amen.

Navigation Systems

SEPTEMBER 7–13, 2009 • JEFFREY A. TAYLOR

MONDAY, SEPTEMBER 7 ~ *Read Proverbs 1:20-33*

I just got a new toy—a GPS navigation system. I could not wait to play with it. I put it on the windshield of my car and initialized it. I was amazed to look at the screen and see an icon representing me sitting right in my driveway, aiming north. I typed in the address for the office, and off I went.

My job involves a great deal of driving. Now Waldo—that's what I named the GPS, after the *Where's Waldo?* books my daughters read when they were young—keeps me on track. At least, Waldo *tries* to keep me on track: "In point four miles, turn left." Sometimes I think I know better than Waldo, and in spite of his warning, I go my own way.

In this passage, Proverbs depicts a different sort of navigation system, the more ancient one of Wisdom—personified, as always, as a woman. Wisdom cries out in the streets and the public squares, telling everybody where they have gone off course. Often, her hearers did not listen. They had been given the ability to understand God, but they refused. When they ended up in trouble and didn't know where to turn, Wisdom taunted them for refusing to listen to God.

But there is a way back: "Those who listen to me [Wisdom] will be secure and will live at ease." That's good news—Wisdom, in effect, recalculates the best route to get us back on the right road.

God is merciful. When we have chosen a path that is inconsistent with God's will, we need only look to God to recalculate. With God's help, we can find our way to God's—not our—intended destination.

God, we thank you for wisdom that gives us direction. Forgive us when we fail to listen and obey. Thank you for grace that leads us safely home. Amen.

President of the United Methodist Foundation of West Virginia, district lay leader, and member of Johnson Memorial United Methodist Church in Huntington, West Virginia

What is the shortest distance between two points? A straight line? Not always.

Recently we traveled from Huntington, West Virginia, to Seattle, Washington. As the crow flies, that's 2100 miles to the northwest. But the first leg of our flight took us 237 miles southeast in the wrong direction. We had to go that far out of our way to make a connection in the Charlotte airport. Intellectually, I can understand that it is sometimes necessary to get to a "hub" in order to make the best connecting flight; conceptually, though, it bothers me to have to go so far out of my way in the wrong direction to get to my destination.

When I make airline reservations, I choose flights based upon arrival and departure times. I choose what is most convenient for the price; it really doesn't matter the flight path. I have to get myself out of the way and trust that the airlines know what they are doing. And they not only choose my flight path, but their pilots and air controllers choose the altitude, the speed, and when to land. I have to let go of the idea that I am in control. There's no question that letting me take control of such details would lead to catastrophe.

When it comes to flying, I give in and go with the flow, relax, and enjoy the flight. I get to my destination intact, pretty much on time, and sometimes I even have my luggage. It works out much better, I admit, than if I have micromanaged each step.

Do we trust God to get us from one leg of life's journey to the next? Or do we try to control, to micromanage the journey ourselves? The choice is ours. Wisdom weighs in with her clear word of counsel: Trust God.

Dear God, give us courage to listen to you and to trust in you so that we will be secure and live at ease, without dread of disaster. Amen.

We have a friend who takes great pictures. She denies that she is a photographer, saying instead that she just carries a camera around, and when she sees God, she takes a picture. She has no training or special equipment—just an inexpensive digital camera and a good eye. They say faith means believing without seeing; somehow, she is able to capture images of faith in pixels. Her art is in her ability to see it and frame it.

The writer of Psalm 19 also has an eye for seeing God. The psalmist communes with God in the majesty of creation. When we can see God right there in front of us, words aren't necessary. There is confirmation all around us of God's splendor.

Too often, I focus only on where I am headed right now. I miss the revelation of God's glory around me. I don't see God because I am not paying attention. But when I do look and see—a sunrise over the ocean or the sunset over the mountains—my immediate response is, "Look at what God has done!"

Creation tells the story of God's glory without words. God gave us the gift of words and of speech to tell that story. The psalmist recognized this and was able to find the words to describe it. The psalmist also recognized the beauty of God's word—more desired than gold, sweeter than honey.

When we understand the relationship between God's creation and the life-giving power of God's word, we arrive at our heart's true desire. Our focus is no longer split among competing claims. We know that God has created us and that we belong to God.

The heavens tell the glory of God. Look around you; use all your senses to experience God's glory, and let your words and actions reveal that glory to others.

Dear God, may all our actions, all our words, and all our hearts reflect your glory. Amen.

The writer of James likens our tongues to a ship's rudder. If he were writing this passage today, perhaps he would compare it to a steering wheel. In relation to the whole car, the steering wheel is a small part. At interstate speeds, however, the slightest error in steering can lead to disastrous consequences. The tongue is a small part of the body, but it can certainly get us into a lot of trouble.

There is power in words. Words can build up and tear down. Unfortunately, the damage done by cruel words is hard to undo. In the news, we have seen the careers of entertainers and public servants ruined because of the words they have chosen to use— words that might have been spoken in anger, or in a poor attempt at humor. I'm sure we've all said things we've regretted; we've wished we'd "held our tongues."

This passage reminds us that the words of teachers—especially religious teachers—will be measured and judged. When people are particularly skilled at "talking the talk" we expect their "walk" to match. People seem to delight at catching a leader, whether an actor, preacher, or politician, in some inconsistency where words and actions do not appear to match.

I think with a little self-control, most of us can practice what we preach. But the writer of James leaves me feeling hopeless about my ability to control my speech. Unlike wild animals, beasts, birds, and sea urchins, "no one can tame the tongue, a restless evil, full of deadly poison."

We can keep our tongues in check if we stay focused on God. If we remember that everything we say will either glorify God or curse God, we might be more apt to steer steadily. The gifts of God build our integrity and give us the strength to overcome the dangers of our human speech.

Dear God, may the words of our mouths and the meditations of our hearts be acceptable to you, our rock and redeemer. Amen.

My daily commute is fifty miles each way. I travel east in the morning and west in the evening, so the sun is in my eyes in both directions. Sometimes it can be annoying, but I do get to see beautiful sunrises and sunsets.

The psalmist wrote about the circuit the sun makes each day, from horizon to horizon. There are many cycles in life. With each month, there is another report to write; with each year another tax return. The cycles can become routine and monotonous. But there is also comfort in knowing that the sun will rise and set each day just as it always has—a reminder of God's presence.

I imagine most people today will remember where they were eight years ago. I had an early morning meeting in a building a few blocks from my office. As the meeting ended, someone startled me when they ran up to me in the hallway shouting, "They've blown up the World Trade Center." Thinking he was crazy or misinformed, I ignored him and kept going. But on the way back to my office, I learned, horrified, that it was true.

The world has changed dramatically since 9/11. For some of us, life has returned to some kind of normalcy. But for those who lost loved ones or who suffered other personal losses in the attacks and their aftermath, the pain is still raw, the wounds slow to heal.

And yet, the words of the psalmist stand, even in the midst of death and pain: "The heavens are telling the glory of God." The sun does still rise in the east and set in the west. And the same sun that occasionally gets in my eyes during my commute shines on all God's creation. It tells the glory of God in West Virginia, in Iraq, in North Korea, and in China. Nothing is hid from its heat. Blessed be the name of the Lord.

Dear God, in these days of loss and pain, comfort us. Remind us of your promise to revive and enlighten us. Make our hearts rejoice again. Amen.

Have you ever placed yourself in the middle of this Gospel story? Imagine that Jesus asks you, "Who do you say that I am?"

If you are like me, you can find the words to describe Jesus. You can say that Jesus is the Messiah, the King of kings, the Son of God, the Redeemer. You can say he is your friend and your savior. He is all that and more. But who do you say Jesus is by the way you behave?

Who do I say Jesus is when I close the gap in traffic to prevent someone else from merging in front of me? Who do I say Jesus is when I get irritated with the restaurant server who didn't get my special order exactly right? Who do I say Jesus is when I avoid a stranger who may ask me for help? Who is Jesus to me when I get comfortable in my own life and neglect the poor and those in need of justice?

Jesus teaches us that we must deny ourselves, take up a cross, and follow him. Sometimes I may be in denial, but I don't know that I really deny my "self" much. So to follow Jesus means we must walk the same kind of journey Jesus walks. Jesus tells Peter and us exactly what this means: To follow him, we must turn our minds away from human things and focus on divine things.

When we meet Jesus face to face, transformation is inevitable. Just as Peter confessed Jesus as the Christ, we come to the realization of who Jesus is, and it changes us. But our transformation is not then finished. Soon after Peter confessed Jesus as the Messiah, Peter was rebuked because he had his mind on things of the world, not on things of God. Peter needed to be reminded to keep his eye on the cross; so must you and I.

Dear God, give us the grace to live so that others can see your glory and know that Jesus is the Messiah. Amen.

The original disciples left everything behind—family, career, their standing in the community—to respond to Jesus' call of "Follow me." Were they impulsive? Had they thought it through? Did they do a risk-return analysis? Or did they take a step or leap of faith?

I wonder what the moment was like when each of the disciples came to know that Jesus was the Messiah. I wonder whether it came as a gradual awakening while they listened to Jesus and saw the miraculous signs or whether it was a sudden epiphany that caught them off guard. But the time must have come when each thought, *He is the One! I've chosen the right path!* Yet at the point of their acceptance of Jesus as Messiah, they didn't want to hear his talk of suffering, rejection, and death on a cross. But just as quickly as they discovered their Messiah, Jesus taught them what it really means to follow him. And that includes the way of the cross.

Jesus shows us how to live. In spite of what some popular religious speakers and "success gospel" authors want their followers to believe, Jesus makes it abundantly clear that there is a cost to being one of his disciples. "For those who want to save their life will lose it, and those who lose their life for my sake, and for the sake of the gospel, will save it." It seems upside down and backwards.

What is the reward for such a cost? Life, and life abundant. This doesn't mean abundant life by the worldly standards of happiness, wealth, or prosperity; it does mean a life of joy that transcends pain and suffering, a peace that surpasses all understanding.

To walk the same path Jesus walks is to set aside what we have and lose our comfortable, secure lives in order to follow Jesus. Are we willing?

Dear God, help keep our minds and hearts focused on divine things and not human things so that we may experience the life you have to offer. Amen.

Greatness

SEPTEMBER 14–20, 2009 • BRIAN K. BAUKNIGHT

MONDAY, SEPTEMBER 14 ~ *Read Proverbs 31:10-31*

Socrates was once reported to have said, "By all means, marry. If you get a good wife, you'll become happy; if you get a bad one, you'll become a philosopher." In much of biblical history, women were considered a commodity. Though not necessarily mistreated, they were considered inferior to men, servants of men, and divorceable by men at the slight provocation. Proverbs 31 is often read in church as a compliment to good women and good wives, but its historical context cannot be ignored.

Jesus changed these preconceptions by befriending women, honoring them, and including them in his inner circle of followers. He quietly but surely broke with the tradition and customs of his time.

My grandmothers were in the Proverbs 31 category with their husbands—toiling faithfully only in the home. My own mother was humbly obedient to my father. Yet she stepped outside just a bit when her children were older, teaching in the public schools. Both of my daughters and both of my daughters-in-law are devoted to husband and family. But they are also fully involved in established careers. They know an equality of personhood that was relatively scarce a few years ago. They keep a working balance among marriage, family, and vocation.

Proverbs 31 is a beautiful tribute written in an ancient context. We can read it with appreciation but not as a defining word for every generation. Thanks be to God for a holistic way of seeing, loving, and living!

Give thanks to God for creating us male and female, equally children of God.

Recently retired after twenty-seven years as senior minister of Christ United Methodist Church in Bethel Park, Pennsylvania

I can still hear my father reading aloud from Psalm 1 in our family Bible. He read with majesty, solemnity, and great authority. I did not know—and still am not sure—why this psalm was so favored by him, but clearly it was.

He always read from the King James Version. The cadence and language was part of his inner being. In my earliest years, that language became part of my being as well: "Blessed is the man that walketh not in the counsel of the ungodly, nor standeth in the way of sinners, nor sitteth in the seat of the scornful. But his delight is in the law of the LORD; and in his law doth he meditate day and night."

Perhaps the focus was upon the joy of right living and avoiding the continuously slippery slope of moving away from God. Perhaps he wanted us to follow the right path—to maintain a disciplined faith journey. Maybe it was the personal delight he found in the Bible and his desire to convey something of that same delight to his children. Or perhaps he wanted us to feel secure when we were thrust into a world of skeptics and scoffers.

All I remember is that he read this psalm over and over to us during our childhood. After a while, we actually began to request this psalm as a favored reading.

Something majestic and thrilling comes in reading the Psalms aloud. Truly, Psalms is the great hymnbook of the Bible. The Psalms were Jesus' hymnbook too. I remember this each time I read Psalm 1.

Read aloud the two opening verses of Psalm 1. Listen to their cadence and power. Hear what the Spirit may be saying to you.

For many years, I have been an amateur vegetable gardener. When space permitted, my garden was fairly large. It was not the size of a farm, by any means, but it was large enough to feed a family of six with plenty left to can or freeze. Today, my garden is small—modeled after something called a "square foot garden."

I have ordered seeds from the same seed company for forty years. My father ordered the seeds from this same company before me. Somehow, I inherently trust this seed company and no other.

I'm especially interested in growing vegetables from what this company's catalogs call "heirloom seeds." These are advertised as "untreated healthy seeds," sometimes labeled "organic" or "open-pollinated" varieties. They are guaranteed to grow, to produce, to succeed. And they do.

I think of heirloom seeds as I read the third verse of Psalm 1. The psalmist describes the faithful believers this way: "They are like trees planted by streams of water, which yield their fruit in its season, and their leaves do not wither."

Surely this is God's design for all of God's children. We are to bear fruit and to live our days in response to the gifts we are given. We are not called to be famous or to become headliners. We are called to be faithful to the One who brought us into being, who guides us along the way, and who receives us into an eternal kingdom in the end.

When you stay close to God, when you seek to grow and give and serve, you find absolute contentment, peace, and fulfillment.

You are an heirloom seed of God's own making. Rejoice in that knowledge, and give thanks.

Read Psalm 1:3 aloud several times. Let God make these words a part of your interior life.

THURSDAY, SEPTEMBER 17 ~ *Read James 3:13–4:3*

What is abundance? How much do you trust God's abundance? Jesus said, "I have come that you might have life abundantly" (John 10:10). Or, as James writes, "Draw near to God and [God] will draw near to you."

The continuing promise of scripture is that God has blessed us with an abundance of whatever we need to do those things we are called to do. Can we rest in the total sufficiency of God? Apparently, many of us cannot. We are caught up in a fear of scarcity rather than a celebration of abundance. So we don't necessarily feel abundantly blessed.

Is this what James is saying to us in the scripture for today? "You ask and do not receive, because you ask wrongly, in order to spend what you get on your pleasures." It may well be.

Craving and coveting—wanting what we don't have or cannot get—lead to war within ourselves and war with others. These conflicts disrupt our relationship with God.

But James writes of godly wisdom versus earthly wisdom, of true abundance versus true scarcity, of peaceableness versus disorder. He urges us to show by the way we live that what we do is born of true wisdom. And the marks of this wisdom are peaceableness, mercy, good fruits, and a harvest of righteousness.

James is, in effect, asking us to realize and "own" our blessings each day. By drawing near to God, we understand that it is out of God's abundance that we are blessed.

Give thanks for your blessings with humility, and draw near to God.

When I was in seminary, we learned about the "hermeneutical arch." These two words describe what happens when you take a passage out of the Bible and "arch" it into the present moment.

Suppose we developed an "arch" from the Proverbs reading today. The passage would then speak of the role of husbands and wives together in the home. The arch might be twofold and say something like this:

Be a God-fearing person! Not terrorized by God or even frightened—but in awe of the reality of God. Be reverent, be gentle, be wise.

Be who God created you to be! This is not the same as the slogan of the US Army: "Be all that you can be." This is, rather, "Be the one God created you to be!" Herein lies the important difference between self-actualization and Spirit actualization. In Spirit actualization, you are directed from above, from outside yourself.

A saint of the church once said, "We shall never succeed in knowing ourselves unless we know Jesus and follow him." We are created to be in the image, form, and model of Jesus of Nazareth in our world. Jesus is God's final design for all humanity. He is the perfect image of God. You and I are made in that same image, and we are called to bring that image to life today.

To be a parent, to be a godly member of a family, is a holy calling. Fear God! And allow yourself to be shaped by the Spirit.

Pray that your life will more and more model that of Jesus and that God will continue to mold you by the Holy Spirit.

Jesus knew the thoughts of the disciples. Jesus heard their quiet murmurings and discussions on the subject of greatness. The disciples did not think he heard their arguing, but he heard.

When the small band reached their stopping place for the night, Jesus confronted them with what he knew. They were embarrassed and a bit sheepish. Mark says, "They were silent." But Jesus had no time for ridicule or put-downs. He launched right into his primary theme. He sat down. (When a rabbi of that time wanted to teach something of importance, he sat. He did not stand.) He called the disciples and told them, 'Whoever wants to be first must be last of all and servant of all.'"

Jesus' words radically reversed everything they knew. Instead of going to the head of the line, you go last. Instead of being waited upon, you serve. This was a deep departure from every human norm.

In the early 1980s, I read Robert Greenleaf's book *Servant Leadership: A Journey into the Nature of Legitimate Power and Greatness*. This book profoundly affected my ministry for the next twenty-five years.

The 1980s vintage leaders of my large-membership church wanted me to be a CEO, much like many of them. I listened and tried for a while. But I became increasingly uncomfortable. Greenleaf's book and a study of scriptures about leadership, changed my understanding of who I was a leader. I developed a style that I call "senior minister as servant leader." I am still learning the meaning and implications of that style for my life.

We are all called to servanthood. Each of us can model Jesus and take the form of a servant—in every venue and turn of life.

Be open today to some small way in which you can be a servant disciple of Christ.

My wife and I have the great privilege of delighting in two sets of grandchildren. At this writing, four of them are almost grown. The other four are under the age of six. Our children have served up grandchildren to us in a superb and gratifying fashion!

Two of the younger set live close to us. We have been blessed by this close proximity with up close and almost daily contact. We have seen what Jesus must have seen and known best: the wide-eyed wonder, the pure joy, the unencumbered sense of play, the unreserved hugs for simple gifts and pleasures, and the ever-present possibilities for exuberant spontaneity.

Jesus knew the dynamic of a child's spirit. All little ones were precious in his sight. He invited children into his arms. He blessed them. He celebrated their capacity for joy. He rebuked anyone who tried to keep children at a distance. Then he said that you and I must receive the kingdom as a child might receive a wonderful surprise—with absolute trust and wide-eyed enthusiasm.

I am not entirely sure of everything Jesus meant in the reading for today. But I think he enjoins us to extend extraordinary hospitality to a child, any child: "Whoever welcomes one such child in my name welcomes me." When we are willing to welcome a child, we are very close to the heart of Jesus.

When we spend time with a child, we find some simple truths of life revealed. We do not need sophisticated knowledge to find or know God. We need the trusting heart of a child, the capacity for sheer surprise, and the ability to listen closely to the still small voice that comes from a high and holy place. To have the trusting heart of a child—this, Jesus says, is true greatness.

Ask God to lead you into the presence of a child today. Watch closely and give thanks for what Jesus sees in that child.

Choices

SEPTEMBER 21–27, 2009 • SUSAN HIBBINS

MONDAY, SEPTEMBER 21 ～ *Read Esther 7:1-6, 9-10*

We all make choices, every day, all our lives. We make choices about important issues that will affect us long term: what job we shall do, where we will live, which person we want to commit to and spend our life with. We make choices about how we live. And we make less significant choices: which breakfast cereal to eat, which suit we wear to the office today.

Esther demonstrates a very different way of making choices. She chooses the brave way—in a dangerous personal situation she reveals her Jewish identity to people who are hostile to her race. No doubt her heart was pounding as she waited for the right moment. But she chose courage: she chose to do the one thing that would save her people. Esther could easily have said nothing. Her own position was secured; she had no need to do what she did. Yet she put herself and her people's future on the line by choosing to speak the truth.

Haman, on the other hand, had chosen the opposite: to betray his people. Unlike Esther, he had chosen to protect his own position, planning the destruction of the Jewish people and having a gallows built for the person who stood in his way. Because of Esther's bravery, however, Haman himself hanged on those gallows instead.

Our choices may not be so dramatic as Esther's nor the results of them so final as Haman's. Nevertheless, we have choices to make: to be selfish or unselfish, to show kindness to others before looking to our own needs; to make choices we know in our hearts are right.

Lord God of all our lives, help us to think before we act, seeking the good and right. Amen.

British editor of the Upper Room Devotional Guide, *assistant editor at Methodist Publishing House, member of the Church of England, attends St. Guthlac's parish church in Peterborough, United Kingdom*

To celebrate their deliverance from a situation that would have destroyed them, the Jewish people celebrate what would later become the Festival of Purim, days set aside to mark a time when they were delivered from their enemies. Two days were spent celebrating to mark the moment when, instead of being crushed by their enemies, they found their sorrow turned into gladness and their mourning into holiday. They gave presents and food to one another, and also chose to include the poor in the general celebration. No one was left out of a time of thanksgiving.

I wonder how the poor felt after two days of being included, of having enough and more to eat? For once they had felt part of a celebration, been given gifts, been one with everyone else. Suddenly, though, the party was over. Did anyone choose to continue looking after them; or did everything go back to normal, and the poor remain the poor?

We have times in our own lives of good fortune or good news when we feel we want to tell everybody about it. We fall in love, and when our love is reciprocated we want to shout it from the rooftops. Maybe we become parents, and we want to celebrate those first moments of joy and new life with everyone we meet. What happens, though, when life calms down, and its problems rise up to meet us? Do we still include everyone in our thinking?

There are times too when the plight of the poor comes under the spotlight in national or international emergencies, and practical giving increases sharply as people respond with what they have. But what happens when the media circus moves on, and the needs of the poor slip out of the headlines? Other things preoccupy us and our daily living. How then do we respond to the needs of the poor?

Lord Jesus, you told us that the poor will always be with us. Help us make the needs of others a daily priority and work to relieve suffering as part of our service to you. Amen.

Two years ago my mother, then aged eighty-three, moved from her home into a residential care home for the elderly. It was a hard decision for her; but because of her frailty, she was no longer safe at home. Because she needed professional care, it was the right decision. To me fell the task of clearing her home of thirty-six years and selling it. It was the hardest thing I have ever had to do. It had been my home as well as my parents', and my mother had continued living there alone after my father's death. I felt as though I was pulling lives apart as well as material possessions, as almost all our family history disappeared in front of me.

I had a date by which the sale had to be completed, and as it drew nearer there was still a lot to do. Tiredness and worry about what I was doing took a toll on my health; but I had no choice but to carry on until it was finished. I had only one prayer during those days, which I spoke when I awoke each morning: "Lord, please get me through this time." And the Lord did. With the help of people who did not let me down and others who came to help as the time ran out, the sale went through on time. My mother was safe, and it was done.

If you have ever faced a time in life when choices were few, then like me I hope you discovered that we always have one choice: to take refuge in our God, to lean on God's strength, and to let God carry us through until we can stand up again and move forward. There is no shame in admitting our weakness to God. If, as we say, we believe that God will always help us, then let us put that belief to the test. "We have escaped like a bird from the snare of the fowlers; the snare is broken, and we have escaped."

Lord, when we feel our choices are few, help us to remember the choice we always have: to find our refuge in you. Amen.

In these verses James talks of what we can do—individually and as a faith community—to build one another up and to keep open our lines of communication with each other and with God. We hear a lot about the need to keep communicating. Diplomatic missions talk to both sides in an international dispute in an effort to resolve it without bloodshed. Counselors talk to warring marriage partners to bring about reconciliation or to parents and children in an attempt to bring them together to talk instead of shouting. Professional mediators listen to both sides in an industrial dispute. The mantra is always: keep talking, keep communicating.

We too can keep communicating with others in our community of faith through prayer. On a more personal level, we communicate our feelings, anxieties, and concerns to God in prayer. So, says James, are you suffering? Then pray about it. Have you got things to be thankful for? Sing songs of praise. Are there people among your community who are sick? Get together to pray, anointing them with the oil of healing and compassion.

We can choose the active or the passive reaction. Suffering and anxiety can result in paralyzing fear and worry. The more we worry the less we are open to finding solutions to our problems. Keeping it all to ourselves makes the burden heavier to bear, whereas sharing it with others in prayer offers a new perspective, allowing grace and healing to flow from God, through others, to us. And we in turn can pray for others, that their burdens might be lifted.

The lines of communication are kept open through our prayers and praises. God's healing power and mercy flow through them to others who are suffering and to ourselves.

Keep talking!

Lord God, may we keep praying in all the circumstances of our lives. We remember your goodness to us in our songs of praise; in our suffering help us reach out to others in your name. Amen.

Who can fathom the results of prayer? James stresses the power of prayer. In situations of human frailty and failing we can pray for each other, to help others feel forgiven, to bring a measure of healing and peace to the sick, to maintain the fellowship of the community of faith. But how much do we pray for one another? Are our intercessory prayers in church reduced to a formal list of petitions and names? Do we assume that God knows people's needs anyway and therefore does not really need our help in the matter?

Similarly, how do we pray for others during our own prayer time? When we say, "I will pray for you" to someone who is in need, do we? How many times, and how often? Do we think that our prayers will help people's situations, and do we keep going in prayer for them?

"The prayer of the righteous is powerful and effective." James goes on to talk about Elijah and his achievements through prayer. We might say, "I am not Elijah. He was one of God's greatest servants, totally dedicating his life to God. He did not have the pressures I have: the rush and tear of twenty-first century life, the problems I have with my boss, my children, my mortgage."

Perhaps Elijah did not have these specific pressures, but James says, "Elijah was a human being like us." He had his own problems and pressures, and yet he persevered in prayer. Life is not simple; it frequently throws us off balance. But we can choose to pray, especially for others in our community of faith. And we can be sure that others within that community are also praying for us. Who knows what the results might be?

Almighty God, when we pray help us remember that you will take our prayers for others and use them for their good. Help us to persevere in prayer, leaving the results in your hands. Amen.

Prayer for others can be one of the most effective things we can do for them. But following on from prayer is the way we treat others practically and the way we work with them. All our lives interact with those of others; it is part of the human condition.

Jesus' disciples complain to him that they have seen someone acting in Jesus' name, not sanctioned by Jesus himself. In other words, they say, "Not one of us." But Jesus says they are not to stop the person; if he is not against Jesus' mission, he is for it. How do we react to other Christians who we feel are not "one of us," perhaps from another church? We might feel suspicious about them, especially if they express their faith in ways very different from ours. Jesus would not agree with us. People may interpret his truth in their own way, but if they were to give us a cup of cold water in his name, their giving would still be honored.

Our hearts have to be big enough to accept all who come to us in Jesus' name. Advancing God's kingdom and helping our neighbor is not solely our preserve. Others are keen to do the same, and there must be room for us all to work together.

Otherwise, as Jesus warns us, we are in danger of becoming a stumbling block to others who love him. If others, especially young people, have new ideas about worship or outreach in the community, do we become stumbling blocks to their faith by being negative about their plans? Or do we encourage, build up, receive from them in Jesus' name? Their ways may be different and unsettling to us, but we need to remember that Jesus is working in their lives as well as our own.

Lord of all who turn to you, help us to accept that others have plans and ways of working that are acceptable in your sight. Persuade us graciously to receive from others, that our own faith may be enriched. In your name we ask it. Amen.

What will you choose, Jesus seems to ask in these verses from Mark. Is it true that Jesus really wants us to maim ourselves physically, rather than have us walk in sin? Or is he saying that if we choose to follow his way for our lives, we might have to make sacrifices that could curtail our lives in the world but will help us walk tall in God's kingdom?

In our Christian lives, sooner or later we are faced with a choice: Is our Christian commitment important enough to us that we make it our sole priority? Are we willing to make the sacrifices we need to in our lifestyle choices to ensure that God is honored, that we serve Christ day by day, that we respond to the Holy Spirit's prompting?

We do not need physically to cut off hands or feet or to put out our eyes to prove our commitment to God. But we may find ourselves in a job that conflicts with our calling; if we give it up, we may suffer financially and in our future career. We may be in a relationship that prevents us from loving others wholeheartedly. It may hurt us grievously to give it up, and our heart may be damaged forever, but is our Christian commitment worth it to us?

If we knew nothing of the skill of surgeons—to cut people open in order to heal them—we would not believe that good can result from what they do. But we know that sometimes the surgeon's knife is the only answer to good health. We may have to go through the rest of our life missing an arm or without a kidney or learning to walk again—but we are alive, and as whole as we can be.

To be salt in the world, says Jesus, we must preserve our saltiness, or we are no good to others. Is the road of sacrifice one that we will choose to tread?

Teach us, Lord Jesus, those things in our lives that we need to get rid of so that we can serve you without holding any part of us back. Help us to become as salt in your kingdom, living in peace with one another and with you. Amen.

Now is the time to order your copy of

The Upper Room
Disciplines
2010

Published for over 50 years, *Disciplines* continues to grow in its appeal to Christians who, like you, desire a more disciplined spiritual life based on scripture.

TO ORDER

CALL
1-800-972-0433
Tell the customer service
representative your source
code is 21D.

WRITE
Customer Service Dept.
The Upper Room
P.O. Box 340004
Nashville, TN 37203-0004

Shipping charges will be added to your invoice.
We accept Visa, Mastercard, checks, and money orders.

REGULAR EDITION (Product #9977)
ENLARGED-PRINT EDITION (Product #9978)

Discussion Guide available

QUANTITY DISCOUNT AVAILABLE!

ALSO AVAILABLE AT CHRISTIAN BOOKSTORES

VISIT OUR WEB SITE: WWW.UPPERROOM.ORG/BOOKSTORE

The Blameless Life

SEPTEMBER 28–OCTOBER 4, 2009 • PAUL MOOTS

MONDAY, SEPTEMBER 28 ~ *Read Psalm 26*

This psalm, attributed to David, begins with an audacious claim: "I have led a blameless life." Really? *Blameless* is an interesting adjective for David to apply to his life. Most famously, he used his power as king to commit adultery with Bathsheba, then to have her husband, Uriah, killed in battle while Bathsheba bore David's child. Ask David's daughter, Tamar, and his sons, Amnon and Absalom, if he was blameless as a parent. David's life is hardly blameless.

Yet David understands what we often do not: true repentance receives true forgiveness. David wrote in Psalm 51: "Wash away my transgressions. . . . For I know my transgressions and my sin is always before me" (vv. 2-3, NIV). David knows he is not blameless; he remembers the evil he has done. But his repentance and God's forgiveness have changed the scale of things. David is blameless because God has made him so.

We often have trouble letting go of sin—our own or the sins of others. When we cannot, we struggle with guilt on the one hand or self-righteousness on the other. If we are blamed rather than blameless, perhaps it is because we choose not to accept the grace of God's forgiveness. Without that forgiveness, we cannot pray David's courageous prayers of confidence and honesty.

Lord, lead us to the true repentance that wipes guilt from our lives and to the true forgiveness that wipes blame from our attitude toward others. Amen.

Pastor of First United Methodist Church in Mt. Sterling, Ohio, and author of Becoming Barnabas: The Ministry of Encouragement

How does this "made blameless" process happen? If we are at all aware of our own sin and need for redemption, this is a question of some immediacy. How can God do for us what God did for David? The author of the epistle to the Hebrews tells us God has not only anticipated our need, God made provision for our rescue at the highest level.

The Gospel of John begins with the Word made flesh. The author of Hebrews simply calls him the Son. The Son has a role to play in the physical universe—God made the world through the Son, the Word we know as Christ Jesus, and Christ continues to hold all things together. He is, according to this passage, the unifying power that physicists discover at the extremes of physical reality but cannot isolate or name ("He holds everything together with his powerful word.") Hebrews joins John's Gospel in making the astonishing claim that this Creator and Sustainer of all that exists is also the means of our salvation: "When the Son made people clean from their sins, he sat down at the right hand of God."

Think about this stunning reality. God, who made all that is— our world and the worlds beyond, worlds seen and unseen—is in the process of restoring creation. Healing humans of the disease of sin is a vital part of the restoration. One "greater than angels," God's own Son, made our healing his mission. When we understand this, we see what God is like—unimaginable love and grace.

Maker of things both immense and miniscule, we are moved to know you care for us. Your love heals and saves us. May we respond with gratitude and joy. Amen.

The most powerful element in this story of "making blameless" is Christ's renunciation of his throne. Like few human kings, the Creator and Sustainer of the universe stepped away from the seat of power to become frail, vulnerable, subject to physical limitations—in a word, *human*. The author of Hebrews writes: "Jesus, who makes people holy, and those who are made holy are from the same family." The Creator of human life *lived* a human life. Again, we are stunned by what Christ has done on our behalf.

In chapter 4, our author will remind us that Jesus was tempted in every way that we are, yet did not sin. Having become human, Jesus felt our frailty morally as well as physically. "Tempted in every way that we are," Jesus felt physical attraction. His desire to do God's will was pulled toward self-centeredness. Feeling anger, Jesus was tempted toward violence and retribution. Yet he resisted these temptations and *every other* temptation we humans experience.

Christ is effective as our high priest because he is our brother. That is, he has shared our life with all the pressures and uncertainties and temptations that come our way. He knows the dangers and fears we face, and he knows the only remedy: absolute reliance on God.

Over and over again in the Gospels, we see Jesus withdraw from his disciples and the crowds, who wanted both to adore him and to use him, so he could seek God in solitude. These were not mere rest breaks; they offered him retreat to seek God's will and to be sustained through prayer. In following his example, perhaps we too will find deliverance from temptation. When we fail, our weakness becomes his strength.

What pulls you from God's way? Follow Jesus' example, and ask God for guidance and strength.

Unfortunately, being made blameless does not keep us humans out of trouble. In this passage from Mark, Jesus' opponents test Jesus with a question about divorce. Today we ask their question with real pain: "Is it lawful for a man to divorce his wife (or a woman her husband)?" The issue for us is not a legal one, of course; divorce is both legal and legally easy to accomplish. Statistics show that Christians are as vulnerable to divorce as non-churched couples. But we ask the question because Jesus' words equating remarriage with adultery haunt us.

Verse 5 suggests that the key sin for Jesus seems to be less adultery than it is hardheartedness. Divorce happens because hearts are hardened against the other. It can certainly be argued that one partner has been less faithful to the marriage vows or more selfish and less honest than the other, and those arguments are sometimes even true. Jesus' words put these arguments in the perspective of human sinfulness: hardheartedness kills the relationship.

We may squirm in discomfort and wish he had spoken differently, but he didn't. The hardheartedness to which he spoke is a powerful, awful thing. Hardheartedness is born of stubbornness, indifference, callousness, insensibility, and a cold self-will. While we may (and should) consider ourselves free of legalistic attitudes that see remarriage as a permanent taint on our relationship with God and the church, we should not take our failure casually. With David, we must accept our responsibility and repent of our hardheartedness; only then can we can be made blameless.

For our own failures in marriage, we ask for forgiveness. For others who have failed, we offer compassion and support.

Hardheartedness is not only at the root of divorce. It is often interwoven with most sin. We become so fixed on our own desires and ambitions that we refuse to acknowledge the needs or hopes or worth of others. If hardheartedness isn't quite our original sin, it's a close relative.

Is there a cure for hardheartedness? Jesus gives us a clue in these verses. The kingdom of God belongs to folks who are like little children. Now I am a big fan of children; I'm also a smitten grandparent. But we shouldn't claim more for children than is true. Innocence wears off children pretty quickly. Yes, children can be enormously generous, but in the next moment they can be just as self-centered and greedy as any adult.

Innocence and generosity, along with a childlike sense of wonder and an ability to live fully in the moment may have something to do with Jesus' assertion about children. Even more important to Jesus than these endearing qualities is the fact of young children's absolute dependence. Without the loving care of adults, young children cannot survive in this world, and they know this. Children cling to parents, grandparents, and other caretakers as though their lives depend on them, because they do.

What happens in those moments when we truly understand our dependence on God? For one thing, we lose the illusion that we are the most important person around; God cares for others as much as for us. For another, we are reminded how much God's love has contributed to our lives, how much it sustains us. The vaccination for hardheartedness—stubbornly clinging to our own self-will—comes from a dose of the reality that we are, in fact, completely dependent on God.

Lord, remind us how much we depend on your love. Reawaken the childlike character and understanding that fits us for your kingdom. Amen.

We find another blameless man in this story, though it is God who calls Job "blameless" rather than Job himself. Job has held fast to his integrity despite the first round of evils visited upon him by Satan. Now, with God's permission, Job receives another disaster, a horrific disease. Job's wife says enough is enough: "Curse God and die." Yet Job answers, "Shall we receive the good at the hand of God, and not receive the bad?"

Although our lives are far from blameless, my wife and I had to wrestle with similar questions last fall and winter. We were in a terrible auto accident, which left Robin's left foot and leg crushed and right femur broken. I had a nasty pilon fracture that detached my left shin from the ankle joint. We both struggled with the "Why us?" question, and we were invited by several well-meaning friends to hold God accountable for our suffering.

Job did not curse God. But he did yearn for—and even demand—that God meet him face-to-face and account for his plight. When God does come, God accepts no accountability. Instead, God comes to Job in all God's glory. Job is overwhelmed with God's majesty, repents his presumption, and admits his lack of knowledge. "I spoke of things I did not understand, things too wonderful for me to know" (Job 42:3, NCV).

Robin and I did not have such a shattering encounter with God. Instead, God revealed God's presence in the heart and skill of our surgeon; the powerful prayer support we received; the loving care of family, friends, and congregation; our rapid recovery; and return to work ahead of anyone's predicted schedule. We discovered, with Job, that life with God brings both good and trouble, and God is with us in both.

Help us trust you, Lord, that we may discover your love and presence both in good times and in troubled. Amen.

So do we have no role to play in being "made blameless"? Are we merely clay in the hands of the Artist? Certainly, making us blameless is God's work and only God can accomplish the task. But God has given us freedom and responsibility as critical characteristics of human life. We have an important part to play in our own rescue.

John Wesley described this process as "sanctification." We cannot make ourselves holy. We can, however, help the process along by making use of the spiritual disciplines Wesley called "the means of grace." Through prayer, study, worship, participation in Christian community, sharing the sacraments, and fasting, we open our hearts and minds to the Spirit within. We share the psalmist's invitation to the Spirit, "Lord, try me and test me; look closely into my heart and mind" (NCV).

By giving ourselves to this process of sanctification, we allow God to change us, to grow us into more mature disciples. We not only learn the necessity of repentance; we experience its joy. With David (and Job), we learn we are not alone in our struggles: "I see your love, and I live by your truth" (NCV). We are clay; but we are living clay, learning from the process of being shaped into new life, feeling joy in our new reality. "I stand in a safe place. LORD, I praise you in the great meeting" (NCV).

Blameless living is God's great gift to us in this life. We will still err. We are still tempted and will sometimes succumb. But, through Christ, we are given the peace of repentance and reconciliation. With David, we can truly say, "I raise my voice in praise and tell of all the miracles you have done" (NCV).

Give thanks for God's good gifts, in this life and in life eternal.

Light at the End of the Tunnel

OCTOBER 5–11, 2009 • SOOZUNG SA RANKIN

MONDAY, OCTOBER 5 ~ *Read Job 23:1-9, 16-17*

I can recount several times in my life when I desperately needed a glimmer of light at the end of the tunnel. My world was crashing. I was emotionally drained. Juggling it all was no longer an option. I wanted to stuff the juggling balls in a big bag and bury it.

It's as if the old joke really is true. Just as I see the glimmer of light, I realize it is not a light at the end of tunnel but a train coming at me!

Job, in search of God, keeps finding darkness. He even finds himself turning away from friends. He feels alone. He laments about his complaining and admits his complaint is also bitter. Job acknowledges God's existence but does not even address God directly anymore. He only speaks of God in the third person. God is that distant for Job.

Finding ourselves alone can be ugly. We may sometimes complain as bitterly as Job did about his life. Cognitively, we know God is present, but we do not feel it. We see only darkness.

Sometimes it's healthy to experience the darkness and just walk through it. Often we're not given permission to do so. We want to walk around it, be rescued from it, or even ignore it. We must learn to embrace these dark times as part of a meaningful process for finding wholeness. In our brokenness we discover our need for healing. In these dark times we find healing. In the dark times we understand God's grace.

In your dark times, how do you experience God? Think of a time when you, like Job, sat in darkness. Who (or what) finally brought some light to you?

Executive director of A United Methodist Witness in Pennsylvania, social justice and advocacy organization of the United Methodist Church; living in Philadelphia, Pennsylvania

One day I suddenly found myself standing in front of a classroom full of fifth graders. *How did I get here?* I wondered.

I honestly believe that nothing prepares you to teach and manage a classroom. Most days teaching felt almost natural to me, but there were days when I questioned my wholeness, sanity, and mental health. One fact was never clearer to me than when I was a classroom teacher: if you don't have your act together, your students will quickly discover everything about you that you don't want them to know. Everything you don't like about yourself comes spilling out, right onto the desk in your classroom for all to see.

When this happened to me, I felt like the psalmist. I found myself crying out for help. I felt helpless and alone. I even felt I needed a time-out. I would have paid someone to do my lunch duty. I needed a break from my students and, surely, they needed a break from me.

Usually when we hear this plea for deliverance from suffering and hostility, we think of Jesus crying out from the cross. I know it doesn't do the scripture reading justice to compare my pain to the pain of the psalmist or to Jesus' suffering, but there is assurance in knowing Jesus was fully human and experienced the pain we have known. The imagery in the psalm is graphic, and some days I can relate to it very personally. Still, the psalmist reminds us, even when we feel completely alone, God has the capacity to save us. Indeed, knowing the greatness of God's power allows us to cry out to God with honesty and candor.

Precious God, just when I feel I am at my wit's end, you remind me of who I am and whose I am. Hear my cry when I feel helpless and hopeless. Amen.

Being in ministry is exciting. Being surrounded by kind people who know the Golden Rule is a treat. These people even know that the Commandments are more than mere suggestions. What a safe place to be. I was certainly conscious this was not how things would always be, but I enjoyed my haven and was grateful daily for it.

But of course, it is inevitable. If we take the risk to be in relationship with people, we will have conflict. We will face criticism. We will experience trouble. Sometimes the trouble we have is with ourselves. We torture ourselves with our thoughts. We get lost in our heads. We feel attacked by others and ourselves.

This is how the psalmist must have felt. Clearly he had been attacked and beaten down. It is also obvious the psalmist knows who his God is. God is strong and capable, eager to save us. It is important to stay the course. Regardless of our actions, God is present, even if we do not feel it. God's work will be carried out. Our human condition may cause a detour, but God is still with us. In searching for help or relief, we may find ourselves having trouble with God, but we know who our God is so we can trust just like the psalmist. In spite of our pain and our trouble, we know God is with us. Such times of suffering are good times to be honest with God and to cry out for deliverance.

Have you ever walked a labyrinth? If there is one near you, go out and walk it. If you are unable to get to a labyrinth, imagine yourself on a walk through a labyrinth. You may discover it helpful to find a picture of a labyrinth, tracing the walk with your finger. Walk, pray, and find yourself centered as you find the labyrinth's center.

God in concert! Live! I love going to concerts and musical performances. There is something immediate, energetic, and moving about the music.

These two verses in Hebrew remind us God's words are living words. God's word is immediate, energetic, and moving. God's word is able to divide the good from the bad. Nothing we do is hidden; we will be judged by this living word. We are exposed. God's word is sharp and piercing like a sword.

Able to separate even soul from spirit, God's word pierces through any subterfuge, any dishonesty within us and lays bare the truth. This is how the living word of God is. It instantly knows what really matters and what does not matter. God's word challenges us every day to continue to be faithful.

We all must stand before God and render an account of our lives. "Account" translates from the Greek logos as word. God's word, then, demands to be answered with a human word. This can be frightening—God as judge, rather than God as creator or liberator. God's judgment is inevitable; we are called to answer for who we are and what we have done—or not done.

Yet we can "hold fast" to our confession because God's judgment never stands alone. God's judgment is always accompanied by God's mercy. God's grace is always there to help in time of need.

God of live and active words, help me to meet you with excitement and encouragement each day. Help me live in a way that I may be open to your judgment and your mercy. Amen.

We are challenged to be bold. To me this also means to live without fear. Do we have to know exactly what our relationship with God is in order to approach the throne boldly? Do we need to feel worthy even to pray? Of course not, because we know grace is available to all. We have a great high priest, and we have access to him.

Jesus is called by many titles. He is the Son of God, the Messiah, our Savior, the Redeemer, the Lamb of God. In Hebrews, Jesus is the great high priest who can sympathize with our weaknesses and our testing. This makes Jesus quite accessible and available to us.

When I am in a tough situation and feel confused or frightened, I seek out someone who has been through what I am facing. Most often, I take great relief in my conversation with that person, I am often consoled and encouraged. This is a great blessing to me, helping to calm my fears and to make me bold.

How much more this is true when the one we go to in our confusion is Jesus, our high priest. Having lived and died as a human being, Jesus is the high priest who will help us be bold as we approach the throne of grace. He is the one who understands and stands by us.

The words of testing and judgment are hard to hear, and yet Hebrews states with conviction: God's judgment never comes without mercy. We will, the letter says, "find grace to help in time of need."

Dear Jesus, thank you for knowing me. Renew my spirit so that I may accept myself as I am. Give me encouragement to approach you with boldness. Amen.

I'm fascinated by the television shows *Clean Sweep* and *While You Were Out*. The goal of these shows is to create a comfortable and ordered living space that will bring out the best in people. To get to this point, however, the people must start by getting rid of much of their "stuff."

I watch in awe as people reveal their clutter and piles of things. I understand when they have difficulty parting with their belongings. Regardless of an object's value, it is clear they have too much stuff, and they hang on to their things tightly. And I know that I too have accumulated much and need to let go of much of it.

If I did give away everything, could I live in complete dependence on others? I remember living this way as a child. I was young when my father began a ministry for the Korean population in Wisconsin. He would accept only a one-dollar check for his annual salary. My parents were completely dependent on others. It's a once-in-a-lifetime experience to see how this works. As part of the family, I was part of the experiment. And I was the recipient of many blessings as well. I can tell you that we never felt poor or hungry. In fact, we felt quite wealthy.

What is wealth? What does it mean to be rich? How does one really enter the kingdom of God? Jesus says it takes a miracle, like getting a camel through the eye of a needle. We cannot flee the world because the world is where our work and ministry are. Therefore, we must rid ourselves of all that takes our focus off Jesus.

Gracious God, help me to know where my real riches lie. Free me from distractions so that I may focus on you. Amen.

I'm reminded of traveling by airplane when I read these verses. When I am the last to board planes, I think, *At least this means I'll be first off*. Or, when I'm at the rear of the plane, I think, *I boarded first, after all, so I'll have to wait my turn to deplane.*

While traveling can bring out the best in people, it can also bring out the worst as well. When the call comes to board the plane, people may push, shove, rush, and cut in line. If you are first, you will quickly take your turn being last.

As I wait, I begin to think about all the stuff I've brought along for the trip and the stress I put on myself because I have over-packed. Will my checked bags arrive? Will my carry-on bags fit? Caught up in my anxiety, I'm certainly not living out these verses with any authenticity. So, I pause to breathe; I reach for some grace, find it, and move on.

The point remains: it's difficult to leave everything to follow Jesus. We hold our stuff too tightly—we value the wrong things; we smother our faith with too much accumulating. It certainly will take a miracle to cajole us toward letting go and following Jesus.

But Jesus is clear: Leave your things and follow me. He tells us, "Many who are first will be last, and the last will be first." We must live into a new way of following Jesus. We must focus on his call and our faith. To do so is to gain the kingdom of heaven.

Take a walk. Leave your cell phone and blackberry at home. Take only your house key and an ID. On your walk, meditate and reflect. What does it mean to shift your focus from posses-sions to your call from Jesus?

Out of Weakness,
Strength and Service

OCTOBER 12–18, 2009 • H. SHARON HOWELL

MONDAY, OCTOBER 12 ~ *Read Joel 2:21-27*

It's Thanksgiving Day in Canada. Our sisters and brothers in Canada have been gathering with family and friends to enjoy a feast and offer gratitude for the year. The proclamation by the Canadian Parliament on January 31, 1957, states that this is "A Day of General Thanksgiving to Almighty God for the bountiful harvest with which Canada has been blessed."

The writer of Joel tells us to "be glad and rejoice, for the LORD has done great things." Every summer my cousins arrived at Granddaddy's East Texas farm filled with awe and wonder as they picked purple-hulled peas, tomatoes, cantaloupe, and watermelons. Every fall Granddaddy hitched the mules to the wagon and gathered the final harvest. The crops were stored in the barn.

Granddaddy's large dining table seemed to expand to the size needed for all of us to sit down together for a bountiful harvest meal. No one could touch a fresh slice of tomato before the prayer was offered. Every grandchild shared something for which they were thankful. God's great creation was named as the young voices shouted—frogs in the pond, tadpoles in the creek, chickens, cows, squirrels, trees to climb, and worms in the catalpa tree. Aunt Janie always closed the prayer with these words: "O Lord of goodness and grace, bless these prayers and all who offer them. Amen."

In a world weary and wounded with hunger, poverty, war, and fractured families, how shall we offer our prayers and thanksgivings for everyone? What do we fear will silence our voices?

President, Scarritt-Bennett Center, Nashville, Tennessee; ordained elder in the Kansas East Conference of the United Methodist Church

TUESDAY, OCTOBER 13 ～ *Read Job 38:1-7*

God finally speaks in chapter 38. To whom is God speaking? Is it to Job? to Job's friend Elihu? Is the divine speech delivered to the whole of creation? The image that frames this scene is the "whirlwind" or "storm" from which God speaks. In other biblical passages "whirlwind" or "storm" refers to divine anger. That fits, doesn't it? Twisting, swirling, or straight force winds do not usually bring calming thoughts. They bring a sense of foreboding, maybe a sense of fear.

Tornado season in Kansas is never taken lightly. For thirty-six years I learned a healthy respect for tornado alerts and warnings. The devastation left behind after a tornado bounces through a community seems to scream "anger." I am still stunned when I see video and aerial pictures of Greensburg, Kansas, which was leveled on May 4, 2007, by a tornado with winds over two hundred miles per hour. The questions the residents of Greensburg raised were not too different from those in the first thirty-six chapters of Job. "Why do the innocent suffer?" and "Why do bad things happen to good people?"

The Lord alerts the hearer to "gird up your loins," get ready, prepare for a direct confrontation. God declares, "I will question you, and you shall declare to me." God initiates a litany of rhetorical questions. I hear them coming in quick, staccato fashion, brushed with urgency. The questions shout: "Do you know who you are in relation to God and God's creation?" and "Do you know who God is?" These straightforward questions bring home the fact that it is God, not us, who has the final word. God does not cause the suffering, but God's wisdom in the middle of that suffering is greater than our wisdom. In acknowledging that truth, we are called to put our trust in God, even in the midst of turmoil. What is our response to God when we hear God speak of a wisdom surpassing ours?

The whirlwind can make unable to hear God's questions for us. Sit quietly; center your thoughts; listen for the voice of God to speak out of life's whirlwind. What questions do you hear?

Job must be the superhero for the culture of entitlement. He was, according to the story, a good person who lost everything that mattered in his life—family, health, wealth, friends. His situation raises questions: Aren't the innocent to be free from suffering? Shouldn't the righteous experience no pain or grief?

The reading for today is frequently seen as a cleverly crafted wisdom poem. God's wisdom skills are extraordinary. The questions are raised in such a manner that they all have the same or similar answer. "Who has the wisdom, knowledge, and understanding to create the heavens and earth?" The question is never really answered. It doesn't need to be. The answer is implied. The answer is God.

Every time I read Job, I am reminded that our wisdom is limited and small. We think too highly of ourselves and believe we are entitled to knowledge and success. We are unsettled seekers, restless searchers, self-absorbed wanderers in the wilderness of life. God is still speaking to us. The questions are framed in such a manner as to engage us in the practice of spiritual discernment.

When I went to my first annual evaluation with the minister who supervised my work, in the spring of 1972, the extravagant and lengthy form that I had to complete prior to the meeting was not, it turns out, the content for our conversation. The first question my district superintendent Dr. Clare Hayes asked me was, "How is your soul?" The question hung in the air between us. How is my soul? What about my church's budget and giving, the new members, our increase in worship attendance?

How is my soul? Dr. Hayes was a very wise man. He knew the proper question to keep a young pastor focused on the right things in ministry. Because of his wisdom, this question has guided and haunted me every year of my ministry.

God, help me find peace in the midst of my life journey. Amen.

I cannot read this creation hymn without hearing the wind whispering through the pine trees in East Texas where I grew up. I never lived in town. We lived in the country. The neighbor's horse could be ridden without a saddle or bridle. The creek was loaded with crawfish that loved the bacon we tied on the string.

The fish in the pond were always safe from our hooks. Flowers and sticker burrs shared the front yard. Blackberries grew wild on the roadway up to Aunt Janie's house. My first paying job was picking strawberries in my cousin's field starting at 5:30 AM.

We were so surrounded by God's creation that we almost took it for granted, even as we carefully tended it. My parents saw to it that God's creation was honored, cared for, and prepared for the next generation. They taught me about stewardship of the earth's resources. My dad rotated crops so that the minerals could be replenished, and he allowed certain fields to lie fallow for a season. Trees were planted. Fields were terraced to stop erosion.

This creation hymn testifies to God's greatness and goodness. I can't read it sitting down or still. I need to stand or move or stretch to the tips of my toes.

There aren't words sufficient or adequate to describe God's creative power. The verses that capture my imagination are, "You make the clouds your chariot, you ride on the wings of the wind, you make the winds your messengers, fire and flame your ministers."

God is still speaking through God's creation. Yet forests are still destroyed in search of riches. Oceans become unbalanced when greed replaces stewardship. Creatures seek new homes as developments displace them. What would it mean for us to take this creation hymn to heart? What would happen if we took God's creation seriously and treated the earth as sacred? How might we become the wise stewards of God's awesome creation?

God, may we be good stewards of your creation. Amen.

I've always wanted to add another line to the Beatitudes: "Blessed are the wounded, for they bind up their wounds one at a time." I know that my understanding of wounded leaders has been influenced by Henri J. M. Nouwen's writing in *The Wounded Healer*. It is not a huge leap for me to connect the "weakness" in our reading from Hebrews and the "wounded" in Nouwen's groundbreaking text.

In my first year at Saint Paul School of Theology, I was part of a small group that spent every Monday at the state mental hospital. We worked under the supervision of Chaplain Paul Kapp. We were sent into different floors and wings for long blocks of time with the express purpose of relating to anyone we encountered.

A few weeks into the semester we complained that we were uncomfortable. Chaplain Kapp listened and kept pushing us about our discomfort. We finally admitted that we felt inadequate to relate to those we were encountering. Chaplain Kapp kept sending us back into the hospital wards with the same assignment.

At last we confessed our attitude and our fear. We had come to the state hospital feeling superior and whole and healthy. We discovered our own weakness and woundedness in the midst of entering into relationship with those who could no longer live without imposed structures, boundaries, and constant support. When we learned to check our all-knowing self-importance at the door and enter into relationships based on honoring the other, we discovered God's overwhelming grace.

It is often difficult for us to acknowledge and name our weaknesses or woundedness. We are encouraged to focus solely on our gifts and strengths. Today's reading suggests that entering into relationship with those who struggle, question, go astray, and wander without hope is what we are called to do. It is out of our weaknesses—not out of our strengths—that we find the resources to be present with others.

God of grace, help us embrace our weakness. Amen.

I started going to church camp as soon as I was old enough. Lakeview Methodist Assembly near Palestine, Texas, was a testimony to the beauty of God's creation and the vision of those who wanted children and youth to have a discipleship experience. It was during a week at camp that I was introduced to the hymn "Are Ye Able?" We had spent the entire week exploring the Gospel readings to see what it would mean to follow Jesus. The hymn became a theme song for the week, and by Friday we could sing with loud volume and heartfelt confidence, "Lord, we are able." Our enthusiasm probably lasted until school started in the fall. We were young believers with so much to learn. We could have been called foolish.

James and John had been a part of the inner circle with Jesus since the beginning. They had witnessed his ministry up close and personal. They still were confused about the difference between success in glory and sacrifice in service. Their request reflected their entitlement desires (we deserve this) to be singled out from and above the other disciples. It was an insensitive and foolish request. Jesus had just predicted his suffering and death. But Jesus didn't rebuke them. Instead, he said to them, "You do not know what you are asking." They were even blind enough to answer, "Yes, we are able." They still saw the ministry of Jesus as that of an all-powerful Christ, not a suffering Christ.

Many days I turn to the Covenant Prayer attributed to John Wesley as my touchstone to say, "Yes, I am able." It's humbling to pray to be "exalted or brought low" for God. It's overwhelming to offer to "be full or empty" for God. That covenant prayer was the vehicle for my call to ministry, reminding me that true faithfulness first goes through the valley of suffering. I pray that this prayer will always remind me to be honest and open to God's leading.

Dear God, give me the strength to be ready and able. Amen.

The Gospel of Mark generally reflects the failure of the disciples to understand the servant nature of Jesus. James and John missed it. In their desire to be recognized in a special manner, they generated an angry response from the other ten disciples. Jesus uses the incident as a teaching moment. It is another explanation of what greatness in the realm of God will mean. It doesn't look like the culture around the disciples where rulers become lords over many. The realm of God equates servanthood with greatness; those wishing to be first must serve everyone else.

How do you define success? The culture and marketplace give us definitions of success. Jesus kept redefining the culture. Jesus didn't ask the disciples or us to be successful. Jesus asked them and us to be faithful. We are not invited to be comfortable; we are asked to share in the baptism of suffering. We are not guaranteed a place of privilege or a reward in the new community; we are told that being a servant of all is the new definition of success or greatness.

What does true servant ministry look like today? The last church I served was First United Methodist in Lawrence, Kansas. We hosted a breakfast program two mornings a week for those who were hungry. Many of the students from nearby Kansas University volunteered in the ministry. It required them to be on site by 6:00 AM.

This meal ministry was designed to serve those coming to eat. It wasn't a food line or a buffet. Each person sat down, ordered their meal of choice from the handwritten menu, and was served by the students. Then, the students were to sit and eat with those they had just served. The students got an important glimpse of God's new community. By becoming servants, by being in a relationship with those served, these students walked in Jesus' footsteps, answering his call to be in service to others in the name of God.

How is God calling you to service and servanthood today?

Discipleship and Vulnerability

OCTOBER 19–25, 2009 • JENNIFER S. GRAVES

MONDAY, OCTOBER 19 ∽ *Read Job 42:1-6*

If you have lived long enough, you have suffered. You have lost people you love dearly. You have lost your health or your faith. You have suffered trauma, or you have journeyed alongside a world that is suffering. You have prayed through your tears and in between gasped for breath.

You know, then, something of the experience of Job. You know the dark nights filled with desperate prayers. You long to know why—if God is powerful and good—this could happen. Why couldn't God prevent it or protect us?

Yet in this passage, we find Job transformed even in his pain. Finally, God answers Job. Job does not get the kind of answer he was looking for, of course. God gives no explanations but says, in effect, "It's just that the rain falls on the just and on the unjust, Job. That's life. Now look up. My creation is vast, and you couldn't understand it if you tried. Breathe it in, because I am God and I made it all in love."

In the middle of his dark night, Job is able to grasp that God is all he has ever had. Job's anguished, clenched fists are transformed into empty, open hands. Job is able to let go of his demand for answers and open up to God's goodness and love.

We endure suffering, and we learn that we are vulnerable. We learn that we are not in control and never were. Indeed, God is all we have. There is space in our hearts for healing and comfort. God can transform our suffering into strength and compassion.

In times of suffering, God, help us grasp the mystery of your love. Fill our hearts with compassion for your suffering world. Amen.

Student at Duke Divinity School and coordinator of the school's Women's Center

Job was a person of faith who lost everything and wound up finding God more mysterious, intimate, and deep than ever before. That was Job's miracle. And then, after all that, God restored Job's blessings twofold.

A friend of mine has been through a divorce, remarriage, and now a recurrence of cancer after several years' remission. She has lost so much in life, and yet she is healthier and has more love in her life than ever before. This time as she faces chemotherapy, she is in touch with her inner strength, her loving community, and the gracious God who carries her through the pain in life. She may not be healed of cancer in this life, but she will tell you that she feels more blessed now than ever. She has grasped God's love for her and for all of creation. She focuses on the resilience of the heart, on nature, and on people who bring her joy.

When we face devastation, we discover that all we have is God; and God is all we need. What has come before is no more, but God endures. And God will help us endure.

We know one day God will heal us and restore us. Until then, let us embrace the gift of discovering new, deeper meaning under the rubble of what we have lost. God promises the gift of God's merciful presence, even in the midst of our suffering.

Gracious God, when we have lost everything, help us hold on to the deep mystery of your love. Amen.

There are times in life simply to give thanks to God for God's deliverance and blessings. I've been fortunate to have been part of Hispanic and Latino ministries in the US; I've also been blessed to have traveled to Central America and seen a small part of life there.

The poverty and desperation in Central America are extreme. Families are often separated in the search for work; a father, brother, or sister will spend years away from the family, living in substandard housing and working exhausting jobs in order to send money back home to support the family.

In Central American and here in the United States, my friends in Latino and Hispanic communities have taught me what it means to worship and give thanks to God. Their praise of God is joyful and genuine. They have suffered much, yet they celebrate each blessing of life. There is no question that the good things in life are from God, and God is to be praised.

When I worship in these congregations, I am often moved from being bogged down in my everyday stress to worshiping God with a joy that passes understanding. We share our sorrows together and our praise. These sisters and brothers of mine revitalize my faith and refix my eyes on Christ. I am thankful to God that God has allowed me to be transformed by their hospitality and worship.

Gradually, because of their example, I give less of my energy over to the stresses of life; I celebrate life's blessings more. I know how intense suffering can be, and I feel intense gratitude for the attentiveness of God and the diversity of the community of faith.

Loving God, I thank you for the blessing of those who have taught me how to worship, trust, and be grateful. Keep my love for you ever in my heart. Amen.

God is attentive, the psalmist says, to the poor and abused. In one moment, we are full of praise for God. In the next, we find ourselves grief-stricken. In one moment we are sure that God is our deliverer, and in the next moment we feel as though injustice has prevailed.

Our world is wracked by death and misery. Innocent children play happily in the street until an IED explodes in the middle of their games. Abused women are terrorized and even killed by those who profess to love them. Senseless suffering from disease, hunger, and violence rocks our world and shakes our belief in justice and peace. The reign of God seems distant.

These verses from Psalm 34 remind us that God knows each of us intimately. They proclaim that God lovingly picks up the broken pieces of our lives and promises to save them all. One day God will put the pieces together again, and each one of us will know healing, justice, and love.

Although it seems there is no justice, God promises otherwise. Evil will eventually destroy itself, and God will prevail. In those times we suffer and it seems injustice has won, let us, like the psalmist, seek refuge in the God who gathers the broken pieces of our world and promises wholeness.

The psalm asserts the firm belief that God will redeem all of God's servants. No one who takes refuge in God will be lost.

Gracious God, grant us your peace in the midst of despair. Hold on to us when we can't hold on to you. Comfort those who mourn with your eternal promises. Amen.

I am finishing seminary, and although I will not be pursuing ordination, I consider myself a Christian minister by virtue of my baptism. I have already had many wonderful opportunities to be in ministry with God's people in a variety of circumstances. I have preached the gospel, visited the sick, and advocated for those who have no voice. I have been in solidarity with the homeless and with battered women. I have faced the seemingly insurmountable challenges of daily life with God's people. I have sometimes spoken truth to power because the vulnerable have spoken their truth to me.

It is easy to be overwhelmed by our call to ministry. The needs are great; God's world cries to be tended, and we often find ourselves exhausted. I am only one person, a baptized Christian with a little church history under my belt. It can be overwhelming.

But then today's scripture speaks: There is a high priest who does have what it takes to heal the world and to sustain us. This priest is Jesus Christ, who "holds his priesthood permanently, because he continues forever." This is the one who can save the world, bind up its wounds, and make it whole.

We are simply those who respond to the high priest's call. We are sustained in our ministry because he is our Savior. We rely on his strength, not our own. And Jesus' strength continues forever.

O God, we need you to remind us daily, sometimes hourly, to rely on you and to trust in Christ Jesus, our Savior. Amen.

It was a busy day on the road to Jerusalem. Everyone was headed into town for Passover. There was a blind man on the side of the road crying out for Jesus. People were telling this man to stop shouting, to be quiet. But Jesus heard him and asked that he be called over. The crowd—the same people who had jeered at the insignificant man—quickly changed their cries and carried Jesus' message to him. "Take heart; get up, he is calling you."

How often it is that Jesus attends to the insignificant people. Here he is, on the way to a grand and final entry into Jerusalem, on his way to the last supper, his betrayal, and his crucifixion. Jesus knows what lies ahead for him, and yet he has time for the blind man.

The crowd in this passage reminds me of our reactions to the homeless. When I come to an intersection where homeless persons are begging, I'm uncomfortable. Sometimes I don't want to look them in the eye. I know some people get angry with these people, throw garbage out their car windows, yell obscenities, and spit at them.

When I got involved in a street ministry, I began to understand these homeless children of God—what their lives were like, what they needed, what they have to give. When we gathered for worship and Communion weekly on the street corner, my own heart was opened. At this table, I learned that the people I had been uncomfortable around, who had been jeered at and spat on, were loved and treasured by God. Learning this, I found myself, like Bartimaeus, healed and claimed by God.

Gracious God, open us to hear the cries of those who need you most desperately. Move us to community with the outsiders and the ones we would like to quiet. Help us to make space at our table for your vulnerable children. Amen.

"What do you want me to do for you?" Jesus asked the blind Bartimaeus. The blind man says he wants to see again. Jesus responds, "Your faith has made you well." Immediately Bartimaeus becomes a follower of Jesus. His request was simple enough. He knows that Jesus can restore his sight. And when Jesus does heal him, his response is remarkable: he follows Jesus on the road to Jerusalem. Sight equals discipleship for Bartimaeus and for us.

With restored sight I have learned that it is not that the poor, the immigrants, and the marginal are invisible; they are all around me. The problem is that *I* am blind. I am blind to my neighbors, those whom Jesus loves with special affection. When I ask God for sight, God opens my eyes to discipleship. God calls me to join God in caring those in special need.

Opening our eyes to see the ones Jesus sees means following Jesus closely—to the places of the poor, the homeless, even the criminal. How easy it is to be blind to the stranger when I am comfortable in my community. How easy it is to be blind to poverty when I have plenty. If Jesus is on the way to Jerusalem, and we have the chance to get his attention, to ask for our eyes to be opened, will we risk it? Will we, as the church and as individuals, make this simple, profound request of our God? Will we then follow Jesus on the road to Jerusalem?

Jesus, Son of David, I want to regain my sight. Amen.

Blessed Assurance, Heaven Is Mine

OCTOBER 26–NOVEMBER 1, 2009 • TIMOTHY J. NADEAU

MONDAY, OCTOBER 26 ~ *Read Isaiah 25:6-9*

The morning headlines are bad: another school shooting, an earthquake with landslides killing hundreds, nine hundred workers to be laid off before the holidays. And then the discouraging report about our patients at the mental health center had left us both shaken. When we finally took a brief break together, my coworker gasped, "I can't wait for Jesus' return. I am so ready!"

We live under the constant threat of attack, capture, and enslavement, just as the Israelites did. Our threats may differ from those back then, but the responses are still often the same. Some lost heart. Others lost faith and turned away from God to worship idols. Isaiah's prophetic ministry was to warn the people of God's punishment for wickedness and disobedience, but his proclamations always included a message of redemption, salvation, and hope. In chapter 25, Isaiah gives us a glorious view of the Messiah's kingdom, a promise to those who await God's salvation and joy.

Many writers in both the Old and New Testaments proclaim the redemption of the faithful and the beginning of the reign of God. But Isaiah 25 carries the promise one step farther: Isaiah is sure that it is not only the faithful of Israel who will be saved; all people and all nations will be saved and delivered. This is the greatness of God's love.

In the face of God's all-encompassing love, can we do anything less than praise God, trust in God, and live our lives as witnesses to God's love and power?

All-powerful God, holy is your name, your kingdom come, your will be done on earth as it is in heaven. Amen.

Registered nurse, with surgical, intensive-care, and psychiatric-care experience; graduate of Abilene Christian University in Texas; attends Calvary Chapel in Albuquerque, New Mexico

The reward of heaven goes to those who trust God despite the hardships of this life. My mother accepted the Lord when she was twelve, and she never looked back. As the wife of an evangelist and missionary to Germany after World War II, she endured many trials. She raised eight children, and she gave all she had to her family. Now, at the age of eighty-three, she has slowed down. She says she feels as though she is a burden to those family and friends around her, despite the fact that we do not agree with her assessment. Through everything, she remains faithful to God.

When you ask what keeps her faithful, my mom is quick to answer: "My parents taught me about a loving God, one that I needed to know as my savior. Even while I raised my children, I made time for devotions every morning. I turned my problems over to God. I knew God was real because God gave me guidance, peace, and comfort. And, or course, I want to go to heaven."

In our lives now, we are burdened by the world's many wars, natural disasters, enticements, and seductions. We sometimes grow tired and discouraged in our faith. But scripture affirms, heaven is a reality. The shroud of our humanity will one day be lifted. We will know God and the things of God with clearer understanding. A feast unequaled by anything here on earth will be served to all. And we will declare with joy, "Surely this is our God." We trusted in God. We have been saved.

I need a lot of encouragement in life, especially in matters of faith. I need the images the scriptures give me—a feast of rich food, tears wiped dry, death swallowed up. These visions, these reassurances, carry me through good days and bad days alike. They strengthen my faith and give me hope.

God of hope, give us strength to persevere the tribulations of this world that we may enjoy the feast and glory of our eternal home with you. In Jesus' name. Amen.

Selah. This word appears over and over again in the Psalms. It is a difficult word to translate, but some say it means "stop and listen" or "pause and think about that." Stop and reflect on God, on God's wonderful creation—the moon, the stars, the sun. Stop and think—who can stand in God's holy place? Stop and think—how does one get clean hands and a pure heart?

The book of Psalms is in essence the music collection of the Bible. Psalm 24 is a song celebrating God's victory over sin and death. It praises God's strength and might. It revels in naming God the "King of glory."

This psalm is often understood as the song of worship written to commemorate and celebrate David's returning the ark of the covenant, the ark of God's presence, to the royal city of Jerusalem. The whole congregation would have sung as they processed with great exuberance into the Temple. For the Israelites, there was no greater pleasure than worshiping God in the Temple. When the psalmist declares, "The earth is the LORD's," he affirms that God is the great creator; but he also reminds the people that their first allegiance is to God and to God alone. Stop and think: this means they can have no other gods, no other loyalties in their lives.

By calling God strong and mighty, the psalmist tells people the good news: God has created a safe place in which we can live. This means God gives consolation when we face death. It also means that God gives us courage to live faithfully in the face of evil.

Surely these are great gifts—gifts precious enough that we join in Israel's hymns of praise and thanksgiving.

Heavenly God, we pause and think about the love you have given us—in creation, in times and places to worship, and in the life and death of Jesus Christ. Keep our hearts pure, focused only on you. Amen.

In her book *On Death and Dying*, Elisabeth Kübler-Ross established a model for understanding grieving. Her studies identified five stages of the grieving process: denial and isolation, anger, bargaining, depression, and acceptance. Since the publication of her findings in 1969, other professionals have determined that one does not necessarily progress through the stages in a linear manner. One might skip from denial to depression and then to anger. There is no set sequence nor is it set that we have to go through each and every stage. Even the length of time that someone stays in a particular stage of grief can vary.

Death is very much a part of life, and we become especially aware of this as we age. No matter how strong our faith or how close we walk with Lord, death will finally come to someone we love. I know that, like Mary in her grief, I challenge God with questions not from a lack of faith but from the depths of grief.

Jesus taught, "I am the resurrection and the life." As kingdom people we believe that. But never are our beliefs, faith, and hope so greatly tested as when a loved one dies. Hardships and tribulations may shake us, but death tests the very foundation of our faith.

Mary, like Martha, and even some cynics in the crowd, believed Jesus could heal their sick brother. But as extraordinary as the raising of Lazarus is, Jesus knows the miracle points to an even greater revelation. Jesus will die on the cross and, by raising him from the dead, God conquers death for all of us.

God of hope and eternal life, you are acquainted with sorrow. Meet us now in our time of grieving. Strengthen our faith in Jesus, the resurrection and the life. Help us celebrate the lives of the saints, sure that we will someday join them. Amen.

Ve believe. Help our unbelief. The words seem odd and contradictory—belief and unbelief, held at one and the same
time. They are contradictory, but they are also true. Our believing
seems to have limits. It's hard for us as finite beings to fathom an
infinite God, even when we see evidence of God's work in our lives.

Martha might have responded the way she did out of the same
belief and unbelief. When Jesus asks for the stone to be rolled away,
Martha's first thought was to warn him, "Lord, already there is a
stench because he has been dead for four days." But the stone was
rolled away, and Lazarus was raised from the dead. It's almost as
though, metaphorically, the tombstone of doubt separated Jesus
from his task of raising Lazarus.

Twice in these last few verses of the Lazarus account, Jesus
admonishes Martha and those around her to believe. Jesus seems to
be asking them to believe beyond what they have heard or seen.
Roll the stone of doubt away, and let the glory of God do its work.

Many had seen Jesus' miracles, but still they found it hard to
believe. Yet Jesus' miracles always pointed to an even greater truth
and not everyone understood. Even the disciples who had been told
by Jesus of his upcoming death and resurrection—even these, who
had traveled so much with him—did not understand that the
raising of Lazarus foreshadowed Jesus' own resurrection.

Our faith will change and grow. The more we study and pray,
the more we seek understanding, the more our faith will grow. The
more time we spend with God and with the community of faith, the
deeper our spiritual life will become. We make our decision to
follow Jesus not once but over and over again.

*All-powerful God, open my eyes and my heart to your miracles
all around me. I want to believe. I want to see your glory. Amen.*

In some traditions, the groom isn't allowed to see the bride on the wedding day until the wedding service begins. She's sequestered away, adorning herself for that moment when the music plays to summon her to the altar to be joined with her betrothed.

I sat in the audience of a wedding recently, waiting and watching as the time drew near. The father of the bride paced with restless anticipation. Finally the groom and his entourage positioned themselves before the altar, confident and proud. And then there was a hush as the music changed and the wedding march began. The church doors opened and the bride stood radiant, ready to walk down the aisle. We, the invited guests and friends, stood in unison. Tears of joy began to flow because the moment had finally arrived when these two would be joined in marriage.

Today's scripture says it will be this way when Christ returns to take us to our heavenly home. Great love exists between Christ and the church. Preparations for leaving the old and starting a new life are made; vows are affirmed and celebration follows.

Heaven's new earth and the holy city, the new Jerusalem, are radiant and beautiful in the eyes of believers. God's love persists until that long-anticipated moment comes—the moment when we are freed from death, fear, and pain. Every tear God wipes away adds to the joyful celebration. This is the prophetic gospel of Jesus Christ. It is an astounding vision. And it is a vision that comforts and surrounds us as we wait for it. God is indeed making all things new.

Dear God, our eternity has already begun. May we be one with Christ and joined with you forever as we wait and anticipate the new Jerusalem. In Jesus' name, we pray. Amen.

ALL SAINTS' DAY

To watch with hope for the heavenly kingdom is a holy thing. This kind of hope is not hope based on wishful thinking. It is hope based on faith and on the word of God, from Genesis to Revelation. Hope is both strong and intangible. It is fragile, yet sturdy.

Isaiah 25 carries a message of hope to a remnant of the faithful: "This is the LORD for whom we have waited; let us be glad and rejoice." The writer of Revelation tells of the hope that comes from understanding, that leads us to a time of decision, whether to believe Jesus and go on to see God's divine glory or to turn our backs on Jesus and be overcome by death.

Revelation offers hope in the beautiful language that describes our future home with God—a place where death, mourning, crying, and pain "will be no more." Psalm 24 sings of hope for the blessing we will receive from the Lord, our strong and mighty King of glory.

Surrounded by so many biblical witnesses, we remember too the witness of many, many others. On All Saints' Day we name and remember the saints who have gone before us. We name and remember those we love who have died and who now rest in God. We name and remember with thanksgiving the strong witness of their lives. And we live in hope for the time we will see them again.

Hope—for the heavenly kingdom. Hope—for our times of decision. Hope—for the time when death will be no more. Hope—for the blessing from our strong and mighty King of glory. This is the hope that nurtures us, sustains us, saves us. Thanks be to God for the gift of hope.

Creator God, I give you thanks for the hope you have put in my heart. Let my life honor you with faithfulness, honor, and obedience. Let me, with all those who have gone before me, rest secure in the hope that ushers me into your arms. Amen.

Unforgettable Themes

NOVEMBER 2–8, 2009 • CHRIS THRON

MONDAY, NOVEMBER 2 ~ *Read Hebrews 9:24-28*

Beethoven's Fifth Symphony opens with the dramatic theme: Da-da-da-*dumm*. These four notes are famous around the world. Millions of people from hundreds of nations recognize them immediately. However, it is not as widely known that this simple four-note theme runs throughout the entire first movement of the symphony. It appears and reappears, until the closing notes.

All of creation is God's symphony, and the Bible is the score from which we read and interpret God's music. In the Bible, one of the great, memorable themes is God's *redemption.*

God's most dramatic statement of redemption comes in the sacrifice of Jesus Christ. In today's passage the melody of redemption is heard in heaven as well as on earth. Just as the high priests of Israel made sacrifices and entered the Holy of Holies in the Temple, so Jesus entered into heaven and into the presence of God to realize our redemption from sin. This salvation means that we can eagerly await Christ's second coming, confident of his presence with us now and at the end of time.

We are musicians in the mighty orchestra of God's eternal symphony of redemption. Let us sing praises to God.

Reflect on these words from a hymn by Fanny Crosby:

I think of my blessed Redeemer, I think of Him all the
day long;
I sing, for I cannot be silent; His love is the theme of my song.

High school teacher, former professor and engineer of communications, member of Bridge-point Fellowship house church in Austin, Texas

Today's passage has a tragic background. Naomi has returned to Israel after losing both her husband and her two sons. One son's widow, faithful Ruth, has left her native country to remain with Naomi. The two penniless widows have found a potential benefactor—Boaz, a relative of Naomi's dead husband. So Naomi instructs Ruth to appeal to Boaz for permanent protection.

Naomi's situation parallels that of the Jewish nation following its destruction by King Nebuchadnezzar of Babylon. After years of exile, the Jews later returned to their homeland broken and destitute. For the next five hundred years they remained for the most part an impoverished and oppressed people, longing for God to redeem them from their bondage. Redemption finally came to Israel through Jesus, the son of Mary—Ruth's direct descendant!

Indeed, parallels exist between Naomi's instructions to Ruth and Jesus' redemptive actions on Israel's behalf (and our behalf as well). Just as Ruth washed herself, so Jesus was baptized by John to fulfill all righteousness. Ruth anointed herself with oil, while Jesus was anointed with the Holy Spirit. Ruth waited at the threshing floor for the meal to finish—while Jesus himself was beaten and his own body became our spiritual meal.

But there's more to the story. Echoes of redemption may *still* be heard in Christ's living disciples. Through Christ we too appeal to God, just as Ruth appealed to Boaz. We have partaken of Christ's broken body and blood; through him we wait in God's presence, confident of God's favorable response to our prayers.

Thank you, God, for the redemption you have lavished on me. Amen.

Ruth's gesture of uncovering Boaz' feet seems strange to us. But to Boaz the meaning was clear: Ruth was seeking a place at his feet, a place in his life, protection, and marriage. And Boaz, though startled at first by her appearance as his side in the middle of the night, responded by making her his wife!

Biblical scholars have written much on the meaning of Ruth's uncovering Boaz's "feet." The Hebrew word often refers to a man's lower body, and this may well be the meaning here. Yet, as with the English word "sleep," the Hebrew "lie down" later in this passage can be used to connote innocence or to imply a sexual relationship.

Given Ruth's need for protection, seeing Boaz's feet as a place of protection make sense. Ruth comes to Boaz seeking rest, provision, and protection.

Just when it seems most hopeless for Naomi and Ruth, God provides for their redemption. With the marriage of Boaz and Ruth, Obed is born—a son to provide protection for Ruth, and also for Naomi in her old age. Obed will do all this and more. Obed will become the grandfather of David, and David will become the king who leads Israel in the ways of faithfulness and justice.

God is able to do all this through the faithfulness and courage of a woman (and a foreigner, at that) whose loyalty to her mother-in-law leads her into a strange land among people to whom she is a stranger. In ways we could not have fathomed, God has moved God's people one more step along the path of redemption. Once again, God works in unexpected ways, through unexpected people, at unexpected times.

God, lead me to trust you and to give thanks for your protection. Amen.

Boaz was Naomi's *redeemer*—he was also her *restorer*. Not only did Boaz release Naomi from penury—he also restored to her all that she had lost: family, honor, and an inheritance in Israel.

God's restoration is the grand theme repeated throughout the Bible. Job's wealth and family were restored to him after his period of testing. The Lord promised restoration to the plague-stricken Israelites. Isaiah called the Messiah the repairer and the restorer. So Christ restores us when we entrust ourselves into his hands.

The Oriental game of *Go* (which is similar to the popular board game *Othello*) serves as an intriguing illustration of God's restoration. The game is played with black and white stones on a board somewhat larger than a chessboard. Two players take turns laying down stones, each attempting to capture the other's stones by surrounding them with his or her own. The game is extremely intricate: one player may scheme to encircle a region, only to discover that his or her own circle has been taken by the other.

God and evil are engaged in a *Go* match of cosmic proportions. Evil continually attempts to encircle us and take us captive. At times it appears evil is successful—but the Lord prevails! In the end, God restores us. God is the master of our lives.

Sing in your heart these words from Martin Luther's hymn "A Mighty Fortress Is Our God":

A mighty fortress is our God, a bulwark never failing; our helper he amid the flood of mortal ills prevailing.

Naomi's name means "pleasant." But during her period of bereavement after the death of her husband and two sons, Naomi called herself *Mara*, meaning "bitter." But what if Naomi had known beforehand that her suffering would end? What if she had known she would regain a family through her adopted daughter, whose descendant would save the entire world?

As we walk through life we too encounter loss and disappointment. There is indeed a time for mourning, but never a time for despair. Weeping is not shameful, for Jesus himself wept. But in Christ, hope always tempers sorrow.

Indeed, the deepest of sorrows often engenders the greatest of triumphs. George Frideric Handel's *Messiah* is an enduring musical masterpiece, one that has remained popular for over two hundred years. At one early performance, the King of England was so awed by the *Hallelujah Chorus* which closes the piece that he felt compelled to stand, starting a tradition that continues until this day.

But *Messiah* was conceived in the throes of misery. Four years earlier, Handel had endured a stroke. He suffered bouts of rheumatism, insomnia, and deep depression. His creativity faltered. Then in August, 1741, he began to work on a new score, writing it in a twenty-four-day creative frenzy. The piece was not performed until almost a year after it was finished. Yet this work, which was almost stillborn, would leave a glorious legacy in the world of music and in the realm of faith! Surely God does redeem us and recover us for salvation.

God, fill me with music this day in thanksgiving for your redemption. Amen.

"Workers of the world unite, you have nothing to lose but your chains." That's the popular paraphrase of Karl Marx, writing in *The Communist Manifesto*. He believed that a worldwide revolution would free all workers from their vain drudgery.

Work is a gift from God, but since the time of Adam and Eve, we have often found work to be a curse. The psalm, a series of wise sayings based on long years of experience, gets to the heart of why we often feel cursed instead of blessed by work. If the Lord builds the house, that work is blessed. But if we try to build on our own—without God—we build in vain; our work is futile and doomed for self-destruction. Human work is only feverish activity if God is not at the center of it.

Galatians says that Christ has redeemed us from the curse of futile work. If we abide in Christ, then our labor is never fruitless (John 15:5). In Christ we receive the freedom that the world can never deliver.

Why then do so many Christians still eat "the bread of anxious toil?" Why are we frustrated and bored by our work? Why are we caught in a mouse wheel, running as fast as we can and going nowhere? Could it be that we are building our own houses our own way, and not the Lord's way?

This is the message from the psalmist: when we are devoted to God's purposes, when we work within God's covenant, our work is good and peaceful and blessed.

Loving God, let my work this day reflect your goodness. Amen.

W e have reflected often this week on redemption. We are the Lord's redeemed; we are God's possession. If we are to walk as Christ did, we must examine our relationship to the possessions in our lives.

Of all our possessions, money is one we most often abuse. Every day in the news we see robbery, fraud, bribery, blackmail, embezzlement, and a host of other money-related crimes. This story, which comes at the very end of Jesus' public ministry, condemns the abuse of money and the abuse of power in striking terms.

Jesus condemns the scribes and their pretentious practices at worship. He points out the unholy contradiction between the scribes' religious practices and their social actions. These scribes are the very ones whose lifestyle oppresses widows like the one Jesus notices at the Temple.

The woman in today's passage, Jesus says, gave wholeheartedly of herself. Her self-giving included money, but it also transcended money.

The woman's gift was exceptional, not because of the amount she gave but because of the heart with which she gave it. Her two small copper coins were, in earthly terms, far outweighed by the donations of wealthier donors, yet Jesus honored her.

Jesus is the redeemer of all things—including money. May we give generously—of our money, certainly, but also of our hearts.

God, I long to give wholeheartedly of myself—my time, my money, my loyalty, and my love. Amen.

Perseverance by the Grace of God

NOVEMBER 9–15, 2009 • HEATHER MORRIS

MONDAY, NOVEMBER 9 ~ *Read Psalm 16*

Heartbreaking, tragic events do happen to those who belong to God. Children die when they are still young. Mothers die on battlefields in war thousands of miles from home. Fathers are taken from their families in plane crashes. Friends fall ill—very ill.

"Protect me, O God," cries the psalmist. The prayer is obviously heartfelt, spoken in circumstances that are dire and threatening. Amidst all our suffering, what does this prayer mean? Let's look at what the psalmist is asking for when he prays for protection.

Scripture has a number of meanings for the word we translate as *protect*. One of these describes the protection of armies who surround a city to keep enemies from doing harm. Here, to protect refers to someone or something that stops bad things happening. But there is another sense in which *protect* is used. It means "to keep close at hand" or "to watch over." Jesus uses the word this way in John 17:11 when he asks God to protect the disciples. Psalm 91 also uses this meaning when it describes God as a shelter for the people.

"Protect me, O God." This is a prayer of trust, a prayer confident in the belief that no matter what happens, God will stay close by.

Our lives are filled with twists and turns. Sometimes disaster does strike. People we love do die. Hearts are broken. Faith is stretched to the breaking point. We face these challenges and more. But we do not face these challenges alone. God protects us. God keeps us close.

Meditate on these words from Psalm 16: "My heart is glad, and my soul rejoices . . . in your presence there is fullness of joy."

Methodist minister and director of ministry (with particular interest in practical care and pastoral theology) at Edgehill Theological College in Belfast, Northern Ireland

My brother ran a marathon last summer, and I cycled some of it beside him. The seventeenth mile was awful. His feet were blistered; his toes ached. At the beginning he had been smiling and chatting. Now the very best he could do was keep going. At one point I tried to encourage him by saying, "Only nine miles to go!" He just looked at me. He knew that the finish line was ahead, but for him it seemed very far away; there were many miles to be traveled before he reached it.

We are deliberately pausing at about the seventeenth mile with Hannah. Read ahead into First Samuel. Before long we discover that she has the child she longs for, but where we pause today she doesn't know. All she knows as she cries out to God in the house of the LORD at Shiloh is that she is heartbroken and that she has been heartbroken for many, many years.

On one level Hannah has much for which to be thankful: she has a home and a husband who loves her. She knows the Lord. But for years Hannah has lived with heartache. She longs for a child but does not conceive, and the situation is made worse by her husband's other wife Peninnah, who taunts her. Year after year, Hannah's suffering continues.

Hannah weeps. And at her seventeenth mile Hannah does all that she can do; she brings her pain and hurt and questions to God.

Allow yourself to pause and remember the presence of God. Abide in the truth that nothing can separate us from the love of God. Let God sustain you. Who encourages you at your seventeenth mile? In what ways might God want you to encourage or stand with a friend or neighbor today who is living with heartache?

There is an old custom in the Methodist Church in Ireland that when ordained ministers reach retirement, they ask permission from the conference not to retire but "to sit down." Their work and travel is now complete, and they can sit.

In these verses the writer of Hebrews contrasts the work of the priests of the old covenant with the work of Christ. Within the old covenant the task of the priest was always unfinished; sacrifices for sin had to be offered day after day after day. With Jesus that dailiness changes. Sin is conquered. Having offered himself "for all time a single sacrifice for sins," Jesus' work is complete. Because of Jesus' offering, sin does not have the final word in our lives or in the world. Having lived for us and died for us, Jesus now sits down at the right hand of God.

So the challenge for today becomes clear. Where in our lives does sin have us in its grip?

When I was eleven, my school took a summer day trip to a seaside town. My parents gave me money for the day, and I spent it all on slot machines. I lied when I got home; I was ashamed that I had wasted the money and gambled. All summer I felt guilty. All summer my relationship with my parents was strained. At last one night I told them. It's a long time now since I was eleven, but I still remember the relief I felt when they forgave me.

God has made it possible for sin to be forgiven. Moreover, God promises to remember our sins no more. We are forgiven and freed for service.

Take time to confess your sin to God. Thank God for the work of Jesus that is complete. Allow yourself to know and feel God forgiving you and releasing you for service.

I think I know much of what there is to know about dieting. I have read many, many diet books; I have accessed diets on the Internet, I have talked to my friends about the latest diet crazes. But that knowledge in itself doesn't make any difference to my waistline. For the diet to work, I must follow the eating plan. I must actually *do* the diet.

Hebrews does a masterful job of helping us to understand the faith. But then the writer shifts gears with the words, "Therefore, my friends. . . . " From this point, on the writer encourages readers to put what they have just read and heard into practice. We have just been reminded that Jesus has dealt finally with sin. *Therefore*, Hebrews says, we can approach God in worship with confidence. Jesus is faithful and trustworthy; *therefore*, we can be confident that we will be sustained as we persevere in faith and in witness. Earlier, in Hebrews 3:1, we were reminded that we are "brothers and sisters, holy partners in a heavenly calling." Now we are to live out that truth in the world daily.

It is vitally important to love God with our minds. And it is vitally important to consider the *therefores*, to think about the ways in which our understanding influences the lives we live. And we must be assured that the Holy Spirit will nudge us when we allow ourselves to slip into thinking that understanding our faith is enough. So with a full assurance of faith, we can hold fast to our confession of hope, encourage one another, and entice others into the faith by our love and good works.

Faithful, guiding God, place in my heart today the desire to live my faith with a passion for integrity. Make my understanding and my deeds match. And let me rest in you when day is done. Amen.

One summer I visited Rome with my younger son. We went to St Peter's in the Vatican. Even David, who was then only eight years old and not usually impressed by buildings, was awestruck with the beauty of that church. We climbed up to the dome, then on narrow stairs to the very top and onto a narrow balcony. From this height we were able to look out over the cathedral and its grounds and farther across the sprawling city.

The temple in Jerusalem at the time of Jesus was a beautiful building. It must have seemed to the disciples the pinnacle of human achievement. It was stable, secure, and beautiful. "Look," the disciples say to Jesus in admiration, "what large stones and what large buildings." Jesus' reply shocked them, "Not one stone will be left here upon another; all will be thrown down."

These words confused his disciples. Four of the disciples ask Jesus the question we might have asked too: "When will this happen?" But Jesus doesn't answer that question because it is the wrong one. Jesus doesn't want them to be concerned about dates and times. He wants them to know how to live in the light of this prophecy.

So he teaches them about watchfulness, perseverance, and the hardships ahead. The destruction of the Temple and the coming challenges for the disciples point to the start of a new kingdom. The disciples, and we, are directed away from questions about when this will happen and redirected to the significant questions: How is the way we live today changed by the fact that this world is the place of our witness but not our final home? How does that truth affect our priorities and relationships? How do we persevere in our faith?

> *Until you come, Lord Jesus, keep us alert to your voice, to your presence, and to the grace that enables us to live lives that speak of your kingdom. Amen.*

The clouds of opposition are gathering in Mark's account of Jesus' life. What had begun as whispering on the edges of the crowd becomes a concerted campaign against Jesus. The cross looms ahead of him.

The first-century Christians who read and heard Mark's Gospel would have identified with that sense of gathering gloom. They faced significant challenges. They were working out what it meant to be a follower of Jesus, what it meant to be a church. The clouds of suffering were gathering for them too. They faced the challenge of remaining faithful to Jesus in every circumstance of a very difficult time.

That is the context into which these verses are written. In response, unreservedly and without apology, Mark brings them—and us—face-to-face with a Messiah who was not saved from suffering; one who faced opposition, trial, and the cross.

As Jesus speaks of wars and rumors of wars, of earthquakes and famine, the challenge is clear. Will believers stay faithful no matter what? It's a crucial question, and one that Jesus even asked of himself. The truth is that amid the scourging and whipping, even on the cross itself, Jesus, their Master, Lord, brother, and friend would remain faithful to them.

Do we have what it takes to be faithful to Jesus? Mark says we must have a discerning spirit so false prophets won't fool us. We must be patient; time and God's kingdom are in God's hands. And we must be hopeful, even in suffering, because suffering does not lead to despair but to hope. All this is given to us. We must only be faithful and persevere.

Thank you, Lord Jesus, for your faithfulness to us. This day may I know the strength to be faithful to you. I pray for strength and encouragement for those who today will suffer for their faith. Amen.

I find myself discomforted by this Bible passage. I believe that God is at work in the world in many different ways and in far more ways, places, and people than we recognize. I believe that God is a God of miracles, who longs to bless. I am thankful to God for answers to prayer that far exceed my hopes and expectations. So I rejoice and thank God as I read about Hannah's answered prayer. My heart leaps as I imagine her joy. I am awestruck as I remember that God, creator of heaven and earth, hears the heartache of individuals.

But in that rejoicing discomfort stirs. I think about those who love the Lord, who cry to God, who pour out their souls before the Lord—and whose situation does not change. I think that I know some of the theological "answers." I know that God gives strength in every situation, that God can work good in situations that seem bleak and hopeless. But I am still uncomfortable.

Could it be that God is at work in that discomfort? Is God calling me deeper into faith and trust? Might God be asking me to trust that I am loved and held even in the darkness, even when I cry out in despair? Perhaps the Holy Spirit is drawing me in my discomfort to an understanding of God that is deeper than my mind can grasp.

Can I truly know that God does love me and that nothing can separate me from that love? I pray for the perseverance that Hannah showed. I pray that I might be as tenacious with my petitions to God as she was with hers.

Lord, we rejoice with those who rejoice today. We pray with those who grieve. In the midst of whatever grief may befall, may we all know your abiding presence. Amen.

If Jesus Shall Reign . . .

NOVEMBER 16–22, 2009 • LAURIE HAYS COFFMAN

MONDAY, NOVEMBER 16 ~ *Read 2 Samuel 23:1-7*

If Jesus shall reign, there may be political implications. "We want a king!" the people of Israel clamored. "Give us a king like other nations, to go and fight for us." Samuel countered their request with the reminder that Yahweh was their sovereign God. Still the people prevailed, seeking security in a human ruler. Reluctantly, the prophet anointed Saul, the mighty warrior who had slain many, and later David, who had slain many more, to rule as king over Israel.

I come from a nation that prides itself in having thrown off the tyranny of a distant king in England and declared ourselves "free." Celebrating freedom is good and worthy, but too much patriotic fervor can taint our religious understanding, tempting us away from God and toward Christian triumphalism. We can be led to distrust God's authority. We forget our dependence on royal mercy.

So it is interesting that we Christians celebrate the Reign of Christ this Sunday. Pope Pius XI declared this a feast day in 1925. The world was facing the fanaticism of dictators and a rising secularism that disregarded Christ's authority. It was obvious that only a just and merciful "king of all kings" could save the world from mutual destruction. And in our own violent, chaotic world, it is also plain. We need one whose kingdom is not of this world—someone like Jesus!

God, thank you for the faith of King David. Help us remember that you alone hold power. When you entrust power to us, help us, like David, to trust in you alone. Amen.

Pastor of Calvary United Methodist Church, a reconciling congregation in Durham, North Carolina

If Jesus shall reign, there could be tribal implications. "Are you the King of the Jews?" asked Pilate. The Roman governor had come to Jerusalem to help keep order at Passover. Now he wanted to know why the locals wanted this man dead. Among themselves, religious leaders considered Jesus a threat and accused him of blasphemy. "You," they said to Jesus, "though only a human being, are making yourself God" (John 10:33). But they knew that such an accusation would not force the hand of a Roman ruler, so they charged him with treason against the state. "We have no king but Caesar." That threat caught the governor's attention. "So you are a king?" Pilate asked.

Never one to be awed by pomp and power, the accused Jesus cross-examined his judge. "Do you ask this on your own, or did others tell you about me?" Pilate stumbled, hardly knowing how to handle this jousting for truth. Caesar's appointee could not find in Jesus a fault worthy of capital punishment, but neither could he find within himself the strength to stand against a hostile crowd. Read John's Gospel to marvel at the irony of establishing true authority and kingship!

"My kingdom is not from this world," Jesus tells him. If it were, his followers would be fighting for his release. Jesus had already chastised his ardent follower Peter for presuming to protect him by taking a sword to Malchus, slave of the high priest (John 18:10-11).

No, the way to victory in this one's royal reign would not be through war and violence. The Prince of Peace trains his troops on a higher ground. If we would follow this king, we must put away the sword and actively imagine and work toward a world without war.

King of Love, you fell the mighty with a word. Help me to find your truth and authority within my own soul and learn the ways that make for peace. Amen.

If Jesus shall reign, there will be cosmic implications. Old King David believed that a kingdom was no better than its king. This is reflected in his last will and testament. The shepherd of Israel had been raised up, exalted by God from humble beginnings, and anointed by Samuel for this work. Through his gift for music and poetry, David often remembered and celebrated his calling, praising God as the source of all power and mercy. Any vocation we have to lead and serve God's people must, like David's call, continually be grounded in the Strong One who summons us.

The impact of a leader's just and faithful service has cosmic as well as communal dimensions. Done well, leadership is like sunshine that breaks through the dark of night, gleaming through the rain. Done poorly, and exercised neglectful of God's covenant, leadership can be thorny, uprooted, subject to being consumed by fire. Whatever our legacy—faithful leadership or leadership that trusts only in its own power—that legacy lives on in our "house" beyond this life. David's tentative language reveals his humility before God, no doubt recalling his troubled family, his tarnished record, his litany of sins. Although David is clear about God's call and covenant, although David strives to be faithful to God, still he bears his human failures.

The long-awaited Son who would sit on David's throne is exalted in Revelation as the faithful witness, incarnated as a human martyr. He is the firstborn of the dead, resurrected as the morning light. He is the ruler of the kings of the earth, returning to serve forever. His leadership alone fulfills the bright expectations that David and we can only aspire to fulfill.

O merciful God, I realize that my whole realm of influence is no better than my own faithfulness to you. Thank you for your everlasting faithfulness to me. I bow before your glory and dominion. Amen.

If Jesus shall reign, there will be communal implications. Kingship costs. Jesus lost his followers to fear and gave his crown for a cross. When we subjects of King Jesus live boldly into our baptism, stepping forward to advocate for God's dream of justice and peace, we also run the risk of being cast out of the community we love.

The writer of Revelation knew the agony of being an outcast. Banished by the Roman emperor to an island in the Aegean Sea, his only consolation came from the resurrected One, "the ruler of the kings of the earth . . . who loves us and freed us from our sins . . . and made us to be a kingdom [of] priests serving his God."

Christ made *us* to be a kingdom! Herein lies Christ's authority. We did not get together and elect him to be our ruler. (If we had, we could also impeach him!) Rather, God gave him heaven's realm, and Jesus gathered *us* to serve in *his* royal domain. By his edict, we are all priests, set apart to pray and sacrifice for others.

As I write, our world is embroiled in military campaigns to determine who will rule resources and peoples. America has engaged in election campaigns and chosen who will be the decider of our communal fate. And the church is beset with competing campaigns for the future direction and scope of our church. Humans want to believe that might and majority rule. But no campaign can put Jesus Christ on the throne. That was done by the One "who is and who was and who is to come."

Christ my King, what an honor to be called a priest in your campaign for the world! Clothe me with righteousness and I will shout for joy. Let me stand with you on the margins where many get lost, so all may be found. Amen.

If Jesus shall reign, there will be personal implications. Jesus was clear about his purpose: announcing the good news of the kingdom of God (Luke 4:43). He was first of all a servant, a representative of God's vast domain. In preaching, he was pointing us to the realm where God's truth rules. In healing, he was demonstrating the Sovereign's compassion. In feeding thousands, he was sharing the benevolent abundance intended for all under the Shepherd's watchful care. And when he was hanging on the tree of shame—still offering forgiveness and a faithful witness—he was exemplifying his persistent trust in God's dream.

"For this I was born and for this I came into the world," Jesus told Pilate, "to testify to the truth." *If only we could all be so clear about the reason for our existence!* But we who see ourselves as having been made into a kingdom for God's sake *do* have some clue as to our purpose. Priests in Christ's kingdom pray. As we become increasingly convinced that Jesus "loves us and freed us from our sins," we too serve as advocates of truth.

Kingdom work is not always glorious. It may lead to suffering. When the prestigious Central Methodist Church in downtown Johannesburg felt a call to confront the injustice of apartheid, many members, unsettled by the demands of such active discipleship, left the church to find ease in the status quo. Others glimpsed a new truth and became truth advocates who changed the world! Faithful, courageous, nonviolent actions of a few "priests" can bring down the corrupt kingdoms of this world. They illumine the in breaking realm of God's justice for all.

King Jesus, I want to walk with you. Wherever your summons takes me, help me respond as faithfully as you did. It is your kingdom, your power, and your glory that will last forever. I'm in! Amen.

I f Christ shall reign, there will be implications for us and our faith community. "Thy kingdom come," we pray. But encountering the heavenly realm in my earthly existence often eludes me. I expect something sensational and find only the ordinary: a common kindness, a purple sky, a puppy's warmth. Wonderful gifts, to be sure, but they remain the stuff of this world.

The dream of God is already here, but it is not yet fully known. Already and always God keeps covenant with us, wooing us homeward and redeeming whatever we have squandered. When I forget this, I grow anxious, hurrying to make it all happen right! When I recall God's faithfulness, I rest in hope.

The realm of God is everywhere, though, to paraphrase Elizabeth Barrett Browning, only those who see take off their shoes. When I keep Sabbath time to still my soul and wait for God, I see.

The reach of God is unfathomed, but sometimes I witness it in wonder. Chris, one of our regular visitors, stood to share his faith: "I've heard for years that God hates people like me. But since coming into this church, I've come to believe . . . " He gulped and reached for his partner's hand. "I now believe God loves me!"

The rule of God is merciful and mighty. It can sweep a woman out of a career and into a vocation. It can require the impossible and then provide what it has required.

The reign of God is palpable. Its victory is made known in the breaking of the bread. I taste wine I did not make and see that forgiveness is good. Lovingkindness reaches across the table. And across the tracks. And over the wall.

The kin-dom (kingdom) of God really *is* in the midst of us. By the grace of Christ, we are it.

I breathe deeply, O God, your spirit of reconciliation. You are making all things new! Ride on, King Jesus. You rule! Amen.

If Christ shall reign, there will be spiritual and social implications. We must be careful when we use "kingdom of God" as a metaphor, for it redefines both kingdom and God. If God is like a king, we imagine an enthroned authority, not the carpenter who sits with sinners. We see a rich and distant ruler, not a friend who sticks closer than a brother or a sister. We know an exalted commander, not a lord who calls his servants friend. We find a demanding collector of tribute, not the suffering servant who pays our way.

Equally dangerous in this image is the sovereignty handed over to earthly kings. The metaphor likens God to rulers, yet we act as though rulers are *like God.* We confess that sometimes we have blindly followed our leaders—even when it led to violence at lunch counters or mass death in gas chambers.

Bishop Peter Storey of South Africa warns us to render to Caesar *only* what is Caesar's and give God what is God's. "It's little wonder that the world pays the church so little attention. *Christians have taken God's house and wrapped it in Caesar's flag. What we ought to do is march to Caesar's house and demand of it God's justice!"*

On this last Sunday of the Christian year, looking to the culmination of all things, we call Christ the King. Yet when the governor of Judea pushed him—"So you are a king?"—Jesus did not rush to claim the title. Instead, he pointed to his kingdom— he pointed to *us*! We the people, his faithful followers, we priests serving God are his real claim to royalty. If Christ is to be king, then his reach and realm will be found in the midst of us.

O Ruler of all, you have made us your dwelling place. Abide with us as our God and our salvation. Amen.

An Honest Faith

NOVEMBER 23–29, 2009 • ENUMA OKORO

MONDAY, NOVEMBER 23 ~ *Read Jeremiah 33:14-16*

These words of promise from Jeremiah come even as God acknowledges Israel's unfaithfulness. Israel has failed to love God with all its heart, mind, and soul. The Israelites have followed false gods and forgotten their identity as children of the God of Abraham and Sarah. Their condition is so bad that the rumor on the street is that God has abandoned Judah and Jerusalem (Jer. 33:24). The Jews are ruled by an unrighteous King Zedekiah, have suffered at the hands of foreign invaders, and persist in their daily disobedience to God's holy standards.

Yet the word of the Lord assures them that God does not abandon them or fail to keep God's promises. God heals and replenishes, forgives and restores, and astounds them with gracious abundance. In the place where unrighteousness has reigned, God will bring righteous authority. In a community governed by injustice, God will bring justice.

But these are promises yet to be fulfilled. God's people have to deal with the reality of their present bondage and disobedience. They have to find courage and faith to hope in God's word, to live into God's forgiveness, and to mold themselves into a community that will not squander what God has given them.

Jeremiah's prophetic words are a message of hope, but they are also a renewed call to accountability. God's righteousness determines our identity. It shapes where justice is done, where promises are kept, and where all seek to live into the character of God.

Lord, your promises give us hope. Help us to imagine a home where justice, righteousness, and security are sought by all people, for all people. Show us how to work for these things. Amen.

Former director for the Center of Theological Writing at Duke University Divinity School; freelance writer and retreat leader; living in Durham, North Carolina

Many think our relationship with God should always be happy and bubbly, but God created us as more complex beings than that. Everything God gives us is gift, and gratitude is our foundation for receiving God's gifts. One thing is certain about our experience as human beings: life includes times of sorrow and personal challenge. Throughout history people have needed reminders of God's faithfulness as they waited for answers and for deliverance. The Psalms are a sobering reflection of our human relationship with God. They remind us that God expects and deserves our honesty. King David surely knew humility before God. Regardless of the things he accomplished in his life and the challenges that came his way, he understood that God's faithfulness did not depend on human faithfulness; this is significant, because we are never as faithful to God or to one another as God is to us.

But even a person like David, chiefly remembered as a devout man fully aware of God's unchanging love, experienced times when he needed to cry out to God in pleading frustration. As this psalm reveals, our times of waiting and uncertainty, and even our frustrations and pleas, can be peppered with remembering that God is good. An honest and growing relationship with the One whose promises never fail also includes our acknowledging that God can handle our pains and our emotions. In the incarnation, God made our pains and emotions the flesh and bone of God's own self. We serve a God who is able to deliver us from all things, even from ourselves.

Faithful God, help us not to cheapen your mercy and grace by withholding our true emotions and struggles from our prayer life. We know that you long to know us intimately and completely. We pray that we may long to know you the same way. Amen.

Paul was writing to a church that knew about sacrifice and temptation. The early church of Thessalonica had set itself apart from the rest of the society to live by gospel standards. Their devotion led to conflict and persecution, which, as Paul says, should never be a surprise to those who choose to follow Christ.

This is a letter of encouragement, urging the Thessalonians to be strong in their faith, to uphold one another with love, and to keep the lifestyle and values they have chosen in Christ. These early Christians faced temptations to return to the "old" way of life. Paul had to remind them that God is faithful and can help them cultivate spiritual practices that produce the fruit of the Spirit, such as love and self-control.

It helps me to know what these early Christians struggled with and how the values of their larger society added to their struggle to be faithful. I think most of us can relate to the feeling of walking between the worlds of faith and culture. My particular struggles revolve around how not to give in to the consumerism that pervades my culture and tells me that having more stuff leads to happiness or that emulating celebrities will make me happy.

Regardless of where we live, we share this one reality as Christians: the coming of Christ doesn't bring immediate peace. It brings conflict between two ways of life. And despite the particular struggles or temptations we face in our different cultures and societies around the world, the message of Christ is the same. We must love one another and encourage one another. We must imitate Christ and cultivate holy disciplines that witness to the kingdom of God and the Messiah whose return we await.

Christ, our Savior, as we wait for your return, help us live as people who recognize your kingdom. May our practices and habits witness to our true citizenship and allegiance. Amen.

Saying thank you is a common practice for most of us, sometimes so much a habit that the routine diminishes the depth of sincerity. Yet the life circumstances of some among us make them deeply aware of giving thanks. The Jews of today's texts were such a people. They knew about widespread famine, natural disasters, and being displaced from their homes. They knew what it was like to have a season of blessing, only then to find themselves in seasons of longing and despair. They knew about prophecies of the end times and the increased suffering that creation would endure.

These folks knew about waiting on God and also about waiting and hoping for their own people to repent and turn to God. And perhaps because they understood life's challenges and human circumstances so well, they also knew how to give thanks in response to God's faithfulness. We can learn much about ourselves and about God from the story of God's turbulent relationship with the Jewish people.

The prayers and prophecies of Joel and the psalmist remind us that God's faithfulness exceeds our imagination and goes far beyond our familiar boundaries. God's faithfulness is deep and wide, and God is moved by our obedience and our genuine attempts to be faithful. These verses remind us that we are in a relationship with a God who has chosen to be in a relationship with us. Our responses to God matter.

In the time of Advent that begins on Sunday, as we look toward our time of waiting for God's promise of the Christ, let us consider how God might also be waiting on us . . . waiting to hear our thanks, waiting to hear our praise, waiting for us to be thankful and faithful people. Let us, on this Thanksgiving Day, raise our voices in praise and our hearts in gratitude to God.

Lord, teach us to say thank you for your continuing presence with us in this world. Amen.

People will faint with fear and nations will be confused. Why such a grim reading when our days just after Thanksgiving are preoccupied with Christmas presents and shopping lists? Why such a grim reading when Advent is only a few days from its start? Luke writes these grim words because Advent is not just about the Christ child. Advent is about the Son of Man returning in clouds of glory bringing redemption, justice, and the fullness of the kingdom of God. This Lukan passage points us to God's faithfulness.

Jesus is calling people to open their eyes and see the world for what it is: falling away without a savior. Instead of losing ourselves in fear and worry, Jesus invites us to see Christ for who Christ is— a faithful Savior who redeems us from ourselves and heals a broken world. This is actually a passage about hope! Some people might say that faith and Christian hope are crutches that keep us from accepting the harsh realities of life, but we know that Jesus doesn't call us to shy away from life's difficulties. He calls us to witness to another reality that exists alongside the reality of this world—the reality of God's faithfulness.

We cannot hope for a better future unless we acknowledge the reality of the present. And once we see the present for what it is, we can act in ways that point toward a better future. What we do today does affect tomorrow; God does call us to play a part in world history. When we see signs of despair and suffering in the world, our knowledge of God's faithfulness and our faith practices help us offer signs of hope and patience and perseverance to an aching world.

Lord, we know that times are hard and sometimes get worse in the world. But we also know that this is not the end of the story. The coming of Christ is the end of this story and the beginning of a new one. Help us keep one another alert, awake, and prayerful. Amen.

Advent begins tomorrow. We usually don't think of missions during Advent. But these words from First Timothy challenge us to action as we wait. There is a difference between waiting around and active waiting. The author of First Timothy advocates active waiting.

If we remember *why* God came into the world as flesh and blood, we can see the connection between Advent and mission. Christ came so that all might hear the good news of God's salvation and redemption. And until Christ comes again we have the responsibility of spreading the word and inviting others to join us in ongoing vigil.

"Supplications, prayers, intercessions, and thanksgivings should be made for everyone." These instructions apply to us today. This text is a reminder of the grace-filled relationship that God has with us. We know that God alone is responsible for the salvation and redemption of creation, yet we have been invited to join in God's work of renewing the broken world.

God bestows on us the gift of praying for others—for people we like, for people we don't, for religious leaders, for political leaders, for people in this country and for those from other countries. Prayer is, indeed, a form of mission. And we must remember that sometimes our own small acts of faithfulness are the way God touches others with grace and love.

Reflect on times when you have said prayers of intercession for a particular person or people. What was it like to lift others in prayer? How do you think God used your prayers? When have you experienced God through the prayers of someone else?

First Sunday in Advent

I imagine that the socioeconomic context from which you hear this passage makes a difference in how you respond to it. If purchasing or growing food and buying clothes is easy for you, then it might also be easy not to worry about food, drink, and clothing. (An aside: Sometimes wealth and affluence can make people worry *more* about sustaining their wealth, rather than less.) If, however, you are unemployed or homeless, working more than one job, a single parent, a refugee of war or natural disaster, a farmer whose land has been taken away by the government, then this text has its added challenges. Yet the words of Matthew are still directed to all who consider themselves Christ's disciples, regardless of life situations.

It helps to remember that this passage is part of Jesus' Sermon on the Mount. He doesn't instruct us to forget about our basic needs simply because God deserves first place in our lives. The instruction is to reprioritize, and the ability to do that is tied to God's wisdom, knowledge, love, and grace. Jesus knows that all our needs are met in God.

Our real challenge lies in expanding our vision of faithfulness and obedience to include economic justice and care for the environment. God's kingdom is about justice, peace, and equality. Clothing the naked, feeding the hungry, and satisfying the thirsty are part of setting our sights on God's kingdom. If we focus on providing for one another, we might find that God has already provided for us.

As Advent begins, let us wait actively with energy. Let us prepare ourselves and our world to receive Christ. As we wait, let us seek God's kingdom and care for God's creatures.

What discipline can you practice this Advent season to remind you that God provides? What prayers will open your eyes and show you how to provide for others? What will help you wait actively and with energy this Advent?

Way Makers

NOVEMBER 30–DECEMBER 6, 2009 • F. DOUGLAS POWE JR.

MONDAY, NOVEMBER 30 ~ *Read Malachi 3:1*

Have you ever been in a situation where you had to prepare the way for someone else, when you were a "way maker" of sorts? There was a time when the circus would send a barker into the town ahead of the circus to prepare the way for the big event. The job of the barker was to get the people excited about the coming of the circus. The barker had to be honest enough, while being exciting enough to encourage people to come to the circus.

In Malachi we are told God will send God's messenger to prepare the way. The one who has to bring God's message has no easy task because the Israelites have not stayed true to the covenant. In fact, God's messenger in this case has a tough task because the people are aware of the covenant and have chosen to ignore it. The messenger has to find a way for them to hear God's message anew.

Sometimes, we find ourselves in the same situation as the Israelites. We need to hear God's message anew. We need someone to prepare the way for us to hear God's word in a fresh way so that we can renew our covenant with God. The way maker in this case has to find a way to connect the importance of loving God and neighbor to our current situation. The good news is that God makes the first move to call us back into relationship. In the text, it is God who sends a messenger to the people and not the Israelites who have to find their way blindly back to God. God does the same for us today, calling us back when we stray.

Holy God, may we respond to your grace that continually calls us into relationship with you. Amen.

Assistant professor of evangelism at Saint Paul School of Theology and a member of Centennial United Methodist Church in Kansas City, Missouri

I am not an artist, but I am fascinated with the process artists go through to get to a finished piece. For example, I observed an artist drawing a sunset, and I thought she was putting on the last few strokes. I commented, "What a beautiful painting!" She smiled and replied, "Thank you! I am just getting started." I was stunned. I asked her what she meant. She explained to me that the basic picture was on the canvas, but now the hard work of integrating all the right colors into the painting would take time. As I watched her paint, I began to notice the difference as she worked to highlight, darken or brighten different parts of the canvas.

This part of Malachi 3 presents God as a stern taskmaster, using the image of fire. Certainly reading the text this way has validity, but another possibility is that God is like the artist who continues to refine the painting by integrating different colors. This image of God continues the idea of God working in our lives to help us become new creatures. The artist I watched emphasized different parts of the painting in the way she used color. I believe God helps us grow as Christians through various means. Relying on only one image of God to capture the way God works in the world is dangerous.

The other side of the equation is, "Are we receptive to God working in our lives to bring about change?" My analogy breaks down at this point because we are not static canvases but dynamic beings who must respond to God's actions. In other words, God can paint and paint or continually refine us with fire; but unless we respond, God's work will not refine us.

Holy God, open us to your brushstrokes on our lives so that we may grow in grace. Amen.

Have you ever heard someone in your church say, "But we've always done it this way"? We hear this comment and sigh, "Here we go again." We know the person is going to remind us how things used to be so great and how the church nowadays is just not the same.

One of the fascinating insights for me in reading Zechariah's prophecy is his ability to make a connection to the past—a connection that gives people hope for the future. Zechariah tells those listening that the covenant God made with Israel a long time ago has not been broken or lost. God is going to do a new thing in the lives of the people that will strengthen the covenant. Zechariah is not clamoring for the past or longing to return to the time of David. Zechariah is looking forward to the future, knowing that God will make a way for the Israelites to serve and live holy lives.

We learn from Zechariah that the past is important, but we do not have to be captive to it. We can move forward knowing that God will empower us even as God empowered those who came before. We can move beyond what has been done before and take risks in our church life. A healthy balance between valuing the past and looking toward the future is not easy to accomplish, but it is the tension we live in as Christians. We remember the resurrection of Jesus even as we look forward to the return of the Christ. Living in this tension requires an understanding of the past that can guide us as we live out our hope for a different future.

Holy God, we need your help to live in the tension between captivity to the past and hope for the future. Help us to live balanced lives. Amen.

The birth of a child is a special event. I imagine Elizabeth and Zechariah made preparations for their child in ways similar to what we do today. Where will the baby sleep? Do we have clothes for the child? I expect Elizabeth and Zechariah also made spiritual preparation for the child. In the first chapter of Luke we learn that Elizabeth and Zechariah will not name the child after his father. Instead, he will be called John. We don't know why this is done, but it is a fair assumption that Elizabeth and Zechariah were communicating with God. The two of them were concerned not only with their own plans; they were also seeking to discern God's plans for John.

For Elizabeth and Zechariah there is not a separation between what we call the sacred and secular in preparing for John's birth. We can learn from the two of them not only about making a way for babies but also about making a way for those new to the faith. This text points to an important way to do this.

By God's tender mercy, Zechariah says, "The dawn from on high will break upon us, to give light to those who sit in darkness and in the shadow of death." And so we can actually enter a new way of life. In response to what God is doing, we can help prepare the way for others to enter into this new life. John came to be a way maker for Jesus, but it was his parents who first made a way for him. God's salvation—which Elizabeth and Zechariah, John and Jesus made way for—will guide us all in the way of peace.

How does your church prepare the way for those new in the faith? How do you help people enter into a new way of life? Pray for God's discernment so you may become a "way maker" for others.

A man often stood nearby our church asking for money or food. We invited him inside to eat, and many of the members learned his name and how he came to fall on tough times. He went to prison for a short time after we had gotten to know him, and while he was in prison church members visited him. When it was time for his release, some of the ministerial staff arranged for his integration back into society. It would have been easy for the members of the church to ignore this person—he was different; he was a stranger; he couldn't "contribute" to the church.

Bible experts interpret the Philippians reference to Paul's imprisonment in various ways, ranging from his literally being in prison to a more allegorical understanding of his imprisonment. But the point Paul is trying to make is not about his imprisonment; it is about those who supported him during a tough time. Those people did not abandon Paul when he needed them the most. And the members of the church I mentioned went further by not abandoning someone who was an outsider—not even a member of the church—during his time of need.

As Christians we are called to make Christ visible more with our actions than our words. We are called to open the doors of the church even to those who make us uncomfortable, to all in need who cross our path. Paul reminds us that God's salvation will be brought to fruition; we are invited every day to participate in that great work.

Think about those around you who need your support. What would be required for your church to welcome these people? How would welcoming these others transform your congregation?

My grandfather always planted a big garden. He would tend the garden every day by pulling weeds, setting the stakes just right, and making sure animals were not eating all of his crops. One year I was with him when he planted the garden, and I soon learned that planting requires more than simply spreading seeds around. I am not a gardener, but I learned from him that the process from beginning to end to produce crops is time-consuming, hard work. When we buy vegetables at the store, we often are oblivious to the process involved in getting food ready for consumption.

In these verses Paul uses the imagery of a harvest of righteousness. We should notice that Paul does not believe this harvest of righteousness will happen by osmosis. He tells those in Philippi that in order to harvest righteousness their "love must overflow more and more with knowledge and full insight." How can love overflow with knowledge and full insight? Paul's statement may seem strange and impractical. But what he means is that the only way for love to overflow is to have the mind of Christ. Paul does not use the specific language "the mind of Christ" in this part of the text, but I believe it is implied. For Paul, being a Christian is a process much like gardening. It does not happen overnight. The harvest of righteousness is not something we should take lightly. We must tend our relationships with God and with neighbor daily. In the same way my grandfather worked daily in his garden, we must be intentional about practices that will help us to grow closer to God and neighbor.

Holy God, we pray that our love will overflow daily. May your love draw us closer to you and to our neighbor. Amen.

SECOND SUNDAY IN ADVENT

One of the wonderful things about scripture is the multiple ways there are to interpret the meaning of a text for our lives today. Many of us are familiar with this text in Luke and often hear people emphasize John as a forerunner of Jesus. I agree with these interpretations, but would like to add a different interpretation: John as a way maker.

The text begins with a long list of those in power over Judea. It starts with Caesar and moves to those immediately over the Israelites. The author of Luke is not simply giving historical data but does this on purpose. He contrasts the power of those who govern with the power of the ministry of John the Baptist. He says John is different. The author of Luke is preparing us for what will make Jesus' power different from the world's power and from John's.

John's call for repentance is not strictly individualistic; it is a call to those in the community to repent for giving in to the Roman power structure. Jesus is the one who can make the crooked straight and the mountains low. In other words, Jesus will stand with the weak against those trying to oppress them. This is good news for those who experience the underside of life and are not a part of the power structures. It is a challenge to all of us who live as part of these power structures.

What is at stake here is nothing less than the salvation of God. John reminds us that the task of making the way for God's salvation in this world is a task the church must not neglect. Salvation—for us and for the rest of the world—depend upon it.

Read Luke 3:1-6 and meditate on John's exhortation to us to get ready for God's salvation to break loose in the world.

Joy Anchored in God's Love

DECEMBER 7–13, 2009 • JONETTE GAY

MONDAY, DECEMBER 7 ~ *Read Isaiah 12:2-6*

With joy you will draw water from the wells of salvation.

When I was a child, there was a spring not far from my house. We would sometimes walk through the woods to that spring to drink its cool water. Water was plentiful in East Texas and the area was filled with wildflowers and trees. We appreciated the abundance of water and the life it nurtured.

When I moved to New Mexico, my relationship with water changed. I began to appreciate water and the lack of it in a different way. I understood better the world of the Israelites in their desert.

So, when Isaiah tells the people, "With joy you will draw water from the wells of salvation," the image speaks to me. I picture the thirst of God's people, and I can feel their joy in knowing that God will provide for them. Isaiah's affirmation—*Surely God is my salvation*—is both a statement of fact and a statement of faith. God *has* redeemed Israel, and God *will* redeem Israel. Those who have seen God's hand at work in their life know that God's promises for the future are trustworthy and reliable. God has quenched their thirst before; God will lead them again to the wells of salvation.

Advent is the time when we who know God's great works wait with joy and anticipate God's continued saving presence in the world. God, who is our strength and might, will come into the world yet again. As we await God's coming, let us proclaim God's name and sing praises to God with joy.

O Holy One, we are thirsty. Show us the path to the well. Teach us to wait with joy for your salvation. Amen.

Ordained elder in the New Mexico Conference of the United Methodist Church, serving as a hospital chaplain in Philadelphia, Pennsylvania

Isaiah says it over and over again: Do not keep God's greatness a secret. "Sing praises to the LORD . . . Shout aloud and sing for joy." Isaiah reminds us that God is our strength, so we can trust that assurance and tell others.

This is an interesting time in our world. We hear much talk about God, and sometimes that talk results in conflicting reports of God's nature and work. But the scriptures tell us that God is known by what God has done in the world. Isaiah writes of God's strength and might—strength that has been used to deliver Israel, might that continues to deliver joy and peace into the world. God's name is exalted because God has lifted up the broken and the poor; God has saved the people from sin and death.

And, in this season of Advent, Isaiah instructs us to "shout aloud and sing for joy," because God continues God's saving, healing work in the world. It is for this we wait: the birth of the Christ child, our Redeemer.

And so we wait. We wait for the Christ to come. As we wait for the coming of the Lord, we are called to tell of God's strength and might for all. "Great in your midst is the Holy One of Israel," Isaiah tells us. God has already done glorious things. As we await God's coming once again this Advent, we need have no fear. God is with us, strong and sure.

Great and mighty is your name, O God of all nations! We cannot keep your deeds a secret. Teach us how to praise you every day as we await the birth of the Christ child. Give us hope without fear this season. Amen.

Afriend of mine once told me, "You hide your tenderness." I am not sure why I do that. I wonder if I do it to defend myself. I wonder if I am trying to protect myself by being tough.

We may think that if we keep our guard up, we will not get hurt. It just doesn't work that way. Trying to protect ourselves sometimes causes the very things we want to avoid: pain and worry.

Gentleness comes from trusting God. This is a time of year that puts many demands on us. We have so many things, people, and responsibilities to juggle. When we are stressed, we lose sight of what's important. These words from Philippians are timely. They speak directly to the anxiety that often overwhelms us in the midst of life.

The apostle Paul gives us a way out of that anxious mind-set. He suggests that we let our gentleness be made known and not to worry about anything. He instructs us to rejoice all the time. He reminds us to pray with gratitude and make our requests known to God.

Then what happens? Do our troubles and problems disappear? Is the way ahead suddenly made smooth? No, not necessarily, says Paul. But what will come is a peace that cannot be overcome by anxiety. The nearness of the Christ child can enable us to keep time in a different way. The peace of God will meet us in our prayers, and a sense of calm will guard our hearts and our minds.

Paul knew something about worry. He knew about hard times and rough paths. But he also knew the peace of God that guards heart and mind. We too may know that peace. Gentleness of spirit and perseverance in prayer—these are the gifts of the season.

God, give me a gentle spirit. Strengthen my life of prayer. Help me to wait in peace for Christ to come. Amen.

One day in my work as a hospital chaplain, I went to my assigned floor and asked the nurses how things were going. I got this response, "We don't need a chaplain today." I left wondering why I wasn't needed; I felt a sense of rejection. My colleague had the same thing experience later that day; he left the floor grateful for the chance to take a break. He and I faced the same circumstances and reacted quite differently to them.

The peace Paul talks about is not about circumstances. Paul, in prison when he wrote these words, was not safe and secure among his friends and community. His words came not from naiveté but from a grounding in harsh reality. Paul wasn't writing from some soft and comfortable home; he was writing from a jail cell. Yet, he wrote eloquently about the peace "which surpasses all understanding." That peace, he was sure, came from a life of prayer and supplication, a life of thanksgiving.

The world told Paul—and tells us—he has every reason to be anxious. Yet he is not. He is guarded by a peace that is beyond understanding, a peace that has little to do with circumstances. It is the peace given to us by God, the peace that guards us as we await the birth of the Christ child.

God doesn't promise us an easy life, free of trouble and heartache. God does promise us a peace that cannot be overcome by those troubles and heartaches. This is God's strong promise to us—during Advent and throughout our lives.

O God, you are with us in small things and in great things, in times of joy and in times of sorrow. Grant us peace as we move through this week toward Christmas. Help us to pray to you and praise you without ceasing. Amen.

Zephaniah, a lesser-known prophet, speaks some of the gloomiest prophecies in the Bible. Judah is in very sad shape; its king is corrupt and the country is so far off the path of God that Zephaniah himself comes near to complete despair.

Then, suddenly, without warning, joy breaks through Zephaniah's message. "Rejoice and exult with all your heart!" He can hardly contain his excitement. The events he most feared for Judah, for the people of God, are not going to happen! Judah's enemies will be turned away. There is no longer any disaster to fear. The lame and the outcast will be saved and gathered.

Judah's shame will be changed into praise and "renown in all the earth." God will, Zephaniah says, bring God's people home. In the face of sure disaster, their mighty and merciful Lord does an astounding and joyous thing: the day becomes not a time of fear but a time of strength and joy. Zephaniah and the people are swept from a day of judgment into a day of anticipation and hope.

As we are filled with anticipation this Advent season, this passage from Zephaniah is a strong reminder that God has moved us from judgment to grace. Anticipating the Christ child brings joy, not condemnation; it brings redemption, not despair.

As a child, I really liked December. I often said, "I can't wait until Christmas." Now that I am an adult, Christmas comes much more quickly each year. When I was very young, just seeing the gifts under the tree was enough to tide me over from Advent to Christmas. Now, I know there is more. These ancient Hebrew texts of the coming day of the Lord bring with it much hope. We have need of a new world, so we wait.

God, we hear the promises of your scripture, and we await your coming with joy and gladness. Help us to proclaim your good news even as we wait for the Christ child's birth. Amen.

Advent is, for me, *not* the time I want to get close to John the Baptist's words in this passage. The words are frightening: *You brood of vipers . . . the ax is lying at the root of the trees . . . cut down and thrown into the fire*. I confess that I rarely preached this text, even though the lectionary gave me the opportunity, time and time again. It just seemed too much to face when the world around me was singing Christmas carols and putting on nativity plays.

We have a lot on our minds at Advent. Gifts to buy, parties to attend, visits with family, and all our other responsibilities—these and more occupy our minds.

But John the Baptist has much more on his mind as he prepares himself and others for the coming of the Lord. He has repentance on his mind. And he says we must have repentance on our minds as well. The consequence for the tree that does not bear good fruit is dire: it will be cut down and thrown into the fire. Who are we John asks, to make a claim on God?

Even John's response to those who wondered whether he might be the Messiah is a little frightening. No, he says, I am not the one. The one who is coming is more powerful. That one will baptize not with water but with the Holy Spirit and fire. This pronouncement must have sent the people into an even deeper examination of who they were and how they lived their lives. John gives them every chance to repent.

And God give us every chance to repent as well. This Advent let us make room in our hearts for repentance, that we may await the coming of the Christ with joy and courage.

O Holy One, we come before you this season with humility and repentance. Hear our prayer; help us to live our life in obedience and anticipation. Amen.

THIRD SUNDAY IN ADVENT

Decorations, Christmas lights, trees, baking, and candy canes are part of the way we prepare for Christmas in my family. John, however, prepares the way of the Lord with a change in life rather than with a change of décor. John's energetic preaching has gotten the people's attention in no uncertain terms. Many are now ready to repent.

After listening to John's fiery words calling people to repentance, the crowd asks, "What then should we do?" What John gives them is an invitation to turn their lives around. Those with two coats must share one. Those who have food must share with those who do not. Tax collectors must stop charging more than they should. Soldiers should quit extorting money from people and be satisfied with their own wages.

Ethical behavior and anticipation of the coming reign of God are, in John's writing, closely tied together. As we await the One who will change the world, we get ready by making changes in our own lives. Repentance gives us the chance to be still and listen to God's examination of us—and to respond by changing our lives so they reflect the life of Christ, whose birth we await.

The call to repent is good news because it points to something we are missing. As we prepare for Christmas, John's words uncover the truth: the something we are missing this season is not about getting one more gift; it is about sharing our hearts and souls with one another and with the world. John may sound harsh to our Christmas-sensitive ears. But what John says is true: good news comes with responsibility. It is our responsibility to ready our lives to welcome the Christ child. God is coming to be in our midst, and we will be renewed. Surely this is good news of the best kind!

Dearest Lord Jesus, show us what to do to prepare our hearts to give to a hurting world during this holy season. Amen.

Finding Fulfillment

DECEMBER 14–20, 2009 • LARRY G. JENT

MONDAY, DECEMBER 14 ~ *Read Micah 5:2-5a*

This prophecy, written by Micah some seven hundred years before the birth of Jesus, is very important to Christians. We see the birth of Jesus as the *fulfillment* of this ancient scripture. A *fulfillment* is much more than a mere prediction.

People make predictions every day. We try to predict the weather, sports scores, or the time of our arrival. Even if we are right, that does not make us prophets. It may simply mean that we have an eye to the sky: when the storm clouds gather, we know it is likely to rain.

Fulfillment is more precious than prediction. When a young mother says, "I thought I knew what life was about, but now that I have my baby I feel so fulfilled," she certainly is not claiming that her life has become predictable. No one with a two-year-old would say that! She is saying that this gift of life has given her a deeper meaning.

On one level, Micah was not making an astonishing prediction. He dreamed of the resurrection of Israel against the Assyrian horde. Of course, that dream must take root in the lineage of David. But this was truly astonishing: The king he dreamed about was not a king of war but of peace. God inspired that dream, and God will not settle for anything less than fulfillment. For more than two thousand years God has been waiting. Will that gift of peace be fulfilled in your heart this Advent?

God, I yearn to find fulfillment in the coming of your Christ child. Forgive me for trying to make you predictable. Set me free to find fulfillment today—and every day of this gift of life. Amen.

Senior pastor of Amelon United Methodist Church, living in Lynchburg, Virginia with his wife, Barbara, and enjoying their grandchildren together

Expectant women speak of feeling their babies move and knowing the promise of life within them. Yet Elizabeth felt something even more profound. At this sacred moment she realized she was in the presence of someone who "believed that there would be a fulfillment" of God's word.

Are we to believe that Elizabeth marveled because Mary believed God's prediction? If God said it, how could she doubt it? After all, how hard would it be for the eternal God to make a prediction about a baby?

But *fulfillment* is much harder—because it requires the cooperation of a human soul. The angel had promised that this child would fulfill the lives of those who knew him. Long before the stone was rolled away, before the nails pierced his hands, before the loaves and fishes were broken—*before he was even born*—people began to find fulfillment when Jesus was near.

Have you known people like this? They are the ones who sense the extraordinary in the ordinary, the profound in the mundane, the light in the darkness, and the promise of God in people like you and me.

Are we the sort of persons who never find fulfillment? Perhaps. The answer is really something that not even God can predict. It all hinges upon this: are we ready to let the Spirit of God overshadow us, to fulfill our life in such a powerful way that others can sense Christ within us?

God is certainly ready to overshadow us—that much is clear. The only question is whether we are ready to yield.

Lord, I have known your power shining through the lives of those who found fulfillment in you. Let your Spirit live in me so that others may see my love for you. Amen.

Blessed? Surely there is no way that Mary could have known the hardships that would accompany her prayer. Our Christmas cards show her seated discreetly and comfortably on a donkey as the holy couple make their way to Bethlehem. The text offers no such comfort. Mary may have walked every step of the way, collapsing in birth pangs as she arrived. She took shelter in a barn and was given a refugee's welcome. She gave birth—not among family and friends but among the beasts.

No sooner had the birthing cries subsided than a band of shepherds came wandering in from the field. An angel had sent them!

Some time later strange visitors arrived, leaving behind costly gifts. It was a blessed moment. Yet before the night was over, Mary knew her family was in danger; they must flee as refugees. Perhaps the gifts bought them safe passage as they fled.

Mary lived to see her baby falsely accused, beaten, and brutally executed. She heard people laugh at his agony and watched as he suffered to death. Mary's life was full of pain—yet all generations do call her blessed. God wove every sorrow, every tear, every heartache into the greatest story ever told. People from every age and station of life have been redeemed by that story.

Blessed!

If God could do that much with a story like hers, then how much can God do with the story of our lives? Can anyone look upon us and call us blessed? They can—and they will—when we allow them to see God at work through our joys and sorrows alike.

God, grant me the courage to pray with Mary in trust. Let all generations see your work fulfilled in me and call me blessed. Amen.

Mary's prayer runs contrary to all the things that promise us fulfillment in this world. Worldly wisdom and power and wealth and strength—these are what we crave and December is the time the world promises to deliver. Toys are not just toys. They promise to bring us together as happy families, sharing golden moments of joy. Automobiles promise to make us secure and safe. Underarm deodorants promise to make us confident. Toothpaste promises to make us sexy. 'Tis the season to buy fulfillment.

Of course, we know that every one of those promises has been broken. The toys we bought last year are long since forgotten. The car we bought last year is already looking old. We still sweat. No one swoons when we brush our teeth. Yet the world keeps promising, and we keep consuming.

Fulfillment will never come from the stuff we think we own. If we allow it, the world will keep us too busy even to look for a deeper satisfaction. But we cannot blame the world for our shallow lives. The problem is that we are not looking. God will always answer when we take time to seek.

The Christ child within is still the answer to our yearning—yet not even God can bring an answer to those who will not recognize their need. If you and I are ready to confess, then we are ready for the fulfillment that only Christ can bring.

Lord, you fill the hungry with good things, but I have been sent away empty. I have been too distracted to admit my own need or to seek true fulfillment. All I can offer is empty-handed need. All I need is your love. Amen.

From the cradle, we want our desires to be fulfilled immediately, but God knows that it is not always good for children to receive instant gratification. Waiting and wanting are healthy disciplines. Yearning teaches us to treasure the gifts we receive. It can also show us the difference between true needs and empty wants.

Like Micah, the psalmist knew a lot about faithful yearning. In language too raw for most Sunday services, this passage aches for an answer to prayer. I find that most Christians are quite well-acquainted with unanswered yearning as well. We make our petitions but are quick to remind ourselves that God always answers—just that sometimes the answer is no.

This psalm will not allow such an easy exit strategy. This persistent soul is not embarrassed to wait for—even to demand—an answer. Imagine that you have caught your fingers in the latch of your car's trunk. You probably will not be polite in your requests for help. No one who loves you would expect you to quietly recite, "Verily, verily, if it be thy will, please open this latch and release my fingers." You would demand action—and keep on demanding action until a friend answered your call.

We may need a good dose of that kind of urgent patience. When our prayers are not instantly satisfied, that does not mean that it is time to sigh and move on. God aches for us to cry out as one trusted friend to another. God is waiting for us to remove all formality, to cry out for an answer until the answer comes. God knows that the more we yearn, the more we treasure the fulfillment of our prayers.

O God, I have been embarrassed to cry out for an answer to prayer. Teach me to trust you, to cry out to you until the answer comes, and to treasure the fulfillment you give. Amen.

Merry Christmas! Have you been sanctified today? That may seem to be a strange question, but it is not. To be sanctified means to be set aside for God's use. Are we available for God's use today? If so, then we have been sanctified. If we have been too busy or too tired or too angry or too far behind schedule—then we have not. It does not matter how much we know about the Bible or how accurate our theology might be or how much we might look like Christians. If God cannot use us, then we are not sanctified.

In Solomon's temple there were shovels set aside for the priests. Those shovels were used in God's service, so they were called sanctified—even though they looked like humble shovels. On the bookshelves of many homes are fancy Bibles that are never opened. If God never gets any use out of those books then they are not sanctified, no matter how many times we write "holy" on the cover. God's word finds fulfillment in the human heart, not the bookshelf.

Through the eternal gift of Jesus Christ, we are sanctified. As we pass that gift on to others by sharing our possessions, words, deeds, automobiles, homes, thoughts—our whole selves—each day we fulfill the gift of Christmas.

It is not that complicated. All we need to do is show God's love to the least, the last, and the lost, just as Christ showed love toward us. That is the gift of Christmas. That is the gift of fulfillment.

O God, sanctify me for your will, and let your purpose be fulfilled in me today! Amen.

Fourth Sunday in Advent

The manger is the scandal of Christianity. Our God was a real child, swaddled with real cloth, that really needed to be changed. The dangerous truth is this: if God dwelled with us once, then God can do it again.

God could be in the eyes of the next refugee child whose image flits across our television screens. God could be knocking on our door, asking for a room. God could be hunkered down in a barn, begging for a clean cloth. The world says that paying attention to these invisible souls is a waste of time. Jesus says that caring for one of the least of these is caring for Christ himself—that this fulfills the kingdom of God. Which will you believe?

Most of us think we added to our list of possessions on Christmas day—but that is only an illusion. The only things we truly own are the items we can take with us when we die. That includes our relationship with God and our relationships with other people—nothing else. All the other stuff in our inventory is only held in trust until our days are complete. God has loaned us this stuff to build relationships—our only true possessions.

God says that when we use our stuff to care for the least, the last, and the lost, we actually build our relationship with Christ. We find fulfillment. It is scandalous but true. The way we use these possessions can help us find God in our midst.

May you use God's gifts so well in this world that you are richly fulfilled in the world to come.

O God, come into this world, come into my life. Let me see you around the next corner in the eyes of the least, the last, and the lost. Let me live as one who knows fulfillment in giving. Amen.

Responding to God's Gifts

DECEMBER 21–27, 2009 • SAM CLARK

MONDAY, DECEMBER 21 ~ *Read 1 Samuel 2:18-20, 26*

The boy Samuel is God's gift to Hannah. He is the answer to Hannah's desperate prayer at the house of the LORD in Shiloh. Hannah, though dearly loved by her husband Elkanah, is barren. She longed to become a mother. When Samuel is born, she offers him to God as a way of showing her gratitude. When Samuel was three years old, she took the young boy to the temple where Samuel was to be trained for priesthood by the elderly high priest Eli.

Hannah and Elkanah come each year for their annual visit to Shiloh to make sacrifices. Hannah visits with her son and gives him the new robe she made for him. As Samuel's parents depart, Eli blesses them. In one translation Eli says, "The Lord give you children by this woman for the *loan* which she lent to the Lord" (RSV). In another translation, he says "May the Lord repay you with children by this woman for the *gift* that she made to the Lord" (NSRV).

There is a clear difference between the two translations. Hannah did not "lend" Samuel to God, expecting to get him back with interest. She *gives* him to God because God gave Samuel to her. The gift of her son is her way of saying thank you to God. Like Hannah, we want to be faithful to the gifts God has given us.

God does not need a loan from us. We do not lend God our lives. We offer our lives to God so that every act and word may be a response to the love and grace we receive from Jesus Christ and the Holy Spirit.

God, accept our lives as our gratitude for the love you have given us in the gift of Jesus. Amen.

Retired United Methodist minister teaching at the Dillard United Methodist Church, living in the mountains of northeast Georgia

Each year when I was growing up, our family gathered on Christmas at the home of my grandparents to share gifts and to eat a sumptuous meal. My mother always insisted that I dress nicely, so I had to take off my traditional jeans and put on some of my new Christmas clothes.

The Colossians are urged to put on new clothing, new virtues, so that they can celebrate their new life in the Christian community. They are to remember their baptism when they put away the clothing that represented the old life and put on a fresh new robe to symbolize the changed life.

The most important article in that new wardrobe, however, wasn't the fresh robe. It was, the letter to the Colossians says, love. Like a belt, love binds all of the other virtues together.

A friend of mine, a pianist, illustrated to his son the difference between a self-centered life and a life of love. First the father banged on the keyboard with his fist. Then, with his fingers, he played a beautiful chord. "Life without faith is discordant," he told his son. "A life of faith and love brings harmony."

Love enables us to bear with people whose insensitivity and aggressiveness can be irritating. We learn to accept them for who they are and to love them because we remember how we have been loved and forgiven by Christ. Our response to the forgiveness we have experienced frees us to forgive others. This forgiveness is not a burden but a joyful expression of our gratitude to Christ.

Because of Christ we can live without fearing the opinions of others and without needing to defend ourselves. We are grateful for the peace in our hearts, but that peace reaches beyond us. It spreads throughout the church. And so we give thanks for the gifts of love and peace, the best Christmas gifts.

Clothe us, God, in love, so that we can serve you and our neighbor in joyful response to your gifts. Amen.

The Christmas music made me decide to join the church choir. I wanted to sing the joyful songs of the season. I was not an accomplished singer, but when I was standing beside a good tenor, I could memorize my part. Our choir director told us that we should sing with all of our heart and give God our best. "Our music is our way of offering thanksgiving to Christ, our way of sharing in the spiritual life of our church," she said.

The church is a community in which each person shares in his or her own way so that we learn from one another. We are guided by the word of Christ, which becomes central in all of our lives. It is not the sole responsibility of the minister to proclaim the gospel. Each of us is called both to teach and to be accountable to our brothers and sisters in the family of faith.

When everyone participates, worship becomes more joyful, a song of praise and thanksgiving. Such spiritual worship enables us to continue that melody in our daily lives with no disconnection between our worship on Sunday and the way we live our lives each day.

During my missionary years in Peru, I worked closely with two Jesuit priests. Both wore medallions on chains around their necks. When I asked what their medallions meant, they showed me one. On one side was a likeness of Ignatius Loyola, the founder of their religious order. On the other were three Latin words: *Age quod agis.* One of them translated for me: "The words mean, 'Do what you are doing.'" This means that if you really act and speak with your whole heart and offer each deed and word to God, your entire life can become a prayer." Everything in our life can be a song of thanksgiving.

As we near the birth of Jesus, may we sing with all of our hearts and live each day as an act of praise. Amen.

CHRISTMAS EVE

Mary and Joseph are alone. No midwife is mentioned, so they seem to have struggled with the birth themselves.

Though angels do not come to help Mary and Joseph, they do come to shepherds in a nearby field. Why to them? There had been heroic shepherds like Moses, David and Amos, but in Jesus' time shepherds were socially on the bottom of the barrel. They often grazed their sheep on other people's property. They were uneducated and usually dirty. They had no way to keep dietary or purification laws. Their job was one that nobody wanted. It didn't pay much, but somebody had to do it, and usually that meant that poor people did the shepherding.

It was for these shepherds another night on a tedious job, but then something extraordinary happens. Suddenly there's a brightness like midday. One angel speaks, then many sing. They tell the shepherds of the birth of a true savior—not like Caesar—who was called "a Savior, who is the Messiah." This new savior has come to bring life and joy to all people.

The shepherds tell Mary and Joseph about the angelic visit. This motley crew become the first evangelists. They wonder. Mary ponders.

Scripture says that all the people were amazed. Who else is present? People from upstairs? We don't know. Maybe this is how we get into the story. Usually, we are spectators at Christmas Eve worship. We enjoy the story, the carols, the candlelight. If, however, we are among those who really hear the shepherds' story, we become participants. We can step into the stable, and let the child change our lives.

Enable us, God, to experience new birth in both Bethlehem and in our own lives. Amen.

_{CHRISTMAS DAY}

In 1969 an earthquake destroyed Chimbote, Peru. The missionary working in that city, Agnes Malloy, suffered with her church members and moved into a tent alongside the survivors. When I became a missionary in that same city in 1974, Agnes came for a visit. At Sunday worship, people rushed up to her, embracing her and talking excitedly, One of the church members said, "We love her because she pitched her tent beside us."

John 1:14 tells us, "The Word became flesh and lived among us; and we have seen his glory." The words "lived among us" can also be translated "pitched a tent among us." The eternal Word identifies with humans, becoming one of us. Taking on human life makes Jesus vulnerable, open to pain and confusion, experiencing the common problems and joys of everyday life.

Who could be more needy than a newborn baby? Who could be more suspect than one who lives among the poor and liberates those who are oppressed? The incarnation of the Word in Jesus is the good news of Christmas and the very meaning of Emmanuel, God with us.

"We have seen his glory." *We* have seen it, but not everyone has. His glory was hidden to many. Can you see glory in the humility and serving love of Jesus? Religious leaders, then and now, often miss this kind of glory. They expect a triumphant display of power and ceremony, so they cannot recognize the quiet glory of Jesus.

There is birth imagery in today's text, but we are the ones being born anew. We are given the gift of faith so that we hear God's word to us from Jesus. We become children of God, made new by the incarnate Word.

We pray to Christ in the words of the carol, "Be born in us today." Amen.

What an appropriate reading for the second day of Christmas! Psalm 148 is one of the last five psalms. These psalms are known as Hallelujah Psalms, because each of them both begins and ends with the word "Hallelu-yah," meaning "Praise the LORD!" These psalms form a doxology to the entire Psalter.

In Psalm 148 all of God's creations in heaven and on earth are called to sing praise to the God who created them. What we hear is a universal hallelujah chorus. We still hear the angels singing to the amazed shepherds, "Glory to God in the highest heaven, and on earth peace among those whom [God] favors" (Luke 2:14).

The psalmist calls everything that exists to sing praise to God. Beginning at God's throne, the angels who serve God are singing, descending to sun, moon, and shining stars. Then the poet calls to the deep sea and ascends through all creatures to the humans, both high and low, young and old, calling them to join in the song.

This psalm inspired Francis of Assisi's *Canticle of the Sun*. Francis hears the great chorus and likens it to God's family singing. The song rings through all time and space.

As a missionary in Peru, I once followed a guide through the dense jungle that surrounds the Amazon River. Suddenly, I heard voices singing. "Who is singing?" I asked. The guide smiled, then said, "The trees are singing." Actually a small hut that served as a church was nearby, and the worshipers were singing. But I'm sure that the trees really were singing, joining the human singers in a chorus of praise.

When we sing at worship, we join the great choir of all creation, blending our voices with heaven and earth. We are partners with everything God called into being.

God, take our weak, unsteady voices and join them in the great melody of your creation. We sing each day in gratitude for your love. Amen.

Traveling with children is often difficult. When they are very young, we don't want them out of our sight. By the time a child is twelve, we can make arrangements to meet if we get separated.

When Jesus goes to Jerusalem for Passover with Mary and Joseph, he becomes fascinated to discover an open-air classroom in the outer court of the Temple. Scholarly rabbis give a question-and-answer teaching session during Passover. Jesus becomes so involved in what he is hearing and learning that he forgets about everything else. He has found his place.

When his parents begin the return journey to Nazareth, they eventually realize that Jesus is not with them. Frantically they return to find him.

When they find him they ask Jesus why he has treated them like this, he answers with a question. It's a simple question, but one that can be translated in different ways: "Did you not know that I must be about my Father's business?" Or, "That I must be in my Father's house?" Or, "That I must be among my Father's people?" No matter which translation we choose, Jesus seems to be saying quite clearly: "I am coming to understand my special relationship with God." Of course, he also realizes that his parents are seeking to do God's will, so he does nothing to break the family unity. He goes home with them to learn how to obey God by loving and obeying his earthly parents.

Just as Mary and Joseph had to be open to raising a son who had a special calling, so our families must be open to the callings of each family member. Mary and Joseph understand that their son does not belong only to them. He is God's gift to them and to the world. This is the good news for us at Christmastime.

Teach us, God, to walk each day in grateful love for your gift of Jesus. May we and all in our home serve Christ with gladness. Amen.

Overwhelmed with Joy

DECEMBER 28-31, 2009 • BETH A. RICHARDSON

MONDAY, DECEMBER 28 ~ *Read Matthew 2:1-12*

W e enter this last week of the year in the season of Christmas but peeking ahead to Epiphany, when the Wise Ones find the Christ child. This scripture sets our theme. "When they saw that the star had stopped, they were *overwhelmed with joy*" (emphasis added). They were finally coming face-to-face with the child for whom they had been searching, and they were overwhelmed at the sight of him.

Many of us have been overwhelmed a lot lately. Overwhelmed with food, with shopping, with houseguests, with Christmas preparation and cleanup. Some of us have been overwhelmed with grief or depression.

But in the midst of the clutter of Christmas, we come face-to-face with the holy and we too are overwhelmed with joy. We hear the giggle of a child. The sights and sounds of a worship service bring tears to our eyes. In a quiet time, we realize our deep gratitude for abundant gifts, and our heart wells up with joy. We feel the presence of one who has passed away, and we know in a new way that we are not alone. In a moment of pure grace, we are filled with the knowledge that no matter who we are or what we have done, God loves us as beloved children.

The Wise Ones found the baby in a stable in Bethlehem—overwhelming joy in an unexpected place. During these remaining days of Christmas, keep searching for the holy. You will discover it too and be overwhelmed with joy.

Loving God, we have been searching for you. Today may we find you and be overwhelmed with joy. Amen.

An ordained deacon of the United Methodist Church, on staff at The Upper Room, and serving at Edgehill United Methodist Church in Nashville, Tennessee

A few years ago I served as the worship leader for a retreat for adults living with HIV and AIDS. We were a diverse, rather ragtag group—from health professionals to homeless; from Baptists to United Methodists to those who hadn't been to church in years; people of all different colors, life experiences, and economic levels.

For me, the high point of each day was gathering for morning and evening prayer. One morning, sleepy faces greeted me as we sang together, "Blessed assurance, Jesus is mine! O what a foretaste of glory divine!" These words of comfort wrapped us in God's abundant grace.

Reading the scripture was like pouring water on a hard, dried-up sponge. The worshippers soaked up the words, their ears and hearts listening intently. I read from the psalm: "[God] delivers the needy when they call, the poor and those who have no helper. . . . From oppression and violence God redeems their life; and precious is their blood in his sight."

God's voice came through the psalmist, proclaiming a special word of comfort and grace to each person in the room. The air was charged with love and joy. I finished reading the scripture, and everyone in the room began to clap. What better response could be given but praise, offered in this basic human action. All clapped with conviction as we said together, "The word of God for the people of God."

We were overwhelmed with the joy of God's message of grace and love and promise borne out in the scripture reading. All of us, especially "the poor and those who have no helper," are precious and beloved children of God. Worn-out, thirsty souls heard this message and were filled to overflowing with God's love.

God of justice, show me how to bring your message of love, hope, and grace to those who are thirsty for your word. Amen.

The Isaiah passage was written for the Israelites, returned home to a ruined Jerusalem after years of devastating exile. The message to these broken people was one of light, hope, and abundance. "Arise, shine; for your light has come, and the glory of the LORD has risen upon you."

During this week between Christmas and Epiphany, we too need this message of hope. Despite our efforts for peace, our world remains torn apart by warring nations. In the midst of great wealth and abundance, men and women and children are hungry, homeless, and hopeless. Christmas celebrations do not diminish the grief and sadness of those who face great loss.

A number of years ago I was overwhelmed by sadness and despair. God's words of light, hope, and abundance could not reach me in the darkness I was experiencing. But I was surrounded by friends who were people of hope and love. These people would not let me go. They would not leave me alone in that dark place. My friends stayed beside me, loving me, hoping and believing on my behalf, until I was able to come out of my despair.

I like to think of the author of Isaiah doing the same for the people of Israel. The prophet affirmed the promise of light and abundance to a people drowning in despair. "Don't give up! There may be deep darkness and destruction, but God's light and healing will break through. Then you'll be overwhelmed with joy at all that God will do for you."

The prophet speaks to us today: "Don't give up hope. Just because you can't see the light doesn't mean it's not there. Keep praying, trusting, and reaching toward the light of God's love."

Brilliant God, shine your light into the shadows of our world and the corners of our hearts. Help us to be hope for friends in despair. You are our hope and our light. Amen.

In today's reading, the writer explains that God's gift of grace through Jesus Christ has come not only for the Jews but also for the Gentiles, that we are "members of the same body."

On this New Year's Eve, when earth rings out one year and welcomes another, we are especially in tune with this gift. We are beloved children of God, living on this planet together.

Members of the same body, we struggle with our differences over religion, politics, and worldview. But we find that despite these differences, we are more alike than we are different.

We have at our fingertips stories and news from the farthest corners of the earth. We rejoice together when a cure for disease has been discovered. We mourn together when lives are devastated by an earthquake, hurricane, or terrorist attack.

We see pictures of earth from space, a blue-green orb suspended in a vast universe, and we know ourselves as members of the same body here on this planet. We are one body on this fragile earth, seeking to save it from such perils as climate change, nuclear and biological threat, starvation, polluted water, and devastating war.

We are, all of us, connected. The decisions that I make—my level of consumption, my treatment of the environment, or my love of my neighbor—have an effect on the whole. I can no longer think of myself as separate and my actions and decisions as affecting only my life. I am a member of the same body, called to be God's love to those around me, both near and far.

May I learn, in the coming year, to be conscious of my connection to the whole human family. And may I learn to live as a loving and responsible member of the whole body.

In the coming year, how are you being called to be a more graceful member of the same body?

The Revised Common Lectionary* for 2009
Year B – Advent / Christmas Year C
(Disciplines Edition)

January 1–4
NEW YEAR'S DAY
Ecclesiastes 3:1-13
Psalm 8
Revelation 21:1-6*a*
Matthew 25:31-46

January 6
EPIPHANY
Isaiah 60:1-6
Psalm 72:1-7, 10-14
Ephesians 3:1-12
Matthew 2:1-12

January 5–11
BAPTISM OF THE LORD
Genesis 1:1-5
Psalm 29
Acts 19:1-7
Mark 1:4-11

January 12–18
1 Samuel 3:1-20
Psalm 139:1-6, 13-18
1 Corinthians 6:12-20
John 1:43-51

January 19–25
Jonah 3:1-5, 10
Psalm 62:5-12
1 Corinthians 7:29-31
Mark 1:14-20

January 26—February 1
Deuteronomy 18:15-20
Psalm 111
1 Corinthians 8:1-13
Mark 1:21-28

February 2–8
Isaiah 40:21-31
Psalm 147:1-11, 20c
1 Corinthians 9:16-23
Mark 1:29-39

February 9–15
2 Kings 5:1-14
Psalm 30
1 Corinthians 9:24-27
Mark 1:40-45

February 16–22
TRANSFIGURATION
2 Kings 2:1-12
Psalm 50:1-6
2 Corinthians 4:3-6
Mark 9:2-9

February 23—March 1
FIRST SUNDAY IN LENT
Genesis 9:8-17
Psalm 25:1-10
1 Peter 3:18-22
Mark 1:9-15

February 25
ASH WEDNESDAY
Joel 2:1-2, 12-17 (*or* Isaiah 58:1-12)
Psalm 51:1-17
2 Corinthians 5:20b–6:10
Matthew 6:1-6, 16-21

March 2–8
SECOND SUNDAY IN LENT
Genesis 17:1-7, 15-16
Psalm 22:23-31
Romans 4:13-25
Mark 8:31-38 (or Mark 9:2-9)

March 9–15
THIRD SUNDAY IN LENT
Exodus 20:1-17
Psalm 19
1 Corinthians 1:18-25
John 2:13-22

March 16–22
FOURTH SUNDAY IN LENT
Numbers 21:4-9
Psalm 107:1-3, 17-22
Ephesians 2:1-10
John 3:14-21

March 23–29
FIFTH SUNDAY IN LENT
Jeremiah 31:31-34
Psalm 51:1-12
  (*or* Psalm 119:9-16)
Hebrews 5:5-10
John 12:20-33

March 30—April 5
PASSION/PALM SUNDAY

Liturgy of the Palms
Mark 11:1-11
(*or* John 12:12-16)
Psalm 118:1-2, 19-29

Liturgy of the Passion
Isaiah 50:4-9a
Psalm 31:9-16
Philippians 2:5-11
Mark 14:1–15:47
  (*or* Mark 15:1-47)

April 6–12
HOLY WEEK

Holy Monday
Isaiah 42:1-9
Psalm 36:5-11
Hebrews 9:11-15
John 12:1-11

Holy Tuesday
Isaiah 49:1-7
Psalm 71:1-14
1 Corinthians 1:18-31
John 12:20-36

Holy Wednesday
Isaiah 50:4-9a
Psalm 70
Hebrews 12:1-3
John 13:21-32

Maundy Thursday
Exodus 12:1-14
Psalm 116:1-4, 12-19
1 Corinthians 11:23-26
John 13:1-17, 31b-35

Good Friday
Isaiah 52:13–53:12
Psalm 22
Hebrews 10:16-25
John 18:1–19:42

Holy Saturday
Job 14:1-14
Psalm 31:1-4, 15-16
1 Peter 4:1-8
Matthew 27:57-66
  or John 19:38-42

Easter
Acts 10:34-43
Psalm 118:1-2, 14-24
1 Corinthians 15:1-11
John 20:1-18
   (or Mark 16:1-8)

April 13–19
Acts 4:32-35
Psalm 133
1 John 1:1–2:2
John 20:19-31

April 20–26
Acts 3:12-19
Psalm 4
1 John 3:1-7
Luke 24:36b-48

April 27–May 3
Acts 4:5-12
Psalm 23
1 John 3:16-24
John 10:11-18

May 4–10
Acts 8:26-40
Psalm 22:25-31
1 John 4:7-21
John 15:1-8

May 11–17
Acts 10:44-48
Psalm 98
1 John 5:1-6
John 15:9-17

May 18–24
Acts 1:15-17, 21-26
Psalm 1
1 John 5:9-13
John 17:6-19

May 21
ASCENSION DAY
Acts 1:1-11
Psalm 47
Ephesians 1:15-23
Luke 24:44-53

May 25–31
PENTECOST
Acts 2:1-21
Psalm 104:24-34, 35*b*
Romans 8:22-27
John 15:26-27; 16:4*b*-15

June 1–7
TRINITY
Isaiah 6:1-8
Psalm 29
Romans 8:12-17
John 3:1-17

June 8–14
1 Samuel 15:34–16:13
Psalm 20
2 Corinthians 5:6-17
Mark 4:26-34

June 15–21
1 Samuel 17:1*a*, 4-11,
   19-23, 32-49
Psalm 9:9-20
2 Corinthians 6:1-13
Mark 4:35-41

June 22–28
2 Samuel 1:1, 17-27
Psalm 130
2 Corinthians 8:7-15
Mark 5:21-43

June 29—July 5
2 Samuel 5:1-5, 9-10
Psalm 48
2 Corinthians 12:2-10
Mark 6:1-13

July 6–12
2 Samuel 6:1-5, 12b-19
Psalm 24
Ephesians 1:3-14
Mark 6:14-29

July 13–19
2 Samuel 7:1-14a
Psalm 89:20-37
Ephesians 2:11-22
Mark 6:30-34, 53-56

July 20–26
2 Samuel 11:1-15
Psalm 14
Ephesians 3:14-21
John 6:1-21

July 27–August 2
2 Samuel 11:26–12:13a
Psalm 51:1-12
Ephesians 4:1-16
John 6:24-35

August 3–9
2 Samuel 18:5-9, 15, 31-33
Psalm 130
Ephesians 4:25–5:2
John 6:35, 41-51

August 10–16
1 Kings 2:10-12; 3:3-14
Psalm 111
Ephesians 5:15-20
John 6:51-58

August 17–23
1 Kings 8:1, 6, 10-11,
  22-30, 41-43
Psalm 84
Ephesians 6:10-20
John 6:56-69

August 24–30
Song of Solomon 2:8-13
Psalm 45:1-2, 6-9
James 1:17-27
Mark 7:1-8, 14-15, 21-23

August 31—September 6
Proverbs 22:1-2, 8-9, 22-23
Psalm 125
James 2:1-17
Mark 7:24-37

September 7–13
Proverbs 1:20-33
Psalm 19
James 3:1-12
Mark 8:27-38

September 14–20
Proverbs 31:10-31
Psalm 1
  (*or* Psalm 54)
James 3:13–4:3, 7-8a
Mark 9:30-37

September 21–28
Esther 7:1-6, 9-10; 9:20-22
Psalm 124
James 5:13-20
Mark 9:38-50

September 29—October 4
Job 1:1; 2:1-10
Psalm 26
Hebrews 1:1-4; 2:5-12
Mark 10:2-16

October 5–11
Job 23:1-9, 16-17
Psalm 22:1-15
Hebrews 4:12-16
Mark 10:17-31

October 12
THANKSGIVING DAY CANADA
Joel 2:21-27
Psalm 126
1 Timothy 2:1-7
Matthew 6:25-33

October 12–18
Job 38:1-7, 34-41
Psalm 104:1-9, 24, 35c
Hebrews 5:1-10
Mark 10:35-45

October 19–25
Job 42:1-6, 10-17
Psalm 34:1-8, 19-22
Hebrews 7:23-28
Mark 10:46-52

October 26–November 1
Isaiah 25:6-9
Psalm 24
Revelation 21:1-6a
John 11:32-44

November 1
ALL SAINTS DAY

November 2–8
Ruth 3:1-5; 4:13-17
Psalm 127
Hebrews 9:24-28
Mark 12:38-44

November 9–15
1 Samuel 1:4-20
Psalm 16
Hebrews 10:11-25
Mark 13:1-8

November 16–22
THE REIGN OF CHRIST
2 Samuel 23:1-7
Psalm 132:1-12
Revelation 1:4b-8
John 18:33-37

November 26
THANKSGIVING DAY, USA
Joel 2:21-27
Psalm 126
1 Timothy 2:1-7
Matthew 6:25-33

November 23–29
FIRST SUNDAY OF ADVENT
Jeremiah 33:14-16
Psalm 25:1-10
1 Thessalonians 3:9-13
Luke 21:25-36

November 30—December 6
SECOND SUNDAY OF ADVENT
Malachi 3:1-4
Luke 1:68-79
Philippians 1:3-11
Luke 3:1-6

December 7–13
THIRD SUNDAY OF ADVENT
Zephaniah 3:14-20
Isaiah 12:2-6
Philippians 4:4-7
Luke 3:7-18

December 14–20
FOURTH SUNDAY OF ADVENT
Micah 5:2-5*a*
Luke 1:47-55
 (*or* Psalm 80:1-7)
Hebrews 10:5-10
Luke 1:39-45

December 21–27

December 24
CHRISTMAS EVE
Isaiah 9:2-7
Psalm 96
Titus 2:11-14
Luke 2:1-20

December 25
CHRISTMAS DAY
Isaiah 52:7-10
Psalm 98
Hebrews 1:1-12
John 1:1-14

December 27
FIRST SUNDAY AFTER
CHRISTMAS
1 Samuel 2:18-20, 26
Psalm 148
Colossians 3:12-17
Luke 2:41-52

December 28–31
Isaiah 60:1-6
Psalm 72:1-7, 10-14
Ephesians 3:1-12
Matthew 2:1-12